POLLEN STREET

THE COOKBOOK

Dedication

With the magnitude of this book and what it's taken to complete all of the recipes, the photography, the pages; there have been so many people involved that to dedicate this book to just one person would be unfair and unjust.

It's very important to me that this dedication is given to so many people who are important to me. I dedicate this book to my immediate family; my wife Irha, without her trust and dedication to my life's work, a book like this could never exist. She is my rock and the love of my life, everything that I am is through her support. Of course, it goes without saying that I also dedicate this to my two little daughters, Keziah and Jemimah. I can't stress enough how becoming a father and role model to my children is the very essence of who I am; so this is to my very own personal two 'Michelin' stars, who I love dearly and who will always be the two most important people in my life.

I'd also like to dedicate this book to my parents, who I wouldn't be here without. My mum, dad and stepfather, who believed in me as a child and told me to follow my dreams when everyone else thought I was crazy, they believed in me and trusted my decision.

Also, I'd like to dedicate this book to all of the team who have worked at Pollen Street Social, past and present. To all those who have been part of Pollen Street Social's journey, and those that continue to be. All of those people know who they are, whose hard work and graft at this restaurant has made it what it is today.

But a special shout out to Dale Bainbridge, my Chef de Cuisine, who works tirelessly to maintain my high standards. To Michael West who has ensured the service is pitch perfect since day one when we opened the doors. To Agnieszka Swiecka and Laure Patry who have lead the wine list to sheer perfection. To Kostas Papathanasiou who works as Dale's number two in the kitchen and always maintains super-high standards.

To everyone who has believed in the restaurant and to all of our customers, our suppliers and everyone who is dedicated to our restaurant, I thank you from the bottom of my heart.

POLLEN STREET

THE COOKBOOK

JASON aTHERTON

WITH PHOTOGRAPHY BY

JOHN CAREY

Jason is a marvellous chef that feeds the soul and leads the way for many young chefs, demonstrating what it is to be a chef in the 21st century.

Ferran Adrià

Jason has mastered the art of creating social places, where people feel good and eat well, and which could be seen as the essence of deformalised dining. A visionary in his own right with a clear grasp of today's international restaurant scene.

Alain Ducasse

Jason is a remarkable fellow. He is a great chef and a restaurateur. Better, he's a kind man and a true friend. He loves cooking, but he also has a boundless curiosity about all aspects of food that keeps him fresh. I've never seen a flash of an Atherton ego, in spite of his prodigious success. He's so much his own man, with a core of tough independence that keeps his feet firmly on the ground. That's the Yorkshireman in him!

Matthew Fort

Jason is one of the most talented, hard-working chefs I know. He's an obsessive and it shows, creating remarkably delicious and approachable dishes that come from an intense passion for the craft of cooking.

Daniel Humm

Chefs cook to nurture people and Jason understands this first hand. His approachability and warmth extend to his cuisine, making him one of the best young chefs working today. Just like his restaurant, Pollen Street will wow its readers with both simplicity and finesse.

Thomas Keller

Jason is a gentleman chef. He cooks with quiet authority and lets his food do the talking.

Pierre Koffmann

Jason spent two years in my kitchen at Chez Nico at Ninety Park Lane. Two things stood out during this period. First his complete assurance and then his blinding determination. Add to this his talent and you have a young chef who now straddles the catering scene with panache and brilliance.

Nico Ladenis

Jason is a chef turned restaurateur that bridges a gap between generations. He has the privilege to have worked alongside some modern classic masters and the wisdom to engage with, invest in and inspire today's future talent… Luck has played no role in Jason's journey. Only determination, ambition, knowledge, self-discipline and humility.

Stephen Terry

Jason Atherton is a realist not a fantasist. He has turned his dreams into reality.

Marco Pierre White

Contents

Introduction

Pollen Street Social is simply the biggest gamble we have ever taken. I remember the night well. It was 2010 and I had arrived home late at night (again) after a long day at work as Executive Chef at Maze. Irha was waiting for me as usual, newly pregnant with Jemimah. Keziah was fast asleep, getting her rest for school. I was extremely nervous and tired, but at the same time excited by this single-minded decision I had made. I burst through the door and announced, 'I'm leaving Maze. We're going to set up our own restaurant!'

Irha looked at me, with a cup of tea in her hand, and said, 'You're crazy! What are you talking about?!' I told her that I couldn't go on any longer and that I had to know.

'Know what?'

'I've been cooking for the last 23 years, most of it with the best chefs in the world. Why can't we do it for ourselves?'

Irha went quiet, as she often does, being the sensible one in the family. I could see she was weighing up the pros and cons in her mind.

She said, 'It's a gamble. How will we afford it?' The magnitude of the risk was everything that we had: our house, our life savings, money we had to borrow from investors. But I was determined that I had come this far, and I wasn't going to fail. After the countless years of double shifts, the mess-ups, the scoldings and the sheer effort to survive for so long in some of the toughest kitchens in the world, the question was killing me – was I good enough to open a restaurant of my own? Did I really have what it took to come out of the shadows and shine?

I was so scared, but I was going to turn this into a positive. It took all my energy, but I wasn't going to let anything get in my way. We set about finding a site. I was told about a pub on Pollen Street, which was in complete disrepair. When you walked through the door it stank. It needed a lot of love. When I said, 'This is the one!', everyone thought I was mad!

It was a big site and a big gamble, but to me it was perfect. We asked Lyndon and Rosanna of the famed Neri & Hu to design it. For me, the restaurant had to be 'Contemporary Mayfair'. I wanted it to have lots of beautiful leather, beautiful brass and woods, contemporary artwork.

Then, we needed a name.

No one knew where Pollen Street was, not even the famous London taxi drivers who know every street! Because of this, I knew I had to use 'Pollen Street' in the name of the restaurant to get it on the radar.

The word 'social' had a lot of meaning for me as a Northern lad. A 'social' means a local meeting point – for drinks, for happy times. A 'social' is where people's grandfathers play snooker and locals play darts, a place where people and communities get together.

So I said, 'How about Pollen Street Social? It says where it is and what it's about.' And so it was and it has now become one of the most iconic restaurants in London!

But the name to Irha and I means one other thing: it means freedom. It's something that gave new meaning to us and our family. It allows us to cook and serve our customers every day to the standard we want and expect.

It's our life, it's our history, it's our legacy – it's Pollen Street Social!

Jason Atherton
London, 2018

Canapés

'Fairy Cakes'
20

Beetroot & Celeriac Tart
24

Smoked Salmon
28

New Forest
Mushroom Tea
30

'Fish & Chips'
38

Foie Gras Eccles Cake
42

Roasted Artichoke Skins
46

'Fairy Cakes'

with
pickled
cucumber
and
dill &
spinach
cream

MAKES 20–30

SWEETCORN MUFFINS

4 large eggs
100g caster sugar
200g plain flour
1½ teaspoons fine sea salt
½ teaspoon baking powder
75g fresh sweetcorn kernels
140ml extra virgin olive oil

Whisk the eggs with the sugar in
a free-standing electric mixer until
pale, light and fluffy. Sift together
the flour, salt and baking powder,
then fold this mixture into the
whisked eggs in 2 batches, taking
care not to over-fold the mixture.
Fold in the sweetcorn followed by
the olive oil. Leave the mixture to
rest for about 10 minutes while you
preheat the oven to 160°C/140°C
fan/Gas Mark 3 and lightly butter
two or three 12-hole mini
muffin tins.

Spoon the mixture into the holes
and bake for about 12 minutes or
until the muffins have risen and are
golden brown. Leave to cool on a
wire rack.

PICKLED CUCUMBER &
CUCUMBER POWDER

1 small cucumber
50ml Salt Pickling Liquid (see
page 376)
Maldon sea salt

Peel the cucumber, reserving
the skin. Put the cucumber in a
vacuum bag with the pickling liquid.
Vacuum-seal the bag and leave in the
fridge to pickle for 4 hours.

Dry the cucumber skin in a
dehydrator at 75°C for 3 hours, then
blitz with a pinch of salt to a powder.

DILL & SPINACH CREAM

2 bunches of dill, about 200g,
   leaves picked
250g blanched large leaf spinach,
   drained and squeezed dry
25ml extra virgin olive oil
250ml double cream
Maldon sea salt

Put the dill, spinach and olive oil
into a blender and blitz until smooth.
Pass the mixture through a fine sieve
into a bowl set over a larger bowl
of iced water (keeping the mixture
chilled like this helps to preserve
the vibrant green colour).

In a large bowl, whip the cream to
soft peaks and season well with salt.
Fold in about 50ml of the dill and
spinach purée, adding more if you
would like the colour and flavour to
be more intense. Transfer the cream
to a piping bag fitted with a 1cm star
nozzle and keep in the fridge until
needed. Put the remaining dill and
spinach purée into a squeezy bottle.

ASSEMBLY

Chive & Dill Oil (see page 381)
1 small can (30g) Ossetra caviar

To assemble the 'fairy cakes', top
each sweetcorn muffin with a little
pickled cucumber, then pipe a
generous layer of dill and spinach
cream over each and squeeze over
a little dill and spinach purée.
Sprinkle with cucumber powder
and the chive and dill oil. Top each
'cake' with a little spoonful of caviar
and serve.

Beetroot & Celeriac Tart

with
fresh
blackberries

MAKES 24

TART CASES

250g plain flour, plus extra
   for dusting
65g type '00' flour
1 teaspoon fine sea salt
155g unsalted butter, softened
a sprig of thyme, leaves picked
1 large egg
1 large egg yolk
25ml cold water

Sift the flours and salt together into a large mixing bowl. Add the butter and mix into the flour with a spatula until the mixture resembles fine breadcrumbs. Add the thyme leaves and mix well. Beat the egg, egg yolk and water together in a small bowl. Add three-quarters of this to the flour mixture and stir until it comes together into a dough. If the mixture is too dry to come together, add a little more beaten egg. Shape the dough into a ball, wrap in clingfilm and chill for at least an hour to firm up.

Preheat the oven to 160°C/140°C fan/Gas Mark 2. Lightly dust a work surface with flour, then roll out the dough thinly (about 2mm thickness). With an 8–9cm round pastry cutter, stamp out 24 discs. Use these to line 24 mini tartlet tins, leaving a little pastry hanging over the rim. Line each pastry case with a small piece of baking parchment, then fill with baking beans.

Set the tartlet tins on a baking tray and bake for 15–16 minutes or until the pastry is light golden brown around the edges. Remove the baking beans and parchment, then return the pastry cases to the oven to bake for a further 3–4 minutes until cooked through. Leave to cool for a few minutes before trimming off the excess pastry with a sharp knife. Set aside to cool completely before removing from the tins.

FILLING

2 large purple beetroots, peeled
1 garlic clove, sliced
a few sprigs of thyme
a few knobs of unsalted butter
¼ celeriac
olive oil, for cooking
a splash of blackberry vinegar
Maldon sea salt and black pepper

Put the peeled beetroots into a vacuum bag along with the garlic, thyme, butter and a little salt and pepper. Vacuum-seal the bag, then lower it into a sous vide machine (or water bath) heated to 85°C. Cook the beetroots for 8 hours or until soft.

Peel the celeriac and chop into a rough dice. Heat a little olive oil in a large frying pan over a medium heat, add the celeriac with a little seasoning, and cook, tossing occasionally, for 10–12 minutes or until tender. Grate the beetroot and add to the pan with its cooking juices and cook until all the liquid has evaporated and the pan is dry.

Transfer the contents of the pan to a blender and blitz to a very smooth purée. Add a splash of blackberry vinegar and adjust the seasoning with salt and pepper to taste. Pass the purée through a fine sieve into a bowl. Cover and keep in the fridge until needed.

About 15–20 minutes before serving, take the bowl out of the fridge and give the purée a quick stir, then transfer to a squeezy bottle.

ASSEMBLY

24 blackberries

Pipe the beetroot and celeriac purée into the pastry cases, filling them almost to the top. Place a blackberry in the middle and serve immediately.

Smoked Salmon

with
cream
cheese
and
caviar

200ml crème fraîche
finely grated zest and juice
    of 2 lemons
1 loaf of rye bread
280g full-fat cream cheese
a side of long-sliced
    smoked salmon
100g keta salmon roe caviar
Maldon sea salt and black pepper
dill fronds, to garnish

Put the crème fraîche into a colander
or sieve lined with a clean piece of
muslin. Set the colander or sieve in
a bowl. Leave in the fridge to drain
for 6 hours, or overnight, to remove
the excess moisture from the crème
fraîche. Add the lemon zest and juice
to the hung crème fraîche and season
with salt and pepper. Transfer to a
squeezy bottle or piping bag.

Thinly slice the rye loaf lengthways
using a meat slicer set to 5.5mm
thickness. Arrange the slices of
bread on cutting boards in a single
layer. Spread each slice with an even
layer of cream cheese, then drape
the smoked salmon slices on top.
Now, you can either cut the slices
into fingers about 5cm x 2cm, or
stamp out neat discs using a 3cm
round pastry cutter.

Squeeze a few dots of lemon crème
fraîche on to each smoked salmon
canapé, then top with a teaspoonful
of salmon roe. Garnish with dill
fronds and serve.

New Forest Mushroom Tea

with
Parmesan
foam
and
cep powder

SERVES 8–10

MUSHROOM TEA

500g flat mushrooms
500g button mushrooms
olive oil, for cooking
1.5kg mirepoix (1 onion,
    2 celery sticks, 1 leek and
    2 carrots, all diced)
2.5 litres Chicken Stock
    (see page 379)
a small bunch of thyme,
    about 50g
100g dried ceps (porcini)
500ml Madeira
250ml egg whites,
    lightly whisked
about 50ml white soy sauce
Maldon sea salt and black pepper

Preheat the oven to 180°C/160°C fan/Gas Mark 4. Wash and dry the flat and button mushrooms, then spread them in a roasting tin and drizzle over a little olive oil. Roast the mushrooms for about 45 minutes or until they are beginning to brown and any liquid they have released has evaporated.

Meanwhile, heat a drizzle of olive oil in a large, heavy-based saucepan. Add the mirepoix with a pinch each of salt and pepper and fry, stirring frequently, for 8–10 minutes or until the vegetables begin to soften. Pour in the chicken stock and add the thyme and dried ceps. Bring to a simmer.

Take the roasting tin out of the oven and pour in the Madeira. Deglaze the tin by scraping the bottom and sides with a wooden spoon, then pour the contents into the saucepan and stir. Bring back to a simmer and leave to cook gently for 5–6 hours or until the stock is flavourful.

Strain the stock through a fine sieve into a clean saucepan, pressing down on the solids to extract all the flavourful juices; discard the solids. Leave the strained stock to cool to about 40°C.

Now clarify the stock. Add the lightly whisked egg whites and set the pan over a high heat. As the stock heats up to a simmer, the egg whites will form a foamy raft on the surface and capture any impurities. Use a ladle to transfer the stock and raft into a muslin-lined sieve set over another saucepan.

Do not press down on the raft or the stock will become cloudy again. Once all the liquid has strained through, discard the raft. Season the resulting mushroom tea in the saucepan to taste with white soy sauce. Set aside.

For serving, reheat the mushroom tea and pour into a warmed teapot.

———————

PARMESAN FOAM

1 large banana shallot,
 thinly sliced
rind from a small block
 of Parmesan
125ml dry white wine
500ml double cream
2 litres whole milk
2g gel espressa
5.5g agar agar

Put the shallot into a heavy-based saucepan and add the white wine and Parmesan rind. Bring to the boil and reduce until the wine is syrupy. Stir in the cream and milk. As soon as the mixture begins to bubble again, take the pan off the heat and strain the liquid through a fine sieve into a clean saucepan; discard the solids. Leave to cool to about 80°C.

Add the gel espressa and agar agar to the mixture. Return to the heat and cook, stirring constantly, for about 3 minutes or until the gel and agar agar have dissolved. Strain the mixture through a fine sieve into a jug. Leave to cool completely, then keep in the fridge until needed.

———————

ASSEMBLY

1–2 tablespoons freshly
 grated Parmesan
cep (porcini) powder,
 for sprinkling

Warm 500ml of the Parmesan mixture with a little freshly grated Parmesan, then pour into an iSi whipper and charge it with 3 canisters of gas. Give it a few shakes. Dispense a layer of Parmesan foam into individual tea cups and sprinkle over a little cep powder. At the table, pour the mushroom tea into each tea cup and serve at once.

Mountain Foods

I established the foraging business, Mountain Foods, back in 1995 and now operate it alongside the wildfoodcentre.org where I run courses and help chefs develop their knowledge of foraged plants.

I first came across Jason over 20 years ago when he was working with Marco Pierre White at the former Hyde Park Hotel and then again during his time with Gordon Ramsay at Maze. In those days the foraging business was in its infancy. Wild mushrooms had become really popular but wild herbs were still little known about or used. For centuries chefs have had strange folk coming out from the forest with twigs in their hair, carrying odd mushrooms and baskets of wild garlic, but until the mid 1990s nobody was supplying wild vegetables. Creating Mountain Foods, specialising in wild plants, gave me the opportunity to walk through the doors some of our country's finest restaurants.

Chefs like Jason have years of experience working with a huge array of incredible ingredients, so the fact that a plant is wild and foraged is not in itself enough reason for him to use it. It's about the taste, the texture and what it does for the food that he puts it with. That's why I'm constantly challenged to find new interesting plants that I can suggest he consider for his latest creations. Jason and his team at Pollen Street are a great example of the exciting British restaurant scene, pushing boundaries and experimenting with new ingredients.

It's really hard to say which is my favourite wild herb, but wood sorrel (Oxalis acetosella) has to be right up there along with hedge sorrel (Rumex acetosa). Wood sorrel is beautiful, with its groups of three heart-shaped, citrus-tasting leaves. It grows in the heart of the forest through all the seasons but most abundantly in the summer when there is a brief flush of delicate yellow and sometimes white flowers — when popped on your tongue these taste like a burst of lemon sherbet. You can tell the weather by watching this delicate little plant: as dark clouds approach, its leaves gently fold down in anticipation of the storm, protecting themselves from being bruised by the soon-to-come heavy raindrops.

Hedge sorrel has much larger spear-shaped leaves. It is found growing outside of the forest, sheltering on the leeward side of the hedges in lanes and along the sides of fields. This plant is a real player in Nature's larder and a great example of the cross-over where popular foraged plants like this and wild rocket are now farmed. Once a cultivated plant, they become part of the gardener's repertoire and this of course leads to it being available in the shops for mass consumption. However, for flavour, the wild version wins hands down every time.

Sorrel is hugely popular, not just because it looks great on a plate and makes a delicious sauce but because it packs a serious, tangy lemon-like punch. So if you ever want to find some and wonder where it might be growing, imagine a crisp, blue sky on a winter morning, the sun shining and a cold breeze in the air. As you walk the country lanes, along a footpath or the side of a field, you may suddenly find yourself in a sheltered spot, out of the chilly wind and bathed in winter sun. Take a good look around you and you'll probably find this precious plant making the most of these near-perfect conditions.

I can't talk about favourite wild plants without mentioning the estuary and beaches that are home to a vast selection of beautiful succulent sea herbs. One that stands out would have to be rock samphire (Crithmum maritimum). Also known as sea fennel, this plant has been in demand for its incredible aromatic flavour since medieval times, even cited in Shakespeare's King Lear, a scene set above a cliff. '... halfway down hangs one that gathers Samphire'.

Despite the hazards that we foragers have to face, in all weather, scaling cliffs and racing against the tide, gathering plants with such an array of flavours, tastes and textures, in such spectacular landscapes, is worth every minute.

Yun Hider
mountainfood.org

'Fish & Chips'

with
taramasalata,
and
salt & vinegar
powder

MAKES 30

CONFIT POTATO 'CHIPS'

1kg clarified butter
4 large chipping potatoes (such
    as Desirée, King Edward or
    Maris Piper)
vegetable oil, for deep-frying
Maldon sea salt and black pepper

Heat the clarified butter in a
wide, heavy-based pan to 160°C.
Meanwhile, peel and grate the
potatoes, working quickly or they
will start to oxidise and discolour.
Season the grated potatoes, then
add them to the hot butter. Fry for
5–8 minutes or until almost tender,
stirring and moving the potatoes
around the pan frequently to prevent
them from sticking to the bottom
and burning.

Tip the potatoes into a colander or
sieve set over a large bowl. Leave
to drain for about 10 minutes, then
season the potatoes with salt and
pepper to taste (discard the butter
drained into the bowl). Spread
out the potatoes in a thick layer
on a baking tray lined with baking
parchment – you want a 2cm thick
layer once the potatoes have been
pressed. Place another sheet of
baking parchment on top, then
weigh down with another heavy
baking tray. Chill for at least an
hour (or overnight if preparing in
advance) until firmly pressed.

When ready to serve, heat oil for
deep-frying to 180°C. Slice the
chilled pressed potato into 'chips'
5cm long, 2cm wide and 2cm thick.
Deep-fry for a few minutes until
golden and crisp. Drain on a tray
lined with kitchen paper, then dust
with a little salt and vinegar powder.

TARAMASALATA

4 slices of white bread
225g smoked cod's roe
½ garlic clove
600ml whole milk
500ml vegetable oil
a squeeze of lemon juice

Tear the bread slices into smaller pieces directly into a food processor. Add the cod's roe, peeled garlic and milk. Blitz the ingredients together. With the machine running, gradually trickle in the oil. Once the mixture has emulsified, add lemon juice to taste. Spoon into a piping bag fitted with a plain round nozzle and keep in the fridge until needed.

SALT & VINEGAR POWDER

100g malt vinegar powder
20g fine sea salt

Simply mix the two ingredients together. Store in a salt shaker (or an airtight container, if making in advance).

ASSEMBLY

bronze fennel fronds

Pipe 3 dots of taramasalata on each fried 'chip' and garnish each dot with a frond of bronze fennel. Serve immediately.

Foie Gras Eccles Cake

with
poppy seed
& almond
crumb

MAKES ABOUT 20

PASTRY

 plain flour, for dusting
 200g puff pastry

Lightly dust a work surface and a
rolling pin with flour. Cut the pastry
in half, then roll out each half to
about 3mm thickness. Place the
pastry sheets on 2 baking trays and
chill for at least 5 minutes.

Cut the chilled pastry sheets into
neat 8cm x 5cm rectangles. Transfer
the rectangles to a baking tray lined
with greaseproof paper. Chill while
you prepare the stuffing.

STUFFING

 200g foie gras, finely chopped
 200g minced pork shoulder
 50g minced lardo
 50g sultanas, soaked in warm
  water to plump
 50ml Cognac
 2g juniper berries, crushed
 4 egg yolks
 Maldon sea salt and black pepper

In a large mixing bowl, combine
the foie gras, pork mince, lardo,
sultanas, Cognac, crushed juniper
and one egg yolk. Season with salt
and pepper and mix well. (If you
want to check the seasoning, fry
off a little of the stuffing and taste.)
Roll the stuffing into balls weighing
about 25g each.

Place a pastry rectangle on the work
surface and set a ball of stuffing
slightly off-centre on the pastry.
Fold the pastry over to encase the
ball, then pinch the edges together,
making sure there are no air pockets
around the stuffing. Cut off any
excess pastry, then roll into a neat
ball and return to the lined baking

tray. Repeat to make the remaining Eccles cakes. Gently press each down to create a flat base.

Lightly beat the remaining egg yolks in a small bowl. Brush this egg wash over the Eccles cakes. Chill for 10 minutes, then brush again with egg wash. Repeat the chilling and egg wash once more to ensure an even glaze. Chill for at least 20 minutes, or until ready to bake.

CRUMB

1 tablespoon black poppy seeds
1 teaspoon chopped almonds
1 teaspoon chopped dried
   clementine peel
1 teaspoon chopped dried apricot
8 sprigs of thyme, leaves picked

Combine all the ingredients in a bowl and stir until well mixed.

ASSEMBLY

Preheat the oven to 180°C/160°C fan/Gas Mark 4. Sprinkle the crumb mixture evenly over the glazed Eccles cakes, then bake for about 12 minutes or until the pastries are evenly golden brown. Leave to cool slightly on the baking tray for a few minutes before serving hot.

Roasted Artichoke Skins

with
artichoke
ice cream

SERVES 8–10

BAKED ARTICHOKES

  500g white-skin Jerusalem
    artichokes
  2 garlic cloves (unpeeled)
  a few sprigs of thyme
  olive oil, to drizzle
  Maldon sea salt
  vegetable oil, for deep-frying

Preheat the oven to 150°C/130°C
fan/Gas Mark 2. Scrub the
artichokes well, then place them on
a large piece of foil with the garlic
cloves and thyme. Drizzle over a
little olive oil and sprinkle with a
generous pinch of sea salt. Wrap up
the foil around the artichokes and
place the parcel on a baking tray.
Bake for about an hour or until the
artichokes are soft when pierced
with the tip of a knife. Leave the
artichokes to cool, still wrapped
in foil.

Cut the artichokes in half
lengthways. Scoop out the flesh into
a bowl and mash it; set aside for the
artichoke ice cream. Arrange the
artichoke skins on a baking tray and
dry in a dehydrator set to 75°C until
the skins are completely dried out.

Before serving, deep-fry the dried
artichoke skins, in small batches,
in vegetable oil heated to 160°C for
1–2 minutes or until golden and
crisp. Remove to a tray lined with
kitchen paper to drain off the
excess oil.

ARTICHOKE ICE CREAM

  500ml whole milk
  2 large egg yolks
  75g caster sugar
  50g maltodextrin
  Jerusalem artichoke mash
    (see above)

2g fine sea salt
50g Parmesan (preferably aged for
36 months), freshly grated

Put the milk into a heavy-based
saucepan and gently heat to
about 50°C. Meanwhile, whisk
together the egg yolks, sugar and
maltodextrin in a bowl until the
mixture is pale and light. Stir a
third of the warmed milk into the
egg mixture, then pour this into
the saucepan and mix with the
rest of the milk. Stir the mixture
over a medium heat until it reaches
70°C. Regulate the heat to keep the
temperature constant at 70°C and
continue to cook, stirring, for 10
minutes. The mixture will thicken
to a smooth custard.

Remove from the heat and add the
reserved artichoke mash, the salt and
grated Parmesan. Blitz the mixture
using a stick blender (or in a regular
blender) until smooth. Pass through
a fine sieve and cool, then churn in
an ice cream machine until almost
firm. Transfer to a freezerproof
container, cover and freeze for at
least 4 hours or until set. (It is best
to serve the ice cream on the day it
is made.)

ASSEMBLY

hazelnuts
truffle, grated

For each serving, place a neat crisp
artichoke skin in a serving bowl and
spread with a scoop of artichoke ice
cream. Chop a couple of hazelnuts
and a crisp artichoke skins to a rough
crumb, mix with some grated truffle
and sprinkle on top of the ice cream.
Serve immediately.

Starters

Lincolnshire
Smoked Eel
52

Pressed Norfolk Quail
& Duck Liver
58

Saddle of Rabbit
64

Slow-cooked
Heritage Breeds
Farm Egg
70

Roasted Orkney
Scallops
76

Pressed Terrine
of Guinea Fowl
82

Braised Broccoli
88

Tomato Tartare
92

Onion Squash Soup
96

Lincolnshire Smoked Eel

with
buttermilk,
beetroot
and
'jellied eel'

SERVES 4–6

BEETROOT & SMOKED EEL REDUCTION

1kg smoked eel bones
olive oil, for cooking
1 onion, chopped
1 bulb of fennel, chopped
1 celery stick, chopped
1 leek, chopped
2 garlic cloves, chopped
1 teaspoon coriander seeds
1 teaspoon fennel seeds
200ml dry white wine
4 litres Fish Stock (see page 378)
1 litre beetroot juice

In batches, fry the eel bones with a little olive oil in a large, heavy-based pan until they are lightly golden brown. Once all the eel bones have been browned, set them aside. Return the pan to the heat and add a little more oil followed by the onion, fennel, celery, leek and garlic. Fry the vegetables, stirring occasionally, for 5 minutes. Add the coriander and fennel seeds, and continue to fry the mixture for another couple of minutes. Return the browned eel bones to the pan. Deglaze the pan with the white wine, stirring well, then let the wine bubble and reduce by half. Pour in enough fish stock to cover the ingredients and bring to a simmer. Lower the heat and leave to simmer gently for 2 hours.

Remove the pan from the heat and set aside to cool slowly – this will allow the flavours of the ingredients to further infuse the stock. Once cold, strain the stock through a fine sieve; discard the solids. Set aside 500ml of the stock for the jellied eel. Pour the remaining stock into a heavy-based saucepan, bring to the boil and boil until reduced to about a litre. Stir in the beetroot juice and bring back to the boil. Boil until the liquid has reduced to a syrupy consistency. Transfer to a squeezy bottle and keep in the fridge until needed.

'JELLIED EEL'

2 gelatine leaves
500ml eel stock (see above)
1 small shallot
1 Granny Smith apple
a handful of dill, leaves picked

Put the gelatine leaves in a bowl of cold water to soak
and soften. Heat the eel stock in a saucepan until it comes
to a simmer. Drain the gelatine and squeeze out the
excess water, then add to the warm stock. Stir until the
gelatine has melted. Remove from the heat and leave the
stock to cool to room temperature.

Meanwhile, peel and finely dice the shallot and apple,
and put them into a bowl. Chop the dill leaves and add to
the bowl. Mix well, then stir in the cooled eel stock. Pour
the mixture into 4–6 small silicone chocolate moulds
and chill for a few hours or overnight until set.

BUTTERMILK FOAM

500ml buttermilk
juice of 1 lemon
1g Maldon sea salt
50g Sosa ProEspuma Cold
4 teaspoons olive oil

Put all the ingredients into a large jug. Blitz with a stick
blender until well mixed. Transfer the mixture to an iSi
whipper and charge with 2 canisters of gas. Shake, then
set aside until needed.

BUTTERMILK & HORSERADISH PURÉE

250ml buttermilk
1 teaspoon ready-made
   horseradish sauce
7g agar agar powder
a squeeze of lemon juice
Maldon sea salt

Put the buttermilk and horseradish sauce in a small
saucepan and gently heat the mixture to about 70°C. Add
the agar agar and stir over a medium heat for 2 minutes
or until dissolved. Pour the mixture into a flat tray and
leave to cool, then cover with clingfilm and chill for a few
hours until set.

Scrape the set mixture into a blender and blitz to a fine
purée. Add lemon juice and salt to taste, then blend again.
Transfer the purée to a squeezy bottle and keep in the
fridge until needed.

SMOKED FISH SKIN POWDER

skin from 1 side of cod
skin from 1 side of smoked eel

Preheat the oven to 120°C/100°C fan/Gas Mark ½. Line a baking tray with baking parchment. Carefully scrape or slice off any excess fat from the cod and smoked eel skins. Put the skins into a pan and pour in enough cold water to cover. Bring to the boil, then immediately remove the skins from the pan and rinse with cold water. Pat dry with kitchen paper. Lay the skins out flat on the baking tray and toast in the oven for about 30 minutes or until golden brown and crisp.

Transfer the skins to a dehydrator tray, making sure to wipe away any fat with kitchen paper. Leave in the dehydrator overnight or until the skins are completely dried out. The next day, break the dried skins into small pieces and put into a spice grinder with a pinch of salt. Blend to a fine powder. Store the powder in an airtight container.

ASSEMBLY

8–12 tranches of smoked eel
bronze fennel
fine apple batons
2 Pickled Cucumbers &
   Cucumber Powder
   (see page 22)
blanched sea herbs (such as
   sea purslane, rock samphire,
   ice lettuce)
a few sprigs of dill
Chive & Dill Oil (see page 381)

Place 2 tranches of smoked eel on each serving plate. Squeeze a little beetroot and smoked eel reduction around them. Squeeze 2 mounds of buttermilk and horseradish purée on the plate and sprinkle a little bronze fennel over each mound. Garnish with 'jellied eel', apple batons, pickled cucumbers and cucumber powder, sea herbs and dill. Drizzle a few drops of chive and dill oil over the jellied eel. Finally, dispense the buttermilk foam into 4–6 small glasses and sprinkle smoked fish skin powder on top. Serve immediately with the smoked eel.

Pressed Norfolk Quail
& Duck Liver

with
braised
quail taco,
cep purée
and
summer
vegetables

SERVES 4

PRESSED NORFOLK QUAIL & DUCK LIVER

8 skinless, boneless quail breasts
100ml Meat Brine (see Braised West Country
   Ox Cheek recipe, page 232)
a few knobs of unsalted butter
150ml brandy
50ml good-quality Jerez vinegar
2½ teaspoons fine sea salt
1 teaspoon caster sugar
¾ teaspoon pink salt
½ teaspoon crushed white pepper
300g grade A foie gras
80g Périgord truffle

Put the quail breasts into a resealable bag and pour over the meat brine. Seal the bag and set aside in the fridge for an hour. Rinse off the brine and pat the breasts dry. Place them in a vacuum bag with a few knobs of butter. Vacuum-seal the bag. Cook in a sous vide machine (or water bath) heated to 57°C for 45 minutes. Transfer the bag to a bowl of iced water to stop the cooking process. Keep in the fridge, in the bag, until needed.

While the quail breasts are cooking, make a marinade for the foie gras. Heat the brandy and vinegar in a small pan with the fine sea salt, sugar, pink salt and pepper. Swirl the liquid in the pan to help dissolve the salts and sugar. Once dissolved, remove from the heat and leave to cool completely.

Remove and discard any veins from the foie gras using the back of a teaspoon. Remould the foie gras to its original shape and place in a vacuum bag. Pour over the cooled marinade and vacuum-seal the bag. Marinate in the fridge for an hour. Remove the foie gras from the bag and rinse off the marinade. Pat the foie gras dry, then place in another vacuum bag and vacuum-seal it. Cook in a sous vide machine (or water bath) heated to 65°C for 10 minutes. Transfer the bag to a bowl of iced water to cool the foie gras quickly, then keep in the fridge until needed.

Lay a large piece of clingfilm on the work surface. Remove the foie gras from the vacuum bag and pour the fat out into a saucepan to warm slightly. Cut the foie gras into 2 long strips. Thinly slice the Périgord truffle and wrap the slices around the strips of foie gras. Put the 2 truffle-wrapped foie gras strips on the clingfilm, leaving a gap between them. Remove the quail breasts from their vacuum bag and arrange 4 breasts on top of the foie gras strips. Arrange the remaining 4 quail breasts in the gap between the foie gras.

Lightly brush the foie gras and quail breasts with the warmed fat from the foie gras. Use the clingfilm to help press together the foie gras and quail breasts into a neat ballotine wrapped in the clingfilm. Chill to set the shape.

QUAIL TACO

8 quail legs
200g duck fat
2 tablespoons Mushroom Purée (see page 371)
100g mixed pan-roasted wild mushrooms
2 tablespoons reduced Pigeon Sauce (see Roast Squab
    Pigeon recipe, page 252)
4 Romaine lettuce leaves
1 large Périgord truffle, thinly sliced
cep purée (see below)
Lettuce and Seaweed Powder (see page 372)

To confit the quail legs, season them with salt and pepper, then place them
in a pan in which they fit snugly. Add the duck fat and bring to a gentle simmer.
Very gently cook the legs for about 3 hours or until they are very tender and
the meat will fall easily off the bone.

Pull the meat off the bones in chunks and remove any bits of sinew. Put
the meat into a large bowl and mix in the mushroom purée. Roughly chop
the roasted wild mushrooms and add these to the bowl along with the
pigeon sauce. Stir until well combined.

Assemble the quail tacos just before serving. For each one, lay a Romaine
lettuce leaf on a chopping board and use a large pastry cutter to stamp out a
rough round. Fold the lettuce round in half to resemble a taco and place it on
a small side plate. Stuff the 'taco' with the confit quail and mushroom mixture
and a layer of thinly sliced Périgord truffle. Pipe little dots of cep purée on top
of the lettuce then dust generously with the lettuce and seaweed powder.

———————

CEP PURÉE

50g unsalted butter
250g fresh ceps
a sprig of thyme
1 small garlic clove
75ml Chicken Stock (see page 379)
1 tablespoon good-quality Jerez vinegar

Heat half the butter in a medium pan over a medium-high heat. As soon as
the butter begins to foam, toss in the ceps and a little seasoning. Fry for 4–5
minutes or until the ceps are evenly golden brown. Add the rest of the butter
along with the thyme, peeled garlic and chicken stock. Simmer until the liquid
has almost all evaporated. Stir in the vinegar, then take the pan off the heat
and tip the contents into a blender. Blitz until smooth. Pass the purée through
a fine sieve, then transfer to a squeezy bottle or piping bag. Keep in the fridge
if making in advance. Before serving, warm by setting the bottle in a bowl of
hot water.

———————

SUMMER VEGETABLES

a bunch of baby carrots
a bunch of baby fennel bulbs
a bunch of baby leeks
truffle trimmings, chopped
reduced Pigeon Sauce (see Roast Squab Pigeon
recipe, page 252)

Bring a pan of salted water to the boil and have ready a bowl of iced water
on the side. Blanch the vegetables separately for 2 minutes or until they are
just tender when pierced with the tip of a small knife. Use a slotted spoon to
transfer the vegetables to the bowl of iced water to cool them down quickly
and stop the cooking process. Drain well.

When they have all been blanched, cut them into small rondelles. Place them
in a bowl and toss with the truffle trimmings and pigeon sauce.

ASSEMBLY

2 fresh ceps, thinly sliced
1 bulb of baby fennel, thinly sliced
sorrel

For each serving, cut a neat slice of quail and foie gras ballotine, then
remove the clingfilm. Place the ballotine in the centre of a serving plate and
sprinkle over a little sea salt and pepper. Arrange the baby carrot, fennel and
leek rondelles around the ballotine. Top with 3 slices each of raw cep and baby
fennel. Drizzle a little pigeon sauce over the vegetables and ballotine, then
garnish with sorrel. Serve with the quail 'taco'.

Saddle of Rabbit

with
crispy
rabbit leg
croquettes,
mixed
beans, bitter
leaves
and
truffle
dressing

SERVES 4

BALLOTINE OF RABBIT

2 large, or 4 small, boned saddles of rabbit
10–15 slices of Parma ham
meat glue, for dusting
olive oil, for cooking
Maldon sea salt and black pepper

To prepare the ballotine, lay out the saddles on a chopping board and trim off
any sinews. Place a large piece of oven-safe clingfilm on the work surface and
arrange the Parma ham slices, overlapping, on this to form a rectangle large
enough to wrap around the rabbit. (You can also make two smaller ballotines,
in which case lay out 2 rectangles of Parma ham.) Place the saddles side-by-
side on top of the Parma ham. Use any small loin trimmings to fill gaps. Season
with salt and pepper and dust with meat glue.

Using the clingfilm to help, tightly roll up the saddles in the ham to form a
neat log shape. Make sure the rabbit is completely covered by the Parma ham
and the ballotine is tightly wrapped up in the clingfilm. Wrap a second large
sheet of clingfilm around the ballotine.

Lower the ballotine into a sous vide machine (or water bath) heated to 62°C
and cook for 25 minutes. Remove and leave to cool. If making ahead, keep the
ballotine in the fridge.

When ready to serve, preheat the oven to 180°C/160°C fan/Gas Mark 4.
Drizzle a little olive oil into a wide ovenproof pan and set over a high heat.
Unwrap the ballotine and place in the hot pan. Sear for 2 minutes on each side
or until evenly golden brown, then transfer the pan to the oven to roast for 2
minutes. Remove and leave to rest.

CRISPY RABBIT LEG CROQUETTES

4 rabbit legs
100g Salt Cure (see Cumbrian Suckling Pig recipe,
    page 203)
olive oil, for drizzling
100ml Rabbit Sauce (see Roast Lincolnshire Rabbit
    recipe, page 240)
a handful of tarragon and flat-leaf parsley, leaves
    picked and chopped
100g plain flour
100g eggs, lightly beaten
100g Japanese breadcrumbs
oil for deep-frying

Put the rabbit legs into a large bowl or tray and rub them with the salt cure.
Cover with clingfilm and set aside in the fridge to cure for 4 hours.

Rinse the salt cure off the rabbit legs, then pat them dry with kitchen paper. Place the legs in a vacuum bag and drizzle over a little olive oil. Vacuum-seal the bag, then cook the rabbit legs in a sous vide machine (or water bath) heated to 85°C for 3 hours.

Take the rabbit legs from the bag and put them into a large bowl (with the cooking juices and oil). While still warm, shred the meat; discard the bones and any sinew. Mix the shredded meat with the cooking juices and oil, followed by the rabbit sauce and chopped herbs. Taste the mixture and adjust the seasoning with salt and pepper. Transfer to a vacuum bag and flatten the mixture to 1cm thickness, then vacuum-seal it. Place the bag on a tray and weight down with another heavy tray. Chill for a few hours or until firm.

Remove the croquette mixture from the bag and cut out 4 neat 3cm x 7cm rectangles. Place the rectangles on a tray and put into the blast chiller (or freezer) to set the rectangles quickly.

Meanwhile, put the flour, beaten eggs and breadcrumbs into 3 separate wide bowls. When the croquette rectangles are firmly set, coat each one in flour, shaking off any excess, then in egg and, finally, with breadcrumbs. Place the coated rectangles on a tray and keep in the fridge until needed.

When ready to serve, heat oil in a deep-fat fryer to 180°C. Deep-fry the croquettes for 2–3 minutes, turning them frequently, until evenly golden brown and crisp. Remove them to a tray lined with kitchen paper to absorb the excess oil and sprinkle lightly with sea salt. Keep warm.

ASSEMBLY

   about 200g mixed beans (such as blanched fine French
      beans and runner beans, cooked coco beans and
      borlotti beans)
   Truffle Dressing (see page 373)
   100–150g mixed seasonal bitter leaves (such as
      castelfranco, radicchio, wild treviso, lollo rosso)
   Tarragon Mayonnaise (see page 373)
   a handful of foraged herbs (such as sorrel and
      hairy bittercress)
   breakfast radishes, cut into fine matchsticks

Slice the blanched beans into 4–5cm lengths and place them in a bowl with the cooked beans. Add a little truffle dressing and toss to coat. Cut or tear large bitter leaves into smaller pieces, then soak in a bowl of iced water for 1–2 minutes to crisp them up. Drain well and dress lightly with truffle dressing.

Thinly slice the rabbit ballotine and arrange 3 or 4 slices on each warmed serving plate. Place a crispy rabbit croquette in the centre. Squeeze little dots of truffle dressing and tarragon mayonnaise around the plate, then arrange the beans, bitter leaves, herbs and radishes on and around the rabbit ballotine slices and croquette. Serve immediately.

Heritage Breeds

When we first started talking with Jason about working together, the initial quality that resonated with us was his desire to source only the best quality ingredients. This made supplying Jason and Pollen Street Social a perfect fit for us.

Our Heritage Breeds range features hen's, duck's and quail's eggs from genuine special breeds at hand-picked British farms. Our eggs boast rich yolks and exceptional quality whites, and feature a stunning palette of delicate shell colours, from deep brown and pastel blue to porcelain white and speckled grey/brown. They are as beautiful as they are delicious.

Knowing that for Jason the provenance of ingredients is incredibly important, working with him is a natural partnership. Our philosophy at Heritage Breeds is that 'better breeding and higher hen welfare make for impeccable quality eggs'. The welfare of our birds is something that we take particular pride in. Our hens are traditionally reared in smaller flocks on hand-picked British farms, typically a third of the size of standard free-range farms, meaning the birds have considerably more space to roam free outdoors with plenty of shade. All Heritage Breeds birds are fed a wholesome vegetarian diet that has been specifically designed by an animal nutritionist and tailored to the flock's individual needs.

In the autumn of 2017, Jason spent the day with one of our hen farmers, Howard – or as we like to call him, our 'chicken whisperer'. Jason saw first hand how our hens live, what they are fed and how much room they have to roam. It was great for Jason to see why the eggs that are produced are the finest quality.

The eggs have their own distinct characteristics, which can significantly enhance cooking to create impeccable dishes:

- Copper Marans – a deep-brown-shelled hen's egg from the famous French Marans hen breed, with a gorgeous dark yolk and clear egg white. A great all-rounder to elevate any egg dish, great for making Scotch eggs or a classic Huevos Rancheros.

- Royal Legbar – a beautiful pastel-shelled hen's egg from the renowned Legbar family, descended from the rare Araucana breed. The Royal Legbar egg is perfect poached, boiled and fried, making it ideal for brunches.

- Gladys May's – a porcelain-white-shelled duck's egg with a stunning, large golden yolk. Descended from the Aylesbury breed, the eggs from these ducks are much larger than hen's eggs and have thicker whites that hold more air, making them ideal for meringues, soufflés and Yorkshire puddings.

- Speckled Quail – a beautiful miniature quail's egg from the Brown and Golden Coturnix breed, this lends itself to delicate canapé dishes and is delicious when served soft boiled with celery salt.

We are immensely proud to have our Heritage Breeds eggs served at Jason's London restaurants as well as being used as ingredients in this book. The incredible dishes in these pages showcase the depth of the range and will inspire food lovers across the country to cook and enjoy more delicious speciality eggs.

heritagebreeds.co.uk

Slow-cooked Heritage Breeds Farm Egg

with
seaweed
crumb,
chicken legs
and
crispy
chicken skin

SERVES 4

_____

SEAWEED CRUMB

125g Parmesan, freshly grated
200g sourdough bread,
    crusts removed
25g sage leaves
oil for deep-frying
25g dried fujiko seaweed

Preheat the oven to 160°C/140°C fan/Gas Mark 3.
Evenly spread the grated Parmesan on a baking tray
and bake for 8–12 minutes or until the cheese is golden
brown and crisp. Remove from the oven and leave to cool
completely, then break into pieces.

Meanwhile, cut the bread into small cubes and spread
out on another baking tray. Toast in the oven for 10–15
minutes or until dry and crisp. Set aside to cool.

Deep-fry the sage leaves in oil heated to 180°C for
1–2 minutes or until crisp but not too browned. Drain
on kitchen paper.

Rinse the excess salt off the fujiko seaweed, then pat
dry with kitchen paper. Combine the seaweed, bread,
sage and Parmesan on a chopping board and chop all the
ingredients to a crumb, mixing them as you do so. Keep
the crumb in an airtight container until ready to use (it
can be stored for a few days).

_____

CHICKEN GRAVY

olive oil, for cooking
1kg chicken wings
2 carrots, peeled and chopped
1 onion, chopped
1 celery stick, chopped
¼ leek, chopped
½ bulb of garlic, cloves separated
    and chopped
30g tomato paste
250ml dry white wine
rind from a large block
    of Parmesan
1 litre Brown Chicken Stock
    (see page 379)
500ml Veal Stock (see page 380)
1 dried kombu leaf, rinsed in
    cold water
a sprig of sage

2 sprigs of thyme
pared peel from 1 lemon
Maldon sea salt and black pepper

Heat a little olive oil in a large, heavy-based pan, then add the chicken wings. Season with salt and pepper, then fry the wings for 6–8 minutes or until they are a deep golden brown all over. Using tongs, remove the wings to a plate, leaving the fat in the pan.

Add the chopped vegetables and garlic to the pan and fry, stirring occasionally, for 8–10 minutes or until they begin to colour. Stir in the tomato paste and fry for another couple of minutes. Deglaze the pan with the white wine, scraping the bottom and sides to dislodge any browned bits, then boil the wine until reduced by half. Return the chicken wings to the pan and add the Parmesan rind and both stocks. Bring to a simmer, skimming off any froth or scum from the surface, then leave to simmer for 4 hours.

Pass the gravy through a fine sieve into a clean saucepan. Bring to the boil and boil until reduced and slightly thickened. Take the pan off the heat and add the kombu, sage, thyme and lemon peel. Set aside to infuse and cool. Before serving, strain out the aromatics and reheat the gravy.

SLOW-COOKED CHICKEN LEGS

1 litre water
100g fine sea salt
2 bay leaves
2 sprigs of thyme
pared peel from 2 lemons
4 boneless chicken thighs
   (skin on)
olive oil, for cooking

First make a brine. Put the water and salt into a saucepan and bring to the boil, then remove from the heat and add the herbs and lemon zest. Leave to cool and infuse.

Put the chicken thighs into a bowl and pour over the cooled brine. Cover and set aside in the fridge for an hour.

Remove the chicken and rinse off the brine. Put the thighs into a vacuum bag, skin side up, and vacuum-seal the bag. Lower it into a sous vide machine (or water bath) heated to 62°C and cook the chicken for 4 hours.

Remove the vacuum bag and place it on a baking tray so the chicken thighs are skin side down. Set another tray on top and weigh down with a few tins. Leave to press overnight in the fridge.

When ready to serve, remove the chicken thighs from the vacuum bag and pat them dry with kitchen paper. Heat a drizzle of olive oil in a wide pan. Lightly season the chicken, then place them in the hot pan, skin side down. Fry for 2–3 minutes or until the chicken skin is golden brown and crisp. Flip the thighs over and fry the other side for 1–2 minutes. Remove to a plate and leave to rest.

_____

SWEDE PURÉE

1 large swede, peeled and diced
200g unsalted butter

Put the swede into a heavy-based pan with the butter and a pinch each of salt and pepper. Set over a high heat and, as the butter begins to melt, stir so that all the swede dice is coated with butter. Cover the pan with a tight-fitting lid, lower the heat and cook/steam the swede for 15–20 minutes or until it is soft, stirring once or twice.

Tip the swede into a food processor and blitz until very smooth. Taste and adjust the seasoning, then pass the swede purée through a fine sieve back into the saucepan, ready to reheat for serving.

_____

SWEDE & POTATO DISCS

1 small swede, peeled
100ml Pickling Liquid
(see page 376)
2 Desirée potatoes
100g unsalted butter

Very thinly cut the swede into 2.5mm slices using a mandoline. Stack the slices, a few at a time, and use a round 5cm pastry cutter to stamp out neat discs. As you cut each batch, put the discs into a small saucepan with the pickling liquid (this will prevent the swede from discolouring). Gently cook the swede discs in the pickling liquid for 15–18 minutes or until tender. Remove from the heat and set aside, ready to reheat for serving.

Peel and slice the potatoes, then cut discs in the same manner as for the swede. Put the potato discs into a saucepan and pour over just enough water to cover. Add the butter and a generous pinch of salt. Gently cook the potato discs for 10–15 minutes or until tender. Set aside.

_____

CRISPY CHICKEN SKINS

8 pieces of chicken skin (from
a breast)

Preheat the oven to 190°C/170°C fan/Gas Mark 5. Use
a sharp knife to remove any excess fat from the underside
of each piece of chicken skin. Lay out the skins on a
baking tray lined with baking parchment and sprinkle
with a little salt. Place another sheet of baking parchment
on top and weigh down with another heavy baking sheet.
Bake for 40–45 minutes or until the skins are golden
brown and crisp. Transfer to kitchen paper and leave to
cool. If making ahead, store in an airtight container.

————————

SLOW-COOKED EGGS

4 large eggs (ours are from
Heritage Breeds farms)

Slow-cook the eggs in a sous vide machine (or water bath)
at 62°C for 50 minutes. Lift them out and place in a bowl
of iced water to cool. Just before serving, carefully crack
the eggs into a pan of boiling water and heat for 1 minute.
Remove with a flat slotted spoon.

————————

ASSEMBLY

Put a spoonful of swede purée in each large serving
bowl. Arrange the swede and potato discs on top. Slice a
chicken thigh into 2 neat pieces and add to the sides of the
bowl, skin side up. Carefully set a slow-cooked egg in the
centre, then cover it with a generous spoonful of seaweed
crumb. Garnish with a couple of pieces of crispy chicken
skin. Serve at once with an individual jug of chicken
gravy on the side.

Roast Orkney Scallops

with
pommes
soufflés
and
caviar sauce

SERVES 4

LEEK & SHALLOT POWDER

2 shallots, very finely sliced
4 leeks (green parts), very finely
   sliced (save the white parts to
   make the Potato & Leek
   Purée below)

Spread out the shallots on a baking tray. Sprinkle them with a little salt, then place the tray into a dehydrator.

Blanch the leek slices in boiling salted water for 20 seconds, then drain and cool in iced water. Drain again and pat dry with a clean kitchen towel. Spread out the slices on another baking tray and put into the dehydrator with the shallots. Leave to dry out, which may take 8–12 hours. When the shallots and leeks are fully dried, you should be able to snap a slice in half easily.

Use a spice grinder to blitz the dried leeks and shallots with a pinch of sea salt to a fine powder. Store in an airtight container until needed.

ROAST SCALLOPS

4 large, raw Orkney scallops
   (in shell)
olive oil, for cooking
50g unsalted butter
a squeeze of lemon juice
Maldon sea salt and black pepper

To shuck each scallop, insert a shucking knife into the hinge of the shell, then twist to pop it open. Run the knife around the edge of the shell to cut through the membrane holding the shell halves together, then remove the top shell. Run the knife under the scallop meat to remove it. Pull away the dark viscera and skirt (fringe-like membrane), plus the side muscle that attached the scallop to the shell if it is still there and the coral, then rinse the white scallop meat and lay it on a plate lined with kitchen paper to dry (reserve the coral for another recipe). Cover with clingfilm and keep in the fridge until needed.

To pan-roast the scallops, heat a little olive oil in a wide, non-stick frying pan over a high heat. Season the scallops, then place them in the pan, in a ring. Sear for 1–2 minutes or until golden brown on the underside, then flip them over in the order they were added to the pan. Add the butter and, as it melts and foams, spoon it over the scallops while they finish cooking for another minute or so. The scallops are done if they feel slightly springy when pressed. Squeeze a little lemon juice over the scallops, then transfer to a warmed plate.

POTATO & LEEK PURÉE

100g unsalted butter
white part of 4 leeks (reserved
    from Leek & Shallot Powder,
    above), finely sliced
2 shallots, very finely sliced
1 Desirée potato, peeled and
    roughly chopped
200ml Vegetable Stock
    (see page 379)
100ml double cream

Melt the butter in a heavy-based pan and sweat the leeks and shallots, stirring frequently, for about 10 minutes or until the vegetables are soft and translucent but not coloured. Add the potato with a little seasoning. Continue cooking, stirring every so often, until the potato begins to soften. Pour in the vegetable stock and bring to the boil, then boil until reduced by half. Stir in the cream and bring back to the boil. Remove from the heat and pour the contents of the pan into a Thermomix or a strong blender. Blitz until smooth, then check the seasoning. Pass through a fine sieve into a clean pan, ready to reheat for serving.

CONFIT LEMON

100ml water
100g caster sugar
1 lemon

Heat the water and sugar together in a pan, stirring until the sugar has dissolved. Bring to the boil and boil until the syrup reaches around 70°C. Meanwhile, trim the tops and bottoms from the lemon, then peel, removing all the white pith. Cut out the segments from between the membranes. When the sugar syrup has reached temperature, remove from the heat. Gently drop in the lemon segments and leave to cool completely. Transfer to a container, cover and set aside. If making in advance, keep in the fridge but return to room temperature for serving.

POMMES SOUFFLÉS

2 litres vegetable oil
2 large russet potatoes

Divide the oil between two heavy-based pans. Heat one pan of oil to 150°C and the other to 190°C. Meanwhile, peel the potatoes, then slice them very thinly (about 5mm) with a mandoline. Pat them dry with kitchen paper.

It is important to keep the temperature of the oils fairly constant, so work in small batches. Add a batch of potato slices to the first pan of oil (heated to 150°C) and fry, tossing frequently and swirling the potatoes in the oil with a slotted spoon to ensure even cooking. After 3–4 minutes, a skin will have formed around each potato slice. Use the slotted spoon to lift out the potatoes and into the second pan of oil (heated to 190°C). The potatoes will soon begin to puff up. Flip them over to cook the other sides. As soon as they are evenly golden brown, remove them to a tray lined with kitchen paper to drain. Quickly dust the pommes soufflés with a little leek and shallot powder, then keep warm in a low oven until all the potatoes are cooked and you are ready to serve.

CAVIAR SAUCE

50ml Potato & Leek Purée
   (see above)
50ml Petrossian liquid caviar

Gently heat the purée with the liquid caviar in a small saucepan.

ASSEMBLY

extra virgin olive oil, to drizzle

For each serving, place a spoonful of potato and leek purée on a warmed serving plate and set a pan-roasted scallop on top. Drizzle a few drops of extra virgin olive oil around the plate followed by the caviar sauce. Garnish the scallop and plate with a few confit lemon pieces. If you wish, dust the tops of 2 pommes soufflés with a little more leek and shallot powder, then add to the plate, placing one on top of the scallop. Serve immediately.

Pressed Terrine of Guinea Fowl

with
smoked ham
knuckle,
port &
bacon jam
and
summer
vegetables

SERVES 8

HAM KNUCKLE LAYER

2 smoked ham knuckles,
   1–1.2kg each
2 small onions, roughly chopped
1 carrot, peeled and
   roughly chopped
1 celery stick, roughly chopped
1 small garlic clove
2 sprigs of thyme
25g flat-leaf parsley, leaves
   picked and chopped
1–2 tablespoons grain mustard,
   to taste

Put the ham knuckles into a large pan and cover them with cold water. Bring to the boil: the froth that rises to the top will contain all the impurities. Pour away the water and rinse the knuckles under cold, running water. Drain and return to the pan.

Add the chopped vegetables, peeled garlic and thyme to the pan and cover with fresh cold water. Bring to the boil, then leave to simmer gently for 4–5 hours or until the meat is very tender. To check if the knuckles are ready, pull out the small bone close to the large one – it should be loose and come out easily. Take the pan off the heat and leave the knuckles to cool slowly in the stock.

Once cooled, remove the knuckles (reserve the stock) and pull the meat from the bone, leaving it in large pieces. Carefully pick off and discard any remaining fat or sinew. Set the meat aside. Measure out about 1 litre of the stock and strain it into another saucepan. Boil until reduced by half.

Add the knuckle meat and stir to coat. Stir in the chopped parsley and grain mustard to taste. Put the mixture into a vacuum bag measuring 15cm x 20cm and press out the ingredients to form a rectangle 3cm thick. Vacuum-seal the bag and chill to set.

GUINEA FOWL LAYER

2 oven-ready guinea fowl
Meat Brine (see Braised West
   Country Ox Cheek recipe,
   page 232)
1 garlic clove

2 sprigs of thyme
about 200g duck fat, melted
50ml Chicken Gravy (see Slow-
    cooked Heritage Breeds Egg
    recipe, page 71)

Carve out the breasts and legs from the guinea fowl.
Place the breasts and legs in one large resealable bag and
pour over enough meat brine to cover. Seal and leave in
the fridge for an hour. Rinse off the brine and pat the
breasts and legs dry with kitchen paper. Lay them out on
a tray lined with a tea towel and leave to dry out in the
fridge for a couple of hours.

To confit the guinea fowl legs, put them into a pan with
the peeled garlic and thyme and pour over enough duck
fat to cover. Simmer gently over the lowest heat for about
2 hours or until the meat is very tender and falling off the
bone. (When slow-cooking like this, do not let the fat get
too hot or the legs will begin to fry and dry out.) Take
the pan off the heat and leave the legs to cool completely
in the fat. Once cooled, remove the legs and strip off the
skin, fat and any sinew with a knife. Pull the meat away
from the bones and tear it into rough pieces. Place in a
bowl, cover with clingfilm and set aside in the fridge.

To cook the guinea fowl breasts, put them into vacuum
bags and vacuum-seal. Cook in a sous vide machine (or
water bath) heated to 62°C for an hour. Immediately
transfer the bags to a bowl of iced water to stop the
cooking process. Once cooled, remove the breasts from
the bags and cut them in half lengthways.

Gently heat the chicken gravy, then add both the leg and
breast meat and toss to coat. Put the guinea fowl mixture
into a vacuum bag measuring 15cm x 20cm. Press out the
mixture to form a rectangle 3cm thick (the same size as
the knuckle meat mixture). Vacuum-seal it, then chill for
at least an hour or until firm.

PRESSED TERRINE

Remove the ham and guinea fowl layers from their
vacuum bags and place them on a baking sheet. Use a
blowtorch to warm the top of each layer, then carefully
place one on top of the other, with the warmed sides
touching. Cover the assembled terrine with clingfilm,
then weigh it down with a chopping board. Leave in the
fridge to set for at least an hour or until ready to serve.

PORT & BACON JAM

1kg red onions, sliced
100g Alsace smoked bacon
750ml ruby port
50ml red wine vinegar
Maldon sea salt and black pepper

Put the onions, bacon, port and vinegar into a heavy-based pan and bring to a simmer, then cook for 1–1½ hours or until the port has reduced and the onions are soft and sticky. Remove and discard the bacon, then scrape the onions into a blender or food processor and blitz until smooth. Taste and adjust the seasoning with salt and pepper. Pass the onion jam through a fine sieve and store in a clean jar (or a piping bag if using soon).

LEEK & MUSHROOM POWDER

3 leeks
100g dried ceps

Bring a large pan of salted water to the boil and have ready a bowl of iced water on the side. Very finely slice the leeks, then blanch in the boiling salted water for 20 seconds. Drain and immediately refresh them in the iced water. Drain again, then pat dry with a clean tea towel. Spread out the leeks on a baking sheet and place in a dehydrator set to 75°C. Leave for 4 hours or until completely dried out. Transfer the leeks to a spice grinder. Add the dried ceps and a pinch of salt, and grind to a fine powder. Store the powder in an airtight bottle or container.

ASSEMBLY

Summer Vegetables (see Pressed
    Norfolk Quail & Duck Liver
    recipe, page 61, without the
    truffle trimmings)
1 truffle, for slicing
a handful of baby leaves and
    micro herbs

Unwrap the terrine and cut into thick slices, trimming the edges if necessary. Place a slice on each serving plate, then pipe a generous mound of port and bacon jam next to it. Arrange the summer vegetables in a neat row alongside and garnish the vegetables with a few truffle slices, baby leaves and micro herbs. Lightly dust the jam with the leek and mushroom powder.

Braised Broccoli

with
broccoli
purée,
seaweed
powder
and
toasted
almonds

BRAISED BROCCOLI

1kg heads of broccoli
a knob of unsalted butter,
    for emulsion
Seaweed Powder (see below)
Maldon sea salt

Bring a pan of salted water to the boil and have ready a
bowl of iced water. Quarter the broccoli head, cutting
through the stalk, then cut the florets from their stems.
Set the florets aside for the seaweed powder. Peel the
tough skins from the stems (still attached to the stalk)
to reveal the tender core. The peeled stem quarters
will now resemble corals. (Save any broccoli leaves and
trimmings for the seaweed powder.)

Blanch the broccoli stem quarters in the boiling salted
water for 2–3 minutes or until just tender but still green.
Use a slotted spoon or tongs to transfer them to the bowl
of iced water (this will stop the cooking process and
retain the colour). Once cooled, drain well, then lay the
stem quarters out on a tray lined with kitchen paper to
dry. Keep in the fridge until needed.

Before serving, warm up the blanched broccoli quarters
in an emulsion of salted water and butter. When heated
through, use tongs to transfer them to a plate, then dust
liberally with seaweed powder.

SEAWEED POWDER

broccoli leaves and trimmings
    (see above)
100g instant dashi powder
2 sheets of nori

Blanch the reserved broccoli trimmings (including the
florets) in boiling salted water for about 3 minutes or
until tender but still green. Drain and refresh in a bowl
of iced water, then drain again. Spread out on a tray, then
dry in a dehydrator for about 6 hours or until completely
dried out but still green.

Put the dried broccoli trimmings into a spice grinder and
add the dashi powder. Tear the nori sheets into smaller
pieces and add to the grinder as well. Grind to a fine
powder. Store in an airtight container (the powder can be
kept for a week).

BROCCOLI PURÉE

1 large head of broccoli, about 1kg
100ml double cream

Cut off the broccoli florets, then cut them into smaller florets. Trim off any woody parts of the stem and peel it, then chop the stem into small pieces. Blanch the florets and stems in boiling salted water for 3–4 minutes or until tender. At the same time, bring the cream to a simmer in a heavy-based saucepan, then simmer to reduce slightly.

When the broccoli is tender, use a slotted spoon to transfer the florets and stems to a blender. Pour in the hot cream and add a pinch each of salt and pepper. Blitz to a smooth purée. Taste and adjust the seasoning. Pass the purée through a fine sieve into a bowl. Leave to cool completely, then cover and keep in the fridge until needed. Reheat for serving.

―――――――――

TOASTED ALMOND FLAKES

250g unsalted butter
200g flaked almonds

Melt the butter in a heavy-based pan until foaming. Add the almonds and toss to coat. Toast over a medium heat, tossing occasionally, until the almonds are a light golden brown. Tip on to a tray lined with kitchen paper and sprinkle with a little sea salt. If preparing ahead, store the cooled toasted almonds in an airtight jar.

―――――――――

ASSEMBLY

Lemon Purée (see page 384)
1–2 tablespoons chopped
   toasted almonds
2–3 sheets of nori, very
   finely shredded
a handful of wood sorrel leaves
a handful of smoked almonds
extra virgin olive oil, to drizzle

Pipe a line of lemon purée in the centre of each serving plate and top this with a little chopped toasted almond. Place a blanched broccoli quarter on one side of the line and a neat quenelle of broccoli purée on the other. Garnish the broccoli quarter with nori strips and wood sorrel leaves. Top the broccoli purée with 5 toasted almond flakes. Garnish the plate with 5 smoked almonds. Finally, drizzle a little extra virgin olive oil around the plate and serve immediately.

Tomato Tartare

with
verjus
granita
and
sourdough
croutons

SERVES 6

TOMATO TARTARE

12 San Marzano tomatoes
2 teaspoons olive oil
2 shallots, finely diced
1 garlic clove, crushed
Maldon sea salt and black pepper

Bring a large pot of water to the boil and have ready a bowl of iced water.
Score the tops and bottoms of the tomatoes with a sharp knife, removing the
eye of each tomato with the tip of the knife. In 2 batches, blanch the tomatoes
in the boiling water for 10 seconds, then use a slotted spoon to fish them out
and refresh them in the iced water. Once cooled, drain the tomatoes and peel
off the skins. Cut the peeled tomatoes into quarters and remove the seeds
(these can be reserved for soups or sauces). Pat each tomato quarter dry with
kitchen paper then roughly dice into 5mm squares. Set aside.

In a medium pan, heat the olive oil over a medium-low heat, add the shallots
and garlic, and sauté for a few minutes, stirring occasionally. Add the diced
tomatoes and gently cook for about 15 minutes or until the shallots are soft
and any liquid released by the tomatoes has reduced. Use a slotted spoon to
scoop out the tomatoes and shallots into a bowl. Continue to simmer the
liquid remaining in the pan until reduced to a syrupy consistency.

Return the tomatoes and shallots to the pan and mix with the syrupy glaze.
Take the pan off the heat and leave to cool, then season the tomatoes well with
salt and pepper. Keep in a covered bowl in the fridge until ready to serve.

DRESSING

70ml light soy sauce
5 dashes of Tabasco sauce
200ml tomato ketchup
10g ready-made English mustard
2 teaspoons brandy
1 tablespoon Worcestershire sauce

Put all of the ingredients into a bowl and use a stick blender to blend them
together until smooth. Transfer the dressing to a screwtop jar and set aside.

VERJUS GRANITA

200ml Muscat verjus
500ml water
50g caster sugar

Combine the ingredients in a saucepan and stir over a medium heat until the
sugar has dissolved. Pour the mixture into a bowl and leave to cool completely.

Transfer to a freezerproof container, cover and freeze for at least 4–6 hours, or overnight, until set.

———————————

SOURDOUGH CROUTONS

¼ loaf of sourdough bread
olive oil, for drizzling

Freeze the sourdough for 30–45 minutes until firm. Preheat the oven to 160°C/140°C fan/Gas Mark 3. Use a meat slicer to slice the bread very thinly. (If you don't have a meat slicer, use a serrated bread knife to slice it by hand as thinly as possible). Arrange the sliced bread in one layer on a baking tray. Drizzle over a little olive oil and season with salt and pepper. Bake for about 10 minutes or until the sourdough is golden and crisp. Leave to cool before storing in an airtight container.

———————————

ASSEMBLY

tahini paste
6–8 mixed baby heritage tomatoes of various sizes
Black Olive Crumb (see Newquay Day Boat Red
    Mullet recipe, page 171), for sprinkling
mixed summer herbs
edible flowers

Dress the tomato tartare just before you are ready to serve. For every 3 tablespoons of tomato and shallot mixture, add a teaspoon of dressing and a teaspoon of tahini paste. Set aside to allow the flavours to infuse for a few minutes. Meanwhile, cut the mixed baby tomatoes into quarters.

For each serving, place a plain ring cutter (10–12cm in diameter) on a serving plate and spoon in the tomato tartare. Use the back of the spoon to smooth and level the surface. Sprinkle with a little black olive crumb. Lift off the ring cutter and garnish the tartare with the quartered tomatoes and mixed herbs or leaves. Break the sourdough slices into shards and stick a few around the tartare, then garnish with a few flowers. Remove the verjus granita from the freezer and scrape it into crystals with a fork. Place a scoop of granita in a separate small serving bowl and serve immediately with the tomato tartare.

Onion Squash Soup

with
white
asparagus
and
sautéed
mushrooms

SERVES 6

_____

ONION SQUASH SOUP

  2 onion squash
  500ml Vegetable Stock
    (see page 379)
  200ml Vegetarian Dashi
    (see page 377)
  200ml plain yoghurt
  Maldon sea salt and black pepper

Preheat the oven to 160°C/140°C fan/Gas Mark 3. Wash the squash and cut each in half. Scoop out and discard the seeds and fibres, then wrap the squash halves in foil. Place on a baking tray. Bake for about 1 hour or until the squash is soft.

Unwrap the squash and place in a saucepan. Add the stock and dashi. Bring to a simmer and cook for 10–15 minutes or until the squash is very soft, including the skins. Transfer the mixture to a blender and blitz until very smooth. Add the yoghurt and season to taste – you want the soup to have a nice balance of savouriness and acidity. Pass the soup through a fine sieve into a clean saucepan.

Before serving, reheat the soup, then use a stick blender to blitz it until it is light and foamy.

_____

WHITE ASPARAGUS

  4 white asparagus spears
  250ml water
  125g unsalted butter
  1½ teaspoons sherry vinegar
  ½ white onion, sliced
  1 bay leaf
  2 sprigs of thyme, leaves picked
  8g Maldon sea salt
  2 teaspoons caster sugar

Peel the stems of the asparagus using a fine vegetable peeler, then cut them across into finger-length pieces, discarding the woody ends. Put all the remaining ingredients into a saucepan and bring to the boil. Reduce the heat, then add the asparagus and simmer for 3–4 minutes or until just tender. Remove from the heat and leave the asparagus to cool in the cooking liquor. Reheat for serving.

_____

SQUASH BALLS

1 butternut squash
100ml orange juice

Cut the butternut squash in half lengthways. Scoop out the seeds and fibres with a spoon and discard. Use a Parisian scoop to cut out neat balls from the flesh. Put the squash balls into a saucepan and pour in the orange juice. Bring to a simmer and cook until the orange juice has reduced to a syrup and the squash balls are coated in the syrupy glaze. Keep warm.

ASSEMBLY

500ml Parmesan Foam (see New
    Forest Mushroom Tea recipe,
    page 33)
Parmesan, for grating
mixed sautéed mushrooms
    (whatever is in season: girolles,
    morels, ceps, etc)
a handful of purple shamrock or
    sorrel leaves
1 black truffle, for shaving

Put the Parmesan foam mixture into a saucepan and add a grating of parmesan. Reheat until the mixture is hot, then pour it into an iSi whipper canister and charge it with 3 canisters of gas.

Arrange a few sautéed mushrooms, squash balls and drained white asparagus pieces in each of 6 wide serving bowls. Ladle the hot, foamy soup into the bowls, then garnish with a few purple shamrock or sorrel leaves and some truffle shavings.

Shellfish

Dressed
Paignton Harbour Crab
102

Fruits of the Sea
108

Isle of Mull
Langoustine
116

Raw
Orkney Scallop
122

Roast
Orkney Scallops
126

Paignton Harbour Crab
132

St Austell Bay
Lobster
136

St Austell Bay
Mussel Purée
144

Dressed Paignton Harbour Crab

with
crab jelly,
bread foam
and lemon
purée

SERVES 4-6

CRAB JELLY

1kg crab shells
olive oil, for cooking
1 small onion, chopped
1 carrot, peeled and chopped
1½ celery sticks, chopped
1 small bulb of fennel, chopped
2 garlic cloves, chopped
2 bay leaves
1 tablespoon tomato paste
100ml brandy
2.5 litres Fish Stock
   (see page 378)
1 tablespoon white peppercorns
6 large egg whites,
   lightly whisked
a handful of tarragon
2g agar agar powder
Maldon sea salt and black pepper

Crush the crab shells into smaller pieces using the back of a cleaver or rolling pin. Heat a little olive oil in a wide, heavy-based pan until hot, then add the crushed shells. Fry over a high heat, stirring frequently, for 4–5 minutes or until golden brown. Remove the shells to a plate and set aside. Add a little more oil to the pan followed by the chopped vegetables, garlic, bay leaves and tomato paste. Fry, stirring, for 8–10 minutes or until the vegetables are golden brown.

Deglaze the pan with the brandy, scraping the bottom well. Let the brandy boil until reduced by half, then pour in the fish stock and add the peppercorns. Return the crab shells to the pan and top up with a little water if the liquid does not cover the shells. Bring to a simmer, then cook gently for 40 minutes. Take the pan off the heat and leave to cool for about 20 minutes.

Now clarify the stock. Strain it through a fine sieve into a clean saucepan, pressing down on the solids with the back of a ladle to extract all the flavourful juices (discard the solids). Add the egg whites to the stock, then set the pan over a high heat. As the stock begins to simmer, the egg whites will form a foamy raft on the top and trap any impurities in the liquid. Ladle the stock and egg white raft into a fine sieve lined with muslin (do not crush or break up the raft) and allow to strain through into a bowl. Once all the stock has been strained, add the tarragon and leave to cool and infuse.

Measure out 200ml of the clarified stock (discard the tarragon) and mix it with the agar agar powder in a saucepan. Set the pan over a high heat and simmer for about 5 minutes until the agar agar has fully dissolved. Check the seasoning. Pour the stock into a baking tray to make a thin layer (about 2mm deep). Leave to cool completely, then chill for a few hours until set.

CRAB POWDER

250g brown crab meat
a drizzle of soy sauce
a drizzle of mirin

Put the brown crab meat, soy sauce and mirin into a blender and blitz until smooth. Pass the mixture through a fine sieve into a freezerproof container. Cover and freeze for a few hours until the crab purée is solid.

Using a microplane, finely grate the frozen crab purée on to a baking tray lined with a silicone mat. Put the tray into a dehydrator and dry out for 2 hours to a fine powder. Store in an airtight container (can be kept for 3 days).

BREAD FOAM

250g sourdough bread trimmings
    and crusts
125ml balsamic vinegar reduction
50ml olive oil
2 sprigs of thyme
½ bulb of garlic, cloves separated
1 litre whole milk
a squeeze of lime juice

Preheat the oven to 180°C/160°C fan/Gas Mark 4. Chop the sourdough trimmings and place them in a baking tray. Pour over the balsamic vinegar and olive oil, and sprinkle with salt and pepper. Add the thyme and peeled garlic to the tray. Toast the bread in the oven for 10–12 minutes or until the pieces are golden brown.

Tip the bread pieces into a pan. Pour over enough milk to cover the bread, then bring to a simmer over a medium heat. Simmer for 10–12 minutes or until the bread is soft. Transfer the contents of the pan to a blender and add a little more milk, then blitz until smooth. Taste and adjust the seasoning with salt, pepper, balsamic vinegar and lime juice. Pour the mixture into an iSi whipper and charge it with 2 canisters of gas. Keep warm until ready to serve.

DRESSED CRAB

500g white crab meat
mayonnaise, to bind
2 Granny Smith apples
a squeeze of lime juice

Pick out and discard any pieces of shell or cartilage from the crab meat. Put it into a mixing bowl and stir in just enough mayonnaise to bind the crab meat together. Season to taste with salt and pepper.

Peel the apples and cut into 1cm dice. Immediately squeeze over a little lime juice to prevent the apples from oxidising. Add the diced apples to the crab meat and mix well. Keep in the fridge until needed.

ASSEMBLY

picked sea herbs
Lemon Purée (see page 384)
12–18 very thinly sliced
    sourdough croutons, toasted

For each serving, use an 8–9cm round pastry cutter to stamp out a neat disc of crab jelly and carefully place it on a serving plate. Pile a neat spoonful of dressed crab on top of the jelly. Garnish it with picked sea herbs. Squeeze little dots of lemon purée around the plate and add a small mound of bread foam on one side of the plate. Sprinkle crab powder on top of the bread foam. Finally, garnish the dressed crab with 3 slices of toasted sourdough croutons and serve immediately.

Fruits of the Sea

with
oyster ice
cream
and
tomato foam

SERVES 12

OYSTER ICE CREAM

1 litre whole milk
1 litre double cream
300g dextrose
15 large egg yolks
2.8kg shucked drained oysters, puréed
12 cleaned oyster shells, to serve
oyster leaves, to garnish

Pour the milk and cream into a heavy-based saucepan and heat until bubbles appear around the edge. Meanwhile, whisk together the dextrose and egg yolks in a large bowl. When the creamy milk is hot, gradually pour it into the egg mixture, stirring constantly. When fully incorporated, return the mixture to the pan and stir over a medium heat until thickened to a light custard (about 84°C).

Transfer the custard to a blender and add the oyster purée. Blitz until smooth, then pass through a fine sieve. Pour the mixture into an ice cream machine and churn until almost firm. Scrape the oyster ice cream into a freezerproof container, cover and freeze for a few hours until set. (If using a Pacojet machine, freeze the ice cream base in Pacojet containers until solid, then process in the Pacojet machine shortly before serving.)

Just before serving, spoon a neat quenelle of oyster ice cream into each cleaned oyster shell and garnish with an oyster leaf.

TOMATO FOAM

500g vine-ripened plum tomatoes, roughly chopped
150ml spring water
1 small shallot, diced
½ teaspoon caster sugar
2 basil leaves
2 small slices of garlic
1 small dried kombu leaf
1¼ gelatine leaves
100ml double cream
extra virgin olive oil, to drizzle

Put the tomatoes, water, shallot, sugar, basil and garlic into a blender and blitz for a few minutes until smooth. Pour the mixture into a fine sieve lined with a piece of muslin and set over a bowl; gather the muslin into a bag and hang it over the bowl, then let the juices slowly drip through for a few hours or overnight.

Pour the strained juice into a saucepan and bring to the boil. Boil until reduced by half. Add the kombu and take the pan off the heat. Leave to infuse for 15 minutes, then remove the kombu and discard.

Meanwhile, soak the gelatine in cold water for a couple of minutes until soft. Warm up the tomato juice again. Squeeze any excess water from the gelatine, then add to the juice and stir until melted. Strain the tomato mixture through a fine sieve into a bowl.

Pour in the cream. Set the bowl over a larger bowl of ice water and whisk frequently until the mixture is cold. Pour it into an iSi whipper, charge with 2 canisters of gas and shake well. Keep in the fridge until ready to serve.

LETTUCE & CUCUMBER JELLY

125g green lettuce heads
125g peeled, chopped cucumber
1 gelatine leaf
a handful of finely diced pickled cucumber
a handful of dill, leaves picked and chopped
cooked lobster meat, from 1–2 claws, chopped
Tomato Foam (see above)
extra virgin olive oil, to drizzle

Bring a pan of salted water to the boil and have ready a bowl of iced water. Blanch the lettuce heads for a minute, then refresh them in the iced water. Drain the lettuce, then put through a juicer followed by the cucumber. Pour the juice into a fine sieve lined with muslin and set over a bowl. Gather the ends of the muslin to make a bag and hang it over the bowl. Leave to drip through for a few hours or overnight.

Measure out 200ml of the strained lettuce and cucumber juice and pour it into a small saucepan. (Any remaining juice can be used for smoothies.) Soak the gelatine in a bowl of cold water for a few minutes. Gently heat the juice until it is warm. Squeeze excess water from the gelatine, then add to the pan and swirl the liquid until the gelatine has melted. Strain the juice through a fine sieve into a jug.

Mix together the pickled cucumber and dill. Spoon into 12 small individual ramekins or serving bowls (about 90ml capacity). Half-fill the ramekins with the lettuce and cucumber juice. Leave in the fridge for a few hours to set.

Just before serving, top each jelly with a tablespoon of chopped lobster meat, then cover it with a layer of tomato foam. Drizzle a few drops of extra virgin olive oil on top of the foam.

BROWN CRAB BISQUE

olive oil, for cooking
1kg crushed crab shells
4 carrots, peeled and chopped
4 onions, chopped
2 celery sticks, chopped
1 leek, chopped
8 plum tomatoes, chopped

1 bulb of garlic, cloves separated and chopped

½ teaspoon coriander seeds

1 star anise

1 clove

2 tablespoons tomato paste

300ml brandy

1.5 litres Fish Stock (see page 378)

1 litre whole milk

500ml double cream

4 sprigs of tarragon

4 gelatine leaves

100g cooked and picked white crab meat

1 tablespoon crème fraîche

a squeeze of lemon juice

1 small can (30g) Ossetra caviar (we use Petrossian)

Heat a little olive oil in a large, heavy-based pan over a high heat. Add the crushed crab shells and fry, stirring often, for 5–6 minutes or until the shells have turned red and smell fragrant. Remove them to a large plate and set aside.

Add a little more oil to the pan followed by the chopped vegetables, garlic and spices. Cook over a high heat, stirring frequently, for 10–12 minutes or until the vegetables have softened but not browned. Stir in the tomato paste and cook for a further 5 minutes, stirring frequently. Return the crab shells to the pan, then pour in the brandy. Set the brandy alight. Once the flames have died down, add the fish stock, milk and cream. Mix well. Bring to a simmer, then leave to cook gently for 40 minutes.

Remove from the heat. Slightly bruise the tarragon sprigs and add to the hot stock. Leave to cool and infuse for 20 minutes.

Strain the stock through a fine sieve, pushing down with the back of a ladle to extract all the flavourful juices. Discard the solids. Measure out 1 litre of stock and pour it into a clean saucepan. (Any extra stock can be used for soups or sauces.) Soak the gelatine leaves in cold water for a couple of minutes. Meanwhile, gently heat the stock. Squeeze excess water from the gelatine leaves, then add to the hot stock and stir until the gelatine has melted. Strain the stock again through a fine sieve. Pour into 12 small serving bowls or ramekins (50ml capacity) to half fill them. Chill for a few hours until set.

Mix together the crab meat, crème fraîche, lemon juice and salt and pepper to taste in a small bowl. Cover with clingfilm and keep in the fridge until needed.

Just before serving, top each ramekin of brown crab bisque jelly with a layer of the crab mixture, then garnish with a small spoonful of caviar.

RAW SCALLOPS WITH JALAPEÑO GRANITA

¼ small mooli (Japanese daikon)

Pickling Liquid (see page 376)

2 very fresh, large, raw Orkney scallops (in shell)

Wasabi & Yuzu Dressing (see Raw Orkney Scallop
  recipe, page 124)

12 queen scallop shells, cleaned
Black Olive Oil (see page 381)
Lemon Purée (see 384)
a small handful of blanched sea herbs
Jalapeño Granita (see Raw Orkney Scallop recipe,
    page 124)

Peel the mooli and cut into a fine dice, then place in a vacuum bag. Pour in enough pickling liquid to cover the mooli. Vacuum-seal the bag and leave in the fridge to pickle for about 10 minutes.

Prepare the scallops shortly before serving. Shuck and clean them (see Roast Orkney Scallops, page 77); save the coral roe for another dish. Dice the scallops and place them in a bowl. Add a couple of tablespoons of wasabi and yuzu dressing and toss the scallops to coat.

Drain the pickling liquid from the mooli and add a tablespoon of diced mooli to the scallops. Mix well. Spoon the mixture into the queen scallop shells. Dress each one with a little drizzle of black olive oil and lemon purée. Garnish each with a few blanched sea herbs. At the last minute, top each scallop shell with a spoonful of jalapeño granita.

ASSEMBLY

To assemble the dish, fill 6 two-tiered seafood stands with crushed ice (this is served as a sharing dish for 2). Place the scallop shells, lettuce and cucumber jellies, brown crab bisque jellies and oyster ice cream in shells on the ice. Serve immediately.

Keltic Seafare

Since 1992 Keltic Seafare has steadily grown to become Scotland's number one live shellfish supplier.

Our scallops and langoustines are among the most sustainable on the market, and are of the highest quality. Our products are fished daily in the pristine waters of the north-west Highlands, the Inner and Outer Hebrides and the Orkney Islands. The fishing zones range from Mallaig, through the Kyle of Lochalsh and then up past Gairloch, Ullapool, the Summer Isles and to the far north of the Scottish Highlands.

The main season for langoustine is winter, while big scallops are readily available during the summer months.

Our scallops are gathered by divers by hand, which ensures that all scallops under the minimum landing size are left to grow and spawn in later years. Thus the impact on the environment is low and the seabed ecology is protected.

All our live langoustines and lobsters are caught by a fishing method using baited creels, also known as lobster pots. This method involves small fishing boats manned by one or two fishermen baiting and dropping creels, then returning the next day to pull the creels back aboard. The langoustines and lobsters emerge from the creels undamaged and in good, active condition.

We work with Pollen Street Social to supply shellfish of the highest standard and quality, which we know is very much appreciated by a Michelin-starred restaurant. We speak to the chefs Roddy, Roy and Kostas on a daily basis, keeping them updated on availability. If the size they require is not available, we supply them with an alternative product of their choice. We always joke about the weather with Roddy, who is from Oban in Scotland, and so knows all about the Scottish weather conditions – especially the rain!

kelticseafare.com

Isle of Mull Langoustine

with
braised
oxtail
and
Parmesan
rice

SERVES 6

LANGOUSTINE BISQUE & TAILS

    6 extra-large langoustines
    olive oil, for cooking
    1 large white onion, roughly chopped
    1 large donkey carrot, peeled and roughly chopped
    1 celery stick, roughly chopped
    1 leek (white part), roughly chopped
    3 garlic cloves, roughly chopped
    1 lemongrass stick, crushed with a heavy pan
    1 red chilli, cut in half lengthways and deseeded
    50g root ginger, peeled and sliced
    1 teaspoon coriander seeds
    1 teaspoon fennel seeds
    2 tablespoons tomato paste
    100ml brandy
    1 litre Fish Stock (see page 378)
    1 litre whole milk
    500ml double cream
    Maldon sea salt and black pepper

Separate the langoustine heads and claws from the tails; set the heads
and claws aside. Straighten 2 tails and tie them together with the undersides
touching so that they will remain straight during cooking. Repeat to tie 3
more pairs of langoustine tails. Bring a large pan of salted water to a rolling
boil and have a large bowl of iced water on the side. Blanch the langoustine
tails in the boiling water for 10 seconds, then immediately lift them out
and immerse them in the iced water to stop the cooking process. Leave
for 2 minutes, then remove and untie the pairs. Peel off the shells (do this
carefully as the tail meat has not been cooked through at this point and it is
very delicate); reserve the shells. Place the tails on a plate or tray lined with a
kitchen towel, cover with clingfilm and keep in the fridge until ready to cook.

Heat a little oil in a large pot, add the reserved langoustine heads, claws
and shells, and fry, stirring occasionally, for 4–5 minutes or until golden
brown. Remove them to a plate and set aside. Add a little more oil to the pan
followed by the chopped onion, carrot, celery, leek and garlic. Sauté for 8–10
minutes or until the vegetables are golden brown, stirring every once in a
while. Add the lemongrass, chilli, ginger, and coriander and fennel seeds and
stir to mix. Cook for 2 minutes, then stir in the tomato paste and fry for a
couple of minutes. Return all but a few langoustine heads, claws and shells to
the pan and lightly crush them with a wooden spoon or a rolling pin. Deglaze
with the brandy, scraping the bottom of the pan well, and bubble until
reduced by half. Pour in the fish stock, milk and cream. If the liquid does not
cover the ingredients, top up with a little water. Bring to a simmer, then
cook gently for 20 minutes. Take the pan off the heat and leave to cool for
20 minutes.

A ladleful at a time, pass the stock through a mouli into a bowl, crushing all
the vegetables, langoustine heads and claws to extract the flavourful juices.
Strain the stock through a fine sieve into a clean saucepan. Return to the heat

and boil until reduced by half, or to the desired intensity – you want the bisque to have a deep, rich langoustine flavour with a hint of spice in the background. Take the pan off the heat and leave to cool, then set aside until needed.

To cook the langoustine tails for serving, you can use a ridged grill pan, frying pan or barbecue. Spear the tails lengthways on metal skewers, then brush them with a little olive oil and season with salt and pepper. Grill them on a hot pan or barbecue for 1½–2 minutes on each side or until they are opaque, firm and just cooked through. Leave the tails to rest for a couple of minutes.

Before serving the bisque, reheat it with the reserved langoustine heads and shells, then strain. Use a stick blender to froth the bisque.

BRAISED OXTAIL

1 large oxtail, about 1.5kg, cut into chunky pieces
olive oil, for cooking
2 onions, chopped
2 carrots, peeled and chopped
1 bulb of garlic, cloves separated and chopped
500ml red wine
1 litre Veal Stock (see page 380)
1 litre Brown Chicken Stock (see page 379)
2 sprigs of thyme
2 bay leaves

Preheat the oven to 150°C/130°C fan/Gas Mark 2. Heat a little oil in a wide ovenproof pan. Season the oxtail, then brown, in several batches, in the hot oil, searing each side for about 2 minutes or until golden brown. Remove the browned oxtail to a large plate and set aside.

Add a little more oil to the pan. Tip in the chopped vegetables and garlic and sauté, stirring occasionally, for 8–10 minutes or until golden brown. Pour in the red wine and let it boil until reduced by half. Return the oxtail to the pan and pour in the veal and chicken stocks. If the liquid does not cover the oxtail, top up with a little water. Add the thyme and bay leaves. Bring to a simmer, skimming off any froth and scum from the surface, then cover the pan with a lid or foil. Transfer to the oven and braise the oxtail for 5–6 hours or until the meat is very tender.

Remove from the oven and leave to cool slightly, then, wearing kitchen rubber gloves, pull the meat from the bones and shred it into stringy pieces; discard the bones.

Strain the braising liquid through a fine sieve into a clean saucepan. Boil until reduced to a rich, sticky glaze. Take the pan off the heat and add the shredded meat to the sauce, stirring to ensure that the meat is well coated. Cover the pan and set aside, ready to reheat for serving.

LANGOUSTINE STOCK

1kg langoustine heads and shells
2 bulbs of fennel, chopped
2 onions, chopped
1 leek, chopped
1 celery stick, chopped
1 bay leaf
1 tablespoon fennel seeds
1 tablespoon coriander seeds
2 litres water
2 dried kombu leaves
rind of a 1kg piece of 36-month-aged Parmesan
100g bonito flakes

Put the langoustine heads and shells, the vegetables, bay leaf and seeds into
a saucepan and pour in the water. Bring to the boil, skimming off any froth or
scum from the surface. Lower the heat, partially cover the pan with a lid and
leave to simmer gently for an hour. Take the pan off the heat and leave to
cool completely.

Strain the stock through a fine sieve into a clean saucepan, pressing down on
the vegetables and langoustine shells to extract the juices. Bring the stock to
a simmer, then add the kombu and Parmesan rind. Remove from the heat and
let the stock infuse and cool to about 50°C. Stir in the bonito flakes, then leave
to cool completely. Strain through a fine sieve into a measuring jug. Set aside
or keep in the fridge until needed.

PARMESAN RICE

olive oil, for cooking
2 shallots, finely diced
250g 7-year-aged Acquerello risotto rice
100ml dry white wine
200g 36-month-aged Parmesan, finely grated
   with a microplane

Heat 700ml of the langoustine stock in a small saucepan. Meanwhile, heat
a little olive oil in a heavy-based pan over a medium heat, add the shallots and
sweat, stirring frequently, for 5–6 minutes or until they begin to soften and
become translucent. Tip in the rice and increase the heat slightly. Stir for 1
minute to coat the rice grains with oil and shallots. Pour in the white wine
and bubble, stirring, until the wine has reduced by half. Add a ladleful of the
hot stock and cook, stirring constantly, until the stock has almost all been
absorbed by the rice. Continue to add the stock, a ladleful at a time, making
sure that the rice has absorbed each addition before adding the next. It should
take about 15 minutes to cook the risotto. When ready it should be thick and
glossy, with the rice al dente (tender but with a slight bite of texture – you
may not need all the stock). If you want to serve the risotto straight away, stir
in the Parmesan and season to taste with salt and pepper.

If preparing the risotto in advance, as soon as the rice is al dente (before
adding the Parmesan), spread it out on a wide baking tray to cool down

quickly, then cover with clingfilm and put the tray into a blast chiller if you have one, or the freezer for a short time followed by the fridge. Before serving, reheat the risotto and heat the remaining langoustine stock in another saucepan. A ladleful at a time, add the hot stock to the risotto, stirring until the stock has been absorbed – add only enough to loosen the consistency. Then add the Parmesan and seasoning.

ASSEMBLY

For each serving, spoon some risotto into a warmed serving bowl, then arrange braised shredded oxtail around the bowl. Spoon over a little oxtail braising sauce. Arrange langoustine tails on top of the risotto. Froth up the langoustine bisque with a stick blender and add 2 tablespoons of the froth to one side of the bowl. Serve immediately.

Raw Orkney Scallop

with
pear purée,
pickled
turnip
and
jalapeño
granita

SERVES 4

JALAPEÑO GRANITA

125g caster sugar
125ml cold water
300ml fresh lime juice
150ml fresh apple juice
50ml fresh cucumber juice
60g fresh jalapeño peppers, deseeded and diced

Put the sugar and water into a saucepan and stir over a medium heat just until the sugar has dissolved. Leave the sugar syrup to cool. Meanwhile, blitz together all the remaining ingredients in a strong blender until very smooth. Strain the mixture through a fine sieve into a large freezerproof container (with a lid). Stir in the sugar syrup. Cover the container and freeze for a few hours or overnight until solid.

PEAR PURÉE

1kg ready-made pear purée (we use Boivron purées)
2g agar agar powder

Put the purée into a saucepan and bring to a rapid boil. Add the agar agar and boil for another couple of minutes, stirring constantly. Pour and spread the purée on to a baking tray and immediately put the tray into a blast chiller (the purée will discolour if not cooled quickly). When cold, transfer the purée to a blender and blitz until smooth. Pass through a fine sieve, then transfer to a squeezy bottle.

WASABI & YUZU DRESSING

100ml olive oil
2 garlic cloves, finely crushed
60ml yuzu juice
50ml light soy sauce
50ml white soy sauce
20g fresh wasabi, grated

Whisk together all the ingredients in a small bowl. Set aside for 30 minutes to let the flavours meld together, then strain through a fine sieve. Transfer to a squeezy bottle and keep in the fridge until needed.

PICKLED TURNIP

2 Tokyo turnips (or 1 small kohlrabi)
Pickling Liquid (see page 376)

Make the pickled turnips shortly before serving. Peel the turnip and thinly slice using a mandoline. Stack a few slices at a time and stamp out neat discs with a 5cm round pastry cutter. Put the discs into a bowl and pour over enough pickling liquid to cover. Leave to pickle for about 10 minutes, then drain.

———————————

RAW SCALLOPS

8–10 very fresh, large, raw Orkney scallops (in shell)

Shuck and clean the scallops (see Roast Orkney Scallops, page 77); save the coral roe for another dish. Thinly slice each scallop horizontally into 3 or 4 discs of even thickness (you want 28 neat discs in total). Put them into a bowl and squeeze over some wasabi and yuzu dressing. Toss gently, then leave to marinate for a few minutes.

———————————

ASSEMBLY

Chive & Dill Oil (see page 381)
Black Olive Oil (see page 381)
a handful of sea herbs
a handful of bronze fennel

For each serving, squeeze dots of chive and dill oil and black olive oil on to a serving plate. Arrange 7 discs of marinated scallop on top of the oils, then top each scallop disc with a pickled turnip disc. Squeeze a little mound of pear purée on each pickled turnip. Garnish with the sea herbs and bronze fennel. Spoon a little wasabi and yuzu dressing around the plate. Scrape the frozen jalapeño granita with a fork to make a coarse grainy texture, then spoon this into a small individual serving bowl to serve alongside.

Roast Orkney Scallops

with
artichoke &
black olive
soup
and
lemon,
artichoke
& celery
brunoise

SERVES 4

ROAST SCALLOPS

4 large, raw Orkney scallops
   (in shell)
olive oil, for cooking
50g unsalted butter
a squeeze of lemon juice
Maldon sea salt and black pepper

Shuck and clean the scallops (see Roast Orkney Scallops, page 77). Rinse the white scallop meat and lay it on a plate lined with kitchen paper to dry. Cover with clingfilm and keep in the fridge until needed.

To pan-roast the scallops, heat a little olive oil in a wide non-stick pan over a high heat. Season the scallops with salt and pepper, then place in the pan, arranging them in a ring. Sear for 1–2 minutes or until the underside is golden brown. Flip them over, in the same order as you put them into the pan, then add the butter. Cook for another minute or so, basting the scallops with the foaming melted butter as they finish cooking. The scallops are done if they feel slightly springy when pressed. Squeeze over a little lemon juice and take the pan off the heat. Remove the scallops and leave to rest for a few minutes.

ARTICHOKE & BLACK OLIVE SOUP

1kg Jerusalem artichokes
a squeeze of lemon juice
olive oil, for cooking
3 shallots, chopped
2 garlic cloves, chopped
200ml dry white wine
200ml Fish Stock (see page 378)
500ml Chicken Stock
   (see page 379)
2 sprigs of lemon thyme
100ml double cream
a drizzle of Black Olive Oil
   (see page 381)

Peel the artichokes – as you peel each one, immediately submerge it in a bowl of cold water that has been mixed

with a squeeze of the lemon juice (the acidulated water
will prevent the artichokes from turning brown).

Heat a little olive oil in a heavy-based pan and add
the shallots and garlic with a pinch each of salt and
pepper. Sweat the vegetables, stirring occasionally, for
6–8 minutes or until they begin to soften. Meanwhile,
very thinly slice the drained artichokes with a mandoline,
then add them to the pan, working quickly so they don't
oxidise and discolour. Cook for 4–5 minutes, stirring
frequently. Pour in the wine and let it boil until almost all
evaporated before you add the stocks and thyme sprigs.
Bring back to a simmer and cook the artichokes for a
few more minutes until they are very soft.

Pour the contents of the pan into a Thermomix or
a strong blender and blitz until smooth. Pass the soup
through a fine sieve into a clean saucepan, ready to
reheat when needed.

For serving, add the cream to the soup and bring
to a simmer. Taste and adjust the seasoning with salt
and pepper. When the soup is hot, blitz it with a stick
blender until light and frothy. Pour into individual
warmed serving bowls and drizzle over a little
black olive oil.

LEMON, ARTICHOKE & CELERY BRUNOISE

    a squeeze of lemon juice
    1 large Jerusalem artichoke
    1 celery stick
    2 preserved lemons (peel only)
    a drizzle of olive oil

Have ready a bowl of acidulated water (water mixed
with the lemon juice). Peel the artichoke, then slice very
thinly on a mandoline. Drop the slices immediately
into the acidulated water. Slice the celery using the
mandoline, then finely dice. Finely dice the peel of the
preserved lemons to about the same size as the celery.

Put the diced celery and preserved lemon into a pan.
Drain the artichoke slices well, then very finely dice them
and add to the pan. Mix with a drizzle of olive oil and a
small pinch each of salt and black pepper. Set aside, ready
to reheat. Gently warm the mixture before serving.

129

Lemon Purée (see page 384)
30g dehydrated black olives
    (dried out in a dehydrator
    at 75°C for 6 hours),
    finely chopped
a handful of celery leaves, soaked
    in iced water

Place a spoonful of brunoise on each warmed serving
plate and add a scallop alongside. Squeeze a little lemon
purée next to the scallop, then sprinkle with a little
chopped dehydrated black olive. Garnish with a few
celery leaves and serve immediately, with the artichoke
and black olive soup.

Paignton Harbour Crab

with
crab,
yoghurt &
sake sauce
and
mixed
radishes

SERVES 6

CRAB, YOGHURT & SAKE SAUCE

olive oil, for cooking
500g crab shells
2 carrots, peeled and chopped
2 onions, chopped
1 celery stick, chopped
1 small leek (white part), chopped
½ bulb of garlic, cloves separated and chopped
4 plum tomatoes, chopped
a pinch of coriander seeds
1 star anise
1 clove
1 tablespoon tomato paste
150ml brandy
600ml Fish Stock (see page 378)
500ml whole milk
250ml double cream
2 sprigs of tarragon
250 full-fat plain yoghurt
200g toasted almonds
a small bunch of seedless white grapes, picked
20g root ginger, peeled and chopped
a squeeze of lime juice
dry mineral sake
Maldon sea salt and black pepper

Crush the crab shells into smaller pieces using the back of a cleaver or rolling pin. Heat a drizzle of olive oil in a wide, heavy-based pan over a high heat, then add the crushed shells. Fry, stirring frequently, for 4–5 minutes or until golden brown. Remove the shells to a plate and set aside.

Add a little more oil to the pan followed by the chopped vegetables, garlic and tomatoes. Cook over a medium heat, stirring every once in a while, for 8–10 minutes or until the vegetables are soft. Add the coriander seeds, star anise and clove, and cook for a minute more. Stir in the tomato paste and increase the heat slightly. Stir-fry for a further 2 minutes or until the vegetables are golden brown.

Return the crab shells to the pan and pour in the brandy. If you want to flambé the brandy, let the flames die down before you pour in the fish stock, milk and cream. Bring to a simmer, skimming off any froth and scum that rises to the surface. Turn down the heat and simmer for 40 minutes. Remove from the heat and leave the stock to cool for 20 minutes.

Strain the stock through a fine sieve into a large measuring jug; discard the solids. Add the tarragon sprigs to the strained stock and leave to infuse for 20 minutes, then fish out and discard the tarragon.

You should now have about a litre of stock (if you have extra, save it for another use). Pour into a blender and add the yoghurt, toasted almonds, grapes

and ginger. Blend until smooth. Season the mixture with lime juice, sake and
salt to taste. Strain through a fine sieve into a bowl set over a larger bowl of
iced water. Leave to cool, stirring the sauce occasionally, then cover with
clingfilm and keep in the fridge until needed.

CREAMY CRAB MEAT

500g cooked and picked crab claw meat
100g crème fraîche
50ml olive oil
lime juice, to taste

Put the crab meat into a large mixing bowl and pick out and discard any tiny
bits of shell or cartilage. Add the crème fraiche, olive oil and a little lime juice
and salt. Mix well, then taste and adjust the seasoning with a little more salt
and lime juice if needed. Keep in the fridge.

MIXED RADISHES

1 small black mooli
1 watermelon radish
1 blue meat radish
1 Tokyo turnip
Lemon Purée (see page 384)
Crab Powder (see Dressed Paignton Harbour
   Crab recipe, page 104)
1 lime, for zesting

Peel the radishes and turnip. Very finely slice them on a mandoline. Stack
a few slices at a time and stamp out discs using a 3cm round cutter. As they
are cut, immerse the radish discs in iced water to crisp them up. If preparing
in advance, keep in the fridge for up to 1–2 hours.

To finish, drain the radish discs and pat dry with kitchen paper, then lay out
the slices. Pipe a small dot of lemon purée on to the centre of each. Dust with
the crab powder and finely grate over a little lime zest.

ASSEMBLY

Make a neat mound of creamy crab meat in the centre of each serving bowl.
Arrange 6 or 7 mixed radish discs over the creamy crab meat to conceal it.
Serve with the sauce in small individual jugs on the side.

St Austell Bay Lobster

with
yuzu jam
and
savoury
seaweed
custard

SERVES 4

YUZU JAM

50g finely grated lemon zest
500ml water
150g caster sugar
a pinch of saffron threads
9g agar agar powder
130ml yuzu juice

Put the lemon zest, water, sugar
and saffron into a heavy-based
saucepan and bring to the boil. Add
the agar agar and stir well. Cook for
2 minutes or until the agar agar has
dissolved, then remove from the
heat. Leave to cool slightly before
pouring into a container. Cover and
chill for a few hours or until set.

Break up the set lemon jelly with
a spoon before tipping it into a
blender. Blitz until smooth, trickling
in the yuzu juice while the machine
is running. Pass the mixture through
a fine sieve, then transfer to a
squeezy bottle or a piping bag.

PINE SALT

50g picked dehydrated pine
    needles (Douglas fir dried
    out in dehydrator at 75°C
    for 8 hours)
25g Maldon sea salt

Simply blend or grind the pine
needles and sea salt together to a
fine powder, then sift the mixture
through a very fine sieve. Store in
an airtight container until needed.

SAVOURY SEAWEED CUSTARD

3 large eggs
500ml Kombu Dashi (see
    page 377)

Lightly whisk together the eggs
and kombu dashi in a bowl. Divide
the mixture among 8 wide heatproof
bowls, each about 100ml capacity.
Cover each bowl with oven-safe
clingfilm to prevent any water
from dripping into the custard as it
steams. Put the bowls into a steamer
oven set to 100°C and steam for
9–10 minutes or until the custards
are just set, with a slight wobble
in the middle when you shake the
bowls. Remove the bowls from the
steamer and leave to cool.

LOBSTER JELLY

350ml Lobster Consommé
  (see page 378)
2 gelatine leaves
Maldon sea salt and black pepper

Put the lobster consommé into a
saucepan over a medium heat and
add a pinch each of salt and pepper.
Meanwhile, soak the gelatine leaves
in a bowl of cold water for 1–2
minutes to soften, then drain and
squeeze out excess water. Add the
gelatine to the pan and swirl or stir
the consommé until the gelatine has
completely melted. Strain through a
fine sieve into a jug. Allow to cool for
a few minutes, then pour a thin layer
over each savoury seaweed custard.
Chill for 20 minutes or until the
consommé jelly has set. Keep in
the fridge until needed.

LOBSTER TARTARE

400g cooked lobster meat (from
  the claws and tail trimmings)
finely grated lime zest and juice
olive oil, to drizzle

Chop the lobster meat, discarding
any bits of shell you come across.
Put the meat into a bowl and season
with a little salt, pepper, lime zest,
a squeeze of lime juice and olive

oil. Taste and adjust the seasoning
with a little more salt or lime juice
if needed.

———————————

ASSEMBLY

  1 small can (30g) Ossetra caviar
  1 lime, for zesting
  4 cooked lobster tails, cut in half
    and heated on a barbecue

For each serving, gently place a
plain 6cm diameter ring cutter
on the centre of a set jelly-topped
seaweed custard. Spoon a layer of
lobster tartare inside the cutter and
carefully smooth it level with the
back of the spoon. Lift off the ring
cutter. Sprinkle the top with a little
pine salt, then garnish the lobster
tartare with a small spoonful of
caviar. Finely grate over a little lime
zest. Pipe a little yuzu jam on to a
side plate and sprinkle with pine salt,
then place a barbecued lobster tail
on top. Serve immediately.

Wye Valley Asparagus

Wye Valley Produce is grown by fourth-generation farmers, the Chinn family, in the Wye Valley, near Ross-on-Wye in Herefordshire. We planted our first asparagus crop in the spring of 2003, and the Wye Valley brand has since expanded to include rhubarb, blueberries and green beans.

The light, sandy soil and south-facing slopes of the meandering Wye Valley capture the earliest spring sunlight, and create a microclimate that is perfectly formed to produce some of the earliest, and the best, produce in the UK.

Our asparagus is hand-harvested and hydro-cooled down to 2°C within an hour of being picked, ensuring that it retains maximum freshness and flavour. We harvest asparagus from March to July, and September to October.

It is our attention to freshness and quality, as well as the natural advantage of our location, which we believe makes Wye Valley Produce stand out from the rest. We are delighted to supply Pollen Street Social, and a number of restaurants across the country, as well as providing all the British asparagus for Marks & Spencer.

wyevalleyproduce.co.uk

St Austell Bay Mussel Purée

with
braised
white
asparagus
and
pickled
shimeji
mushrooms

SERVES 4

PICKLED SHIMEJI MUSHROOMS

250g Moscatel vinegar
200g white wine vinegar
200g caster sugar
2 star anise
2 cinnamon sticks
6 cloves
2 teaspoon mustard seeds
1kg shimeji mushrooms

Heat the vinegars and sugar together in a small saucepan, stirring to dissolve the sugar, then bring to a simmer. Take pan off the heat, add the spices and leave this pickling liquid to cool completely.

Meanwhile, clean the mushrooms and put them into a sterilised jar. Strain the pickling liquid into a clean pan (discard the spices) and bring to the boil. Pour it over the mushrooms. Cover and leave to cool completely, then leave to pickle in the fridge for a few days before using.

MUSSEL PURÉE

4kg fresh mussels (in shell)
2 celery sticks, chopped
2 carrots, peeled and chopped
2 shallots, chopped
400ml dry white wine
100ml white soy sauce
4g xanthan gum

Wash and scrub the mussels. Heat a drizzle of oil in a large pan, add the celery, carrots and shallots, and sweat for 2 minutes. Add the mussels along with the wine. Cover the pan and steam the mussels open.

Strain the cooking liquid into another pan and boil to reduce to 50ml. Meanwhile, pick the mussels from their shells (you need 500g), adding any liquid to the reducing stock. Put the mussels into a blender and add the soy sauce, xantham gum and reduced stock. Blitz to make a smooth purée. Pass through a sieve. Keep in the fridge until needed.

MUSSEL POWDER

200g mussel purée (see above)

Freeze the mussel purée for a few hours until solid. Finely grate it with a microplane over a baking tray lined with a silicone mat. Put the baking sheet into a dehydrator and dry out the grated mussel purée completely. Grind in a spice grinder to a powder. Store in an airtight container until needed.

BRAISED WHITE ASPARAGUS

8 white asparagus spears
1 litre water
500g unsalted butter
2 tablespoons sherry vinegar
1 white onion, sliced
4 bay leaves
8 sprigs of thyme, leaves picked
30g Maldon sea salt
30g caster sugar

Peel the stalks using a fine vegetable peeler, then cut the asparagus to 8cm lengths. Place the rest of the ingredients in a pan and bring to the boil. Reduce the heat and lower in the asparagus spears. Simmer for 2–3 minutes or until just tender. Remove from the heat and leave the asparagus to cool in the cooking liquor.

DASHI-BRAISED KING OYSTER MUSHROOMS

4 king oyster mushrooms
2 tablespoons red miso paste (we
    use Ichibiki brand)
400ml Kombu Dashi (see
    page 377)
2g xanthan gum

Thinly slice the mushrooms. Stack a few slices at a time and stamp out neat discs using a 2–3cm round pastry cutter. Put the discs into a small bowl. Heat the miso and dashi together in a small saucepan, stirring with a whisk to break up the miso paste. Add the xanthan gum and continue to stir until slightly thickened. Pour the thickened dashi over the mushrooms and mix gently to give each one a nice glaze. Keep warm until ready to serve.

ASSEMBLY

8 button mushrooms,
    thinly sliced
a large handful of bronze fennel
a large handful of sea
    lettuce leaves
a large handful of sea purslane
a large handful of mixed
    sorrel leaves
10 salty fingers

For each serving, place a white asparagus spear on
a serving plate. Arrange a tablespoon of pickled
mushrooms, 5 slices of braised oyster mushroom discs
and a few slices of raw button mushroom around the
asparagus. Garnish with sprigs of bronze fennel, sea
lettuce leaves, sea purslane, sorrel leaves and salty fingers.
Place a neat teaspoonful of mussel purée on the plate and
sprinkle mussel powder on top. Serve immediately.

Fish

Poached Day-netted
South Coast Sea Bass
150

Looe Day Boat Turbot
156

Poached South Coast
John Dory
162

Newquay Day Boat
Red Mullet
168

Isle of Gigah Halibut
174

Long Line-caught
Cornish Cod
180

Brixham Day Boat Brill
186

Newlyn Line-caught
Sea Bass
194

Poached Day-netted South Coast Sea Bass

with
Tokyo
turnip,
Paignton
Harbour
crab
reduction
and
olive oil
mash

JOHN DORY

4 x 120g pieces of sea bass fillet
    (skin on)
750ml Kombu Brine (see
    page 377)
olive oil, to drizzle

Put the John Dory fillets into a wide dish and pour over
the brine. Cover and leave to brine in the fridge for
10 minutes, then rinse the fish fillets and pat dry with
kitchen paper (discard the brine). Put the fillets into
vacuum bags and drizzle with a little olive oil. Vacuum-
seal the bags and keep in the fridge until needed.

To cook the fillets, poach them in a sous-vide machine (or
water bath) heated to 58°C for 8 minutes. Remove and
leave the fish to rest, in the bags, for 2 minutes.

CRAB REDUCTION

4 large crabs (we use Paignton
    Harbour crabs)
olive oil, for cooking
1 large white onion, roughly
    chopped
1 large carrot, peeled and roughly
    chopped
3 garlic cloves, roughly chopped
1 leek (white part), roughly
    chopped
1 celery stick, roughly chopped
1 lemongrass stick, trimmed
    and bashed
1 red chilli, deseeded
    and chopped
50g root ginger, peeled
    and chopped
1 teaspoon coriander seeds
1 teaspoon fennel seeds
2 tablespoons tomato paste
100ml brandy
1 litre Fish Stock (see page 378)
1 litre whole milk
500ml double cream
Maldon sea salt and black pepper

Chop the whole crabs into quarters using a cleaver or a
heavy knife. Heat a little olive oil in a large saucepan, add

the crab pieces and fry, turning the pieces occasionally, for about 10 minutes or until golden brown all over. Remove to a plate and set aside.

Drizzle a little more oil into the pan, then add the onion, carrot, garlic, leek, celery and a pinch each of salt and pepper. Stir over a high heat for 8–10 minutes or until the vegetables are beginning to soften and brown. Add the lemongrass, chilli, ginger, coriander seeds and fennel seeds and stir well. Fry for 2 more minutes, then stir in the tomato paste. Fry for a further 2 minutes until the vegetables are golden brown.

Return all but a few browned crab pieces to the pan (reserve the remaining pieces for reheating the sauce). Pour in the brandy to deglaze, scraping the bottom of the pan to dislodge the browned sediment. Pour in the fish stock, milk and cream and bring to a simmer, skimming off any froth and scum from the surface. Leave to simmer gently for 20 minutes.

Remove the pan from the heat and allow to cool for 20 minutes, then strain the sauce into a bowl. Pass the crab shells and vegetables through a mouli into the bowl. Strain the sauce again through a fine sieve into a clean saucepan. Bring to the boil and boil until reduced by half. Taste the sauce – it should have a deep, rich crab flavour with a hint of spice in the background. Leave to cool, then keep in the fridge until needed.

When ready to serve, add the reserved browned crab shells to the sauce and bring to the boil, then strain the sauce through a fine sieve into a warmed serving jug.

TOKYO TURNIP

1 large Tokyo turnip, about 150g
100g unsalted butter
100g Fish Stock (see page 378)
a sprig of lemon thyme
finely grated zest and juice of
   1 lemon

Bring a pot of salted water to the boil and have ready a bowl of iced water. Peel the turnip, then use a Japanese vegetable spiraliser to create long, thin strips of turnip resembling spaghetti. Rinse the turnip 'spaghetti', then blanch in the boiling water for 10 seconds. Drain and refresh in the bowl of iced water until cooled. Keep in the fridge until needed.

To reheat the Tokyo turnip, heat the butter, stock, thyme, lemon zest and juice, and some salt and pepper in a small saucepan. When the butter has melted, add the turnip and bring to a simmer. Take the pan off the heat.

_____

BROCCOLI DASHI POWDER

    trimmed stems and stalk from a
       head of broccoli, about 200g
    100g dashi powder
    2 sheets of dried nori

Blanch the broccoli stems/stalks in a pan of boiling water for 20 seconds. Remove to a bowl of iced water to stop the cooking process. Once cooled, drain the stems and pat dry with kitchen paper. Place the stems on a baking tray in a dehydrator and dry out for about 6 hours or until completely dry but still green.

Put the broccoli and dashi powder into a blender. Tear or chop the nori sheets into smaller pieces and add to the blender. Blitz the ingredients to a fine powder. Store in an airtight container.

_____

ASSEMBLY

    thin discs of Granny Smith apple
    thin discs of Tokyo turnip
    Pickling Liquid (see page 376)
    Arbequina olive oil, to drizzle
    meat from 4–5 cooked crab
       claws, cut into smaller pieces
    Crab Powder (see Dressed
       Paignton Harbour Crab recipe,
       page 104)
    Olive Oil Mash (see page 371)

Lightly pickle the apple and turnip discs, separately, in pickling liquid to cover for 1 minute.

For each serving, use a fork to twirl a portion of turnip 'spaghetti', then place it in the centre of a warmed serving plate. Drizzle over a little Arbequina olive oil. Place a piece of John Dory on top of the turnip. Arrange 3 pieces of crab claw meat on top of the fish. Dust the pickled apple discs with the broccoli dashi powder and the turnip discs with crab powder. Lay a few of these over the crab meat, on top of the fish fillet. Serve immediately with the crab reduction and olive oil mash on the side.

Looe Day Boat Turbot

with
wild garlic
& cockle
velouté
and
cauliflower,
yoghurt
purée

SERVES 4

_____

WILD GARLIC & COCKLE VELOUTÉ

1 bulb of garlic, cloves separated
   and half of them chopped
100ml olive oil
1 onion, chopped
500g large fresh cockles (in shell),
   thoroughly washed
100ml dry white wine
500g picked wild garlic
Maldon sea salt and black pepper

First confit the peeled whole garlic cloves. Put them into a small saucepan and pour over enough olive oil to cover. Gently simmer over the lowest heat for 40–45 minutes until the garlic is soft.

Meanwhile, set another large pan (with lid) over a medium-high heat. Add a little oil followed by the onions and the chopped garlic. Cook for 2 minutes, stirring occasionally, then add the cockles and white wine. Cover the pan and let the cockles steam for 2 minutes or until they have opened. Immediately remove the pan from the heat and tip the cockles into a colander set over a large bowl to collect the stock. Transfer the cockles to a wide bowl and spread them out so they will cool quickly, then pick the cockle meat from the shells. Keep the meat in the fridge until needed. Strain the cockle stock through a fine sieve into a small saucepan and set aside.

Bring a large pot of salted water to the boil and have ready a bowl of iced water. Blanch the wild garlic in the boiling water for 20 seconds, then fish out with tongs and immerse in the iced water to cool quickly. Drain well.

Add the drained confit garlic and blanched wild garlic to the cockle stock and cook for about 4 minutes or until the wild garlic leaves will break apart when lightly squeezed with your fingers. Transfer the contents of the pan to a blender and blitz to a smooth purée. Taste and adjust the seasoning with salt and pepper. Pass the purée through a fine sieve into a bowl set over an ice bath to cool quickly and retain the vibrant green colour. Stir this velouté occasionally as it cools, then keep in the fridge until needed.

To serve, pour the cockle and wild garlic velouté into a saucepan, add the cockle meat and reheat gently.

_____

CAULIFLOWER & YOGHURT PURÉE

1 head of cauliflower
250ml whole milk
250ml double cream
about 500ml full-fat plain
   yoghurt, hung in muslin
   overnight to drain

Cut the cauliflower into florets and place in a saucepan
with the milk and cream. Add a pinch of salt and set a
cartouche (a circle of baking parchment) on top. Bring to
a simmer and cook the cauliflower for 10–12 minutes or
until very soft and almost falling apart (try not to cook it
for much longer than this or it will begin to discolour).

Drain the cauliflower, reserving the creamy milk, and
tip into a strong blender or Thermomix. Blitz to a silky-
smooth purée, adding a splash of the creamy milk if
needed to get a good blend. Taste and adjust the seasoning
with salt and white pepper. Transfer to a bowl and leave
to cool slightly, then weigh the purée and stir in an equal
amount of hung yoghurt. The mixture should be pale
and thick. Transfer to a squeezy bottle. Before serving,
lightly warm the purée by placing the bottle in a bowl
of hot water.

CAULIFLOWER FLORETS

12 cauliflower florets
olive oil, for cooking
a few knobs of unsalted butter

Lightly blanch the florets in boiling salted water for
2–3 minutes, then drain and refresh in iced water. Drain
again. Keep in the fridge until needed.

To cook, heat a drizzle of oil with a few knobs of butter in
a frying pan, add the florets and toss them in the foaming
butter for 30 seconds. Use tongs to turn each floret top
side down and fry for a further 1–2 minutes or until
the tops are golden brown but the stems are still pale.
Remove to a plate.

BRAISED GIROLLES

olive oil, for cooking
500g girolles, cleaned
100g unsalted butter, diced
50ml dry white wine

250ml Chicken Stock (see
    page 379)
a sprig of thyme

Heat a drizzle of olive oil in a wide frying pan. Add
the girolles, season with a little salt and pepper, and add
a knob of the butter. Cook the girolles, tossing them
frequently to baste them with the foaming butter, until
they begin to brown. Pour in the wine and boil until it
has reduced by half. Add the chicken stock and return
to a simmer, then add the thyme and the rest of the
butter. Swirl the contents of the pan as the butter melts
and emulsifies with the stock. Take the pan off the heat.
Before serving, reheat the girolles in the braising liquor.

TURBOT

4 x 120g skinless turbot fillets
olive oil, for cooking
a few knobs of unsalted butter

Cook the fish just before serving. Heat a little olive oil
in a wide frying pan. Season both sides of the turbot
fillets, then add to the pan, skinned side down. Fry for
2–3 minutes or until the fillets are cooked two-thirds of
the way up and are golden brown on the underside. Add
the butter to the pan and carefully turn the fillets over.
Cook for 30 seconds to a minute or until the fish is just
cooked through. Remove to a plate and leave to rest for
a few minutes.

ASSEMBLY

a handful of picked
    woodland sorrel
8 large shards of Lemon &
    Yoghurt Meringue (see
    page 382)

Place a turbot fillet on each warmed serving plate
and squeeze a mound of cauliflower and yoghurt purée
next to it. Pour a drizzle of cockle and wild garlic velouté
around the purée, then arrange a few cauliflower florets,
cockle meat and girolles over and around the fish.
Garnish with a few sorrel leaves and a couple of lemon
meringue shards. Serve immediately.

Poached South Coast John Dory

with
caramelised
celeriac &
chestnut
purée,
chestnut
gnocchi
and
Périgord
truffle sauce

SERVES 4

CARAMELISED CELERIAC & CHESTNUT PURÉE

1 celeriac
olive oil, for cooking
400g unsalted butter
100g vacuum-packed cooked
  chestnuts
200ml Chicken Stock (see
  page 379)
Maldon sea salt and black pepper

The day before, peel and roughly dice the celeriac, then spread it out on a tray. Leave, uncovered, in the fridge overnight to dry out. (This will help to achieve better caramelisation during cooking.)

The next day, heat a small drizzle of oil in a large pan. When hot, lightly season the celeriac and add to the pan. Keep moving and tossing the celeriac in the pan as it cooks, so that it browns evenly. When it is evenly golden brown, add the butter and stir as it melts to coat the celeriac evenly. Cook for a few minutes, then add the chestnuts and some salt and pepper. Sauté for 2 more minutes or until the chestnuts are roasted.

Tip the celeriac and chestnuts into a colander or sieve set over a bowl, to drain off the excess butter (discard this). Return the chestnuts and celeriac to the pan and pour in the chicken stock. Bring to the boil and boil until the stock has reduced by half. Transfer the contents of the pan to a Thermomix or blender and blitz to a smooth purée. Pass the purée through a sieve into a clean pan, ready to reheat. Once reheated for serving, transfer the purée to a piping bag or squeezy bottle.

POACHED JOHN DORY

1 John Dory, about 2.5–3kg
Kombu Brine (see page 377)
olive oil, for drizzling

Clean and fillet the John Dory; save the bones for the sauce. Cut the fish fillets into 4 individual portions, 120–150g each, trimming the ends to neaten the shapes. Place the fish in a large bowl or tray and pour over enough kombu brine to cover.

Set aside for 10 minutes, then remove the pieces of fish and pat dry with kitchen paper. Place the fillets in vacuum bags and drizzle with a little olive oil. Vacuum-seal, then keep in the fridge until ready to cook.

To cook the fish, simply lower the vacuum bags into a sous vide machine (or water bath) heated to 58°C and poach for 8 minutes. Remove and leave the fish to rest, in the bags, for a couple of minutes.

GARNISHES

a handful of raw chestnuts
Périgord truffles, for shaving

Peel off the outer skins of the raw chestnuts (reserve the skins for the sauce), then very thinly slice the chestnuts on a mandoline. Soak the chestnut discs in iced water to keep them pale and crisp.

Thinly slice the truffles, then stack the slices and stamp out neat discs using a 1cm round pastry cutter. Save the trimmings for the sauce.

PÉRIGORD TRUFFLE SAUCE

olive oil, for cooking
John Dory bones (see above)
2 shallots, sliced
200g chestnut mushrooms, sliced
200ml red wine
500ml Fish Stock (see page 378)
300ml Veal Stock (see page 380)
10 chestnut skins (see above),
    lightly smoked over charcoal
1 tablespoon Cabernet
    Sauvignon vinegar
50ml black truffle vinegar
100g truffle trimmings
    (see above)
50ml extra virgin olive oil

Heat a little olive oil in a large pan. Add the John Dory bones and fry for a few minutes until golden brown all over. Remove from the pan and set aside. Add a little more oil to the pan followed by the shallots. Sweat the shallots for a few minutes, stirring frequently, then add the mushroom and fry over a high heat until the mushrooms begin to colour.

Return the fish bones to the pan and pour in the red wine. Boil until the wine has reduced by half. Add the stocks and chestnut skins and bring back to the boil,

skimming off any froth and scum from the surface.
Lower the heat and leave to simmer for an hour.

Strain the stock through a fine sieve into a clean saucepan.
Boil the stock until reduced to a syrupy consistency that
lightly coats the back of a spoon. Season to taste with the
vinegars, salt and pepper. Set aside in the pan, ready
for reheating.

Put the truffle trimmings on a chopping board and
drizzle over a little extra virgin olive oil . Chop the truffle
to create a paste. Put the paste into a small bowl and
set aside. Before serving, stir the truffle paste into the
warmed sauce.

CHESTNUT GNOCCHI

    rock salt
    500g floury potatoes (such as
        King Edward), scrubbed, dried
        and pricked
    100g chestnut flour
    100g type '00' flour
    1 large egg
    olive oil, for cooking
    a few knobs of unsalted butter

Preheat the oven to 160°C/140°C fan/Gas Mark 3.
Spread a layer of rock salt on a baking tray and set the
potatoes on top. Bake for 45 minutes to an hour or until
tender when pierced with the tip of a knife. Remove from
the oven and, while still hot, peel off the skins. Mash the
potatoes using a mouli, then push the mash through
a fine sieve.

Put the mash into a large bowl and add the flours and
egg. Mix together to make a dough, taking care not to
overwork it (this would make the gnocchi dense and
tough). Divide the dough into 20g portions. Shape each
into a ball, then roll the ball over the ridges of a butter
paddle to give a distinctive gnocchi shape. Dust with a
little flour to prevent the gnocchi from sticking together.

To cook the gnocchi, bring a large pot of salted water to
the boil. Shake off excess flour from the gnocchi, then
drop them into the boiling water. Cook for 2–4 minutes
or until they float to the surface. Scoop out the gnocchi
with a slotted spoon on to a lightly oiled tray.

Heat some oil and butter in a wide pan. Lightly season the gnocchi with salt and pepper, then fry them for a couple of minutes until golden brown.

ASSEMBLY

Spoon a little Périgord truffle sauce on to each warmed serving plate or bowl. Set a piece of poached fish on top. Squeeze little blobs of caramelised celeriac and chestnut purée on top of the fish and plate. Add some chestnut gnocchi to the plate. Garnish with black truffle and raw chestnut discs. Serve immediately.

Newquay Day Boat Red Mullet

with
poached
Orkney
scallops,
black olive
crumb
and
bouillabaisse

SERVES 4

RED MULLET

4 x 120g red mullet fillets
    (skin on)
olive oil, for cooking
lemon juice
Maldon sea salt and black pepper

Run your fingers along each fillet and remove any pin bones. Trim the edges of the fillets to neaten their shape, then lay them on a tray lined with kitchen paper, cover with clingfilm and keep in the fridge until needed.

To cook the fish, heat a little olive oil in a wide frying pan. Season the red mullet fillets with salt and pepper, then add to the pan, skin side down. Pan-roast for 2–3 minutes or until the fish is cooked two-thirds of the way up. Flip the fillets to cook on the other side for a minute. Drizzle over a little lemon juice, then transfer the fish to a plate and keep warm.

POACHED ORKNEY SCALLOPS

4 large, raw Orkney scallops
    (in shell)
200g spinach leaves
200g sea lettuce,
    thoroughly washed
200g unsalted butter, melted
    and cooled
100ml Fish Stock (see page 378)

Shuck and clean the scallops (see Roast Orkney Scallops, page 77). Rinse the white scallop meat and lay it on a plate lined with kitchen paper to dry. Cover with clingfilm and keep in the fridge until ready to cook. Scrub the shells for serving.

For the seaweed butter, blanch the spinach in boiling salted water for 3–4 minutes or until very tender but still green. Drain in a colander or sieve, squeezing lightly to remove excess water. Put the blanched spinach into a blender and add the sea lettuce and 100g of the melted butter. Blitz until the mixture is smooth and emulsified. Taste and season with salt and pepper, then pass through a fine sieve into a bowl. Cover and keep in the fridge until needed.

To cook the scallops, put the remaining butter into a small pan and add the fish stock and a pinch of salt. Bring to a gentle simmer. Lower the scallops into the pan and poach for 1–2 minutes or until just warmed through. Meanwhile, gently heat the seaweed butter in another small pan. With a slotted spoon, transfer the scallops to the pan containing the seaweed butter. Baste the scallops with the butter for a few seconds.

BLACK OLIVE CRUMB

100g unsalted butter
100g stale breadcrumbs
100g dehydrated black olives
    (dried out in a dehydrator
    at 75°C for 6 hours)

Melt the butter in a pan. When it begins to foam, add the breadcrumbs and stir until evenly coated. Cook over a medium-high heat, stirring frequently, until the breadcrumbs are golden and crisp. Turn the breadcrumbs out on to a plate or tray lined with kitchen paper to absorb the excess butter, then tip on to a chopping board. Mix the dry black olives with the breadcrumbs and chop to fine crumbs. Season with a little salt and pepper. Once cooled, store in an airtight container (can be kept for 3 days).

BOUILLABAISSE

1kg fish heads and bones (from
    fish such as bass, gurnard,
    mullet), rinsed and eyes and
    guts removed, then chopped
1 large shallot, chopped
1 small bulb of fennel, chopped
1 small carrot, peeled
    and chopped
½ celery stick, chopped
2 garlic cloves, chopped
1kg over-ripe plum tomatoes,
    roughly chopped
a pinch of saffron threads
5g fennel seeds
5g coriander seeds
1 star anise
250ml dry white wine
100ml Pernod
olive oil, for cooking
½ tablespoon tomato paste

½ teaspoon cayenne pepper

1 litre Fish Stock (see page 378)

Put the fish heads and bones on one side of a large, deep tray or bowl. Add all the chopped vegetables, the garlic, tomatoes, saffron, fennel and coriander seeds, and star anise to the other side (keep the bones separate from the vegetables if you can). Pour the white wine and Pernod over the fish bones and vegetables, then cover with clingfilm and leave in the fridge overnight.

The next day, use a slotted spoon to remove the fish heads and bones to a plate. Heat a wide, heavy-based pan until hot. Add a little olive oil followed by the fish heads and bones. Fry over a high heat for 5–6 minutes or until golden brown. Remove to a plate with the slotted spoon and set aside.

Drain the vegetables and spices (reserve the liquid in the tray) and add to the pan with a little more oil. Fry over a high heat, stirring frequently, for 8–10 minutes or until the vegetables are soft. Stir in the tomato paste and cayenne pepper and cook for a couple more minutes. Return the fish heads and bones to the pan and add the liquid from the tray. Boil until reduced by half, then pour in the fish stock. Bring almost back to the boil, then leave to simmer for 30 minutes.

Strain the stock into a bowl. Pass the ingredients of the stock through a mouli into the bowl (this will extract all the flavour of the ingredients and thicken the soup). Pour the soup back into the pan and boil until reduced and thickened slightly. Taste and adjust the seasoning, then strain the soup through a fine sieve into a clean pan, ready for reheating.

ASSEMBLY

1 cucumber

olive oil, for cooking

Saffron & Garlic Mash (see page 371)

Heat a plancha or ridged grill pan. Trim off the ends of the cucumber, then cut it in half lengthways. Cut each half into small wedges. Drizzle with a little olive oil and sprinkle with salt and pepper. Grill the cucumber on the hot plancha or grill pan for a few minutes on each side. Remove to a plate and keep warm.

For each serving, place a poached scallop in a scallop shell half and cover it with a spoonful of seaweed butter.

Drizzle over a few drops of olive oil. Set the shell on a side plate on a layer of coarse salt.

Spoon or pipe a mound of saffron and garlic mash into each wide serving bowl and sprinkle with a little black olive crumb. Place a red mullet fillet alongside the mash and garnish with a few pieces of grilled cucumber. Bring the fish and scallop to the table with a warmed jug of bouillabaisse soup. Pour a little soup around the fish and mash as you eat.

Isle of Gigah Halibut

with
courgette
and basil
purée,
cockle
minestrone
and
trofie pasta

SERVES 4

COURGETTE & BASIL PURÉE

4 courgettes
olive oil, for cooking
500g baby spinach
4 bunches of basil, about 400g,
  leaves picked
100ml double cream
50g Parmesan, freshly grated
Maldon sea salt and black pepper

Peel the courgettes (reserve the skins) and grate the flesh.
Heat a little olive oil in a heavy-based pan and add the
grated courgettes with a pinch each of salt and pepper.
Cook for 4–6 minutes, stirring frequently, until soft and
any moisture released has evaporated.

Meanwhile, blanch the spinach with the courgette skins
in a pan of boiling water for 2–3 minutes or until the
spinach has wilted but is still bright green. Fish out the
spinach and courgette skins with a slotted spoon and
place in a colander to drain. Add the basil leaves to the
boiling water and blanch for 30 seconds. Drain the basil
in the colander.

Squeeze out the excess water from the spinach, basil
and courgette skins, then add to the pan containing
the grated courgettes. Pour in the cream and bring to
a simmer. Immediately remove the pan from the heat
and transfer the contents of the pan to a blender or
Thermomix. Blitz until very smooth. Add the Parmesan
and blend again. Taste and adjust the seasoning with salt
and pepper.

Pass the purée through a fine sieve into a bowl set over
a larger bowl of iced water. Stir the purée frequently
while it cools, then transfer to a squeezy bottle and set
aside. Before serving, warm the purée by placing the
bottle in a jug of warm water.

COCKLE MINESTRONE

2kg fresh cockles (in shell)
100ml dry white wine
olive oil, for cooking
1kg langoustine (or lobster) heads
  and shells
1 onion, diced
2 carrots, peeled and diced

2 celery sticks, diced

2 garlic cloves, chopped

½ leek, diced

1 teaspoon espelette pepper

1 teaspoon tomato paste

3 courgettes, diced

1.5kg tomatoes, deseeded
   and diced

2 red peppers, deseeded
   and chopped

1 litre Fish Stock (see page 378)

1 litre Chicken Stock (see
   page 379)

4 sprigs of tarragon

4 sprigs of basil

a few knobs of cold unsalted
   butter, diced

4 baby courgettes, finely diced

Leave the cockles in a bowl of cold water for 2–3 hours to purge any sand from the shells, then thoroughly wash them. Heat a large, heavy-based pan until hot. Tip in the cockles and pour in the white wine. Cover the pan and steam the cockles over a high heat for 4 minutes or until they have opened. Tip out the cockles into a fine sieve set over a large bowl. Leave to drain and cool for a few minutes, then pick the cockle meat out of the shells; discard the shells. Save the cockle juices in the bowl for the minestrone. Pick out any remaining dirt or grit from the cockle meat and remove the skirts. Keep the cockles in the fridge until needed.

Heat a little olive oil in a large, heavy-based pan, add the langoustine heads and shells, and fry over a high heat until they are fragrant and lightly browned. Remove the heads and shells to a plate or tray and set aside. Add a little more oil to the hot pan followed by the onion, carrots, celery, garlic and leek. Sweat the vegetables over a medium heat, stirring frequently, for 8–10 minutes or until they are soft. Add the espelette pepper and cook for a few more minutes. Stir in the tomato paste and fry over a high heat for a further 2 minutes or until the vegetables have browned.

Add the diced courgettes, tomatoes and red peppers and sweat them for a few minutes. Return the langoustine heads and shells to the pan and pour in both stocks and the reserved cockle juices. Bring to a simmer, then cook for 30 minutes.

Take the pan off the heat and leave to cool for a few minutes. In batches, scoop out the langoustine heads and shells and vegetables with a slotted spoon and pass through a mouli into a clean pan. Strain the stock through a fine sieve or chinois into the pan. Slightly bruise the tarragon and basil sprigs and stir into the minestrone. Leave to cool and infuse.

SWEETCORN

2 large ears of sweetcorn, husks
    and silk removed
olive oil, for brushing

Heat a Japanese konro barbecue (or grill). Lightly brush the sweetcorn all over with olive oil, then sprinkle with a little salt and pepper. Grill, turning the sweetcorn frequently as they cook, for 10–15 minutes or until the kernels are tender and evenly browned. Leave to cool for a few minutes before cutting the kernels from the cob. Set aside.

HALIBUT

olive oil, for cooking
4 x 120g pieces of skinless,
    boneless halibut fillet
a few knobs of unsalted butter
a splash of Fish Stock (see
    page 378)
a squeeze of lemon juice

Heat a little olive oil in a wide frying pan. Season the fish and place in the pan, skinned side down. Fry for 2–3 minutes or until golden brown and cooked two-thirds of the way up. Flip the fish over and add the butter and a little fish stock. Baste the fish with the foaming butter and stock during the last minute of cooking. Finally, add a squeeze of lemon juice and remove the fish to a plate. Keep warm.

ASSEMBLY

320g fresh trofie pasta
2 tablespoons mixed chopped
    basil and tarragon
bronze fennel leaves
popcorn shoots (micro greens)

Bring a pot of well-salted water to the boil and cook the pasta for 2 minutes or until al dente. Meanwhile, fish out and discard the herb sprigs from the minestrone, then reheat it with a few knobs of butter and a drizzle of olive oil. Taste and adjust the seasoning with salt and pepper.

Blitz the minestrone with a stick blender to create an aerated, foamy sauce. Add the chopped baby courgettes to warm through.

Mix the grilled sweetcorn kernels with the cockle meat in a saucepan. Add a drizzle of olive oil and a pinch of salt and warm through.

Drain the pasta and mix with a little of the minestrone sauce. Divide among warmed small bowls and sprinkle with the chopped basil and tarragon. Spoon over the rest of the aerated minestrone sauce.

Place a piece of fish on each warmed serving plate and add a squeeze of spinach and basil purée alongside. Garnish the fish with the sweetcorn and cockle mixture, bronze fennel and popcorn shoots. Serve immediately, with the pasta.

Long Line-caught Cornish Cod

with
onion squash
purée
and
squid &
seaweed
sauce

SERVES 4

ROAST COD

about 500g skinless cod fillet (from the centre loin)
about 1.5 litres Kombu Brine (see page 377)
200ml olive oil
pared zest from 1 lemon
100ml lemon juice
a handful of soft herbs (such as parsley, mint and
   tarragon leaves)

Trim the cod fillet to neaten the shape and remove any pin bones you come across. Lay the cod in a small, deep tray or dish and pour over enough brine to cover (you could also brine the fish in a sealed vacuum bag). Set aside in the fridge for 40 minutes.

Remove the cod from the brine and pat it dry with kitchen paper. Wrap the fish tightly in oven-safe clingfilm to create a neat log shape. Keep in the fridge until needed.

When ready to cook, preheat the oven to 200°C/180°C fan/Gas Mark 6. Mix together the olive oil, lemon zest and juice, and herb leaves in a small bowl and set aside to infuse for a few minutes. Meanwhile, slice the cod fillet across into four 120g portions, leaving the clingfilm on to preserve the cylindrical shapes. Heat a little olive oil in a wide ovenproof frying pan, then sear the fish on each cut side for about 2 minutes or until golden brown. Remove the clingfilm and transfer the pan to the oven. Roast for a couple of minutes, to finish cooking the fish. Take the pan out of the oven and brush the cod with the lemon and oil mixture. Keep warm.

ONION SQUASH PURÉE

1 onion squash
1 large garlic clove, chopped
a sprig of thyme, leaves stripped
olive oil, for drizzling
100g unsalted butter
grated Parmesan, to taste
Maldon sea salt and black pepper

Preheat the oven to 160°C/140°C fan/Gas Mark 3. Cut the onion squash in half. (Leave the skin on as it gives the purée a deep orange colour.) Scoop out and discard the seeds and fibres. Place the squash halves, cut side up, on a foil-lined baking tray and scatter over the chopped garlic and thyme leaves. Drizzle over a little olive oil and sprinkle with salt and pepper. Cover the tray with another large piece of foil, then bake the squash for about 40 minutes or until completely soft.

While still hot, scrape off the garlic and thyme from the squash, then place it in a food processor or Thermomix. Add the butter and blitz on high speed to a silky-smooth purée. Add grated Parmesan, salt and pepper to taste and blitz again. Pass the purée through a fine sieve, then transfer to a squeezy bottle. Before serving, reheat by placing the bottle in a jug of hot water.

_____

BUTTERNUT SQUASH FONDANT

2 large butternut squash
100g unsalted butter, plus a few extra knobs
a splash of Thai fish sauce
a splash of ready-made shiro dashi (white dashi stock)

Cut each squash across into two pieces to separate the rounded half from the straight -sided half. Reserve the rounded pieces for another dish. Peel the straight pieces, then cut each across into two 3.5cm-thick rounds. Use a small round pastry cutter about 5cm in diameter to stamp out a neat round of squash from each slice. Run a turning knife around the sharp edges of each squash slice to create rounded edges.

Place the squash in a large vacuum bag. Add the 100g butter and a splash of fish sauce. Vacuum-seal the bag and cook in a sous vide machine (or a water bath) heated to 85°C for 15 minutes. Remove and immediately submerge the bag in a bowl of iced water to stop the cooking process. Keep in the fridge (in the bag) until needed.

When ready to serve, remove the butternut squash fondants from the vacuum bag and sear the cut sides in a hot pan with a few knobs of butter until golden brown. Add a splash of shiro dashi to the pan and spoon the butter and dashi over the fondants to glaze them.

_____

SQUID & SEAWEED SAUCE

2 onion squash
500ml Fish Stock (see page 378)
50ml ready-made shiro dashi (white dashi stock)
200g plain yoghurt
30ml noto ishiri (fermented squid sauce) or Thai
    fish sauce
20g diced squid
10g chopped chives
10g chopped sea lettuce

Preheat the oven to 160°C/140°C fan/Gas Mark 3. Cut the onion squash in half (leave the skin on), then scoop out and discard the seeds and fibres. Wrap the squash halves in foil and place on a baking tray. Bake for about 40 minutes or until soft.

Unwrap the squash, put them into a large saucepan and add the fish stock and dashi. Bring to the boil, then simmer for 10–15 minutes or until the squash is very soft, including the skin. Transfer the contents of the pan to a blender or Thermomix and blitz until smooth. Pass the sauce through a fine sieve into a clean saucepan. Add the yoghurt and noto ishiri or fish sauce. Taste and adjust the seasoning with a little more yoghurt (for acidity) or squid sauce (for savouriness). Set aside, ready for reheating.

Before serving, reheat the sauce with the squid, chives and sea lettuce for about 2 minutes or until the squid is cooked, then transfer to individual warmed serving jugs.

SQUID 'RICE'

1 large squid, about 2kg, cleaned
a sprig of thyme
1 garlic clove, crushed
olive oil, for cooking

Use a damp cloth to wipe off any ink or sinew left on the squid, then lay it on a tray lined with kitchen paper. Cover and chill for 12 hours or overnight.

Put the squid into a vacuum bag with the thyme, garlic, some salt and pepper, and a drizzle of olive oil. Vacuum-seal the bag, then cook in a sous vide machine (or water bath) heated to 63°C for 8 minutes. Remove the bag to a bowl of iced water. Once cooled, take the squid out of the bag and cut into a fine dice to resemble grains of rice.

ASSEMBLY

100g blanched sea purslane
Pumpkin & Seaweed Oil (see page 381), for drizzling

Pipe a little onion squash purée on each warmed serving plate. Spoon over a little squid 'rice'. Place a squash fondant and piece of roast cod on the plate, then garnish with a few blanched sea purslane leaves. Squeeze a little pumpkin and seaweed oil around the plate and bring to the table with individual jugs of squid and seaweed sauce. Pour the sauce over the squid rice to serve.

Brixham Day Boat Brill

with
goat's
cheese &
cauliflower
purée,
Maylor
prawns
and
herb sauce

SERVES 4

POACHED BRILL

4 brill fillets, 120–150g each
Kombu Brine (see page 377)
olive oil, to drizzle

Place the fillets in a wide dish and pour over enough
kombu brine to cover. Set aside in the fridge for 20
minutes, then remove the fillets and pat them dry with
kitchen paper (discard the brine). Put the fillets into
vacuum bags and drizzle over a little olive oil. Vacuum-
seal the bags. Keep in the fridge until ready to cook.

About 20 minutes before serving, poach the fish in a
sous vide machine (or water bath) heated to 58°C for 15
minutes, then remove and leave the fish to rest, in the
bags, for a couple of minutes.

GOAT'S CHEESE & CAULIFLOWER PURÉE

½ head of cauliflower
500ml whole milk
250ml double cream
100g goat's cheese
Maldon sea salt and black pepper

Cut the cauliflower into florets and roughly chop
the tender part of the stem (discard the rest). Place the
cauliflower in a heavy-based pan and season with a little
salt and pepper. Pour over the milk and cream. Bring to a
simmer over a medium heat, then cook for 4–6 minutes
or until the cauliflower is soft.

Meanwhile, trim the rind from the goat's cheese, then
leave the cheese in a warm place to soften.

When the cauliflower is ready, tip the contents of the pan
into a blender. Add the goat's cheese. Blitz to a smooth
purée and season well to taste. Pass the purée through a
fine sieve into a clean saucepan, ready to reheat gently
for serving.

HERB SAUCE

4 celery sticks
2 bulbs of fennel
1 large cucumber

2 Granny Smith apples
100g spinach leaves
4 bunches of mint, about 400g
4 bunches of basil, about 400g

Juice the celery, fennel and cucumber through an electric juicer/press. Cut the apples into quarters and remove the core and seeds, then juice the apple quarters. Pour the juices into a Thermomix blender and add the spinach and herbs. Blend at 80°C for 6 minutes. Strain the liquid through a fine sieve lined with muslin into a bowl. The resulting sauce should be a vibrant green. Cover with clingfilm and keep in the fridge until needed. Reheat gently in a pan for serving.

_____

MAYLOR PRAWNS

24 raw Maylor prawns
finely grated zest of 2 limes
3–4 tablespoons plain flour,
   for dusting
vegetable oil, for deep-frying

Remove the heads from the prawns and set aside 12 heads. Peel off the shells from the prawns and devein them. Put the prawns into a bowl and season with the lime zest and a pinch of salt. Take half of the seasoned prawns and use a sharp knife to finely chop them into a paste. Scrape the paste into a small piping bag and pipe into the reserved prawn heads. Cover the stuffed prawn heads and seasoned prawns with clingfilm and keep in the fridge until needed.

When ready to serve, dust the stuffed prawn heads in a little flour, then deep-fry them in oil heated to 180°C for 1–2 minutes, turning them halfway, until golden and crisp. Remove to a tray lined with kitchen paper and sprinkle with a little sea salt.

_____

ASSEMBLY

Put a generous spoonful of the goat's cheese and cauliflower purée into the centre of each serving bowl. Set a poached brill fillet on top, then arrange 3 raw seasoned prawns and 3 stuffed prawn heads on top of the fish. Pour the herb sauce into individual jugs (garnish these with additional herbs, if you like) to serve alongside.

Flying Fish

Flying Fish has been supplying the best seafood in the British Isles to the UK's best chefs since 2006, but I have been in the business for nearly two decades. On leaving school I joined a local seafood supplier and by my mid-twenties had worked my way up the ranks to sales manager. I soon moved to Cornwall to be closer to the source and Flying Fish was born.

I have worked with Jason from the very beginning, in 2011, when he opened Pollen Street Social. We have built up a strong relationship and I understand the exceptionally high quality and standards Jason needs for his restaurants. I always aim to give Pollen Street Social, and the Social Company, the best that is on offer.

Jason is an amazing and passionate chef and has done a great deal of good for the industry so it's a pleasure to work with him and supply his restaurants. My favourite fish to supply him with is our first line-caught sea bass of the season – it's very special to be able to share that with someone who, I know, will get the very best from it.

Apart from the fact that he is a great chef, Jason understands that we care about sustaining our fish stocks in the Cornish waters. Jason is aware that fishing is not a 9-to-5 business with abundant stocks all year round and that the weather has a big impact on our small day-boats' ability to go out. The fish change seasonally, and Jason works with me on what is available and changes his menus to use the fish that are in season and at their peak.

The best day I have ever had was when he came down to Cornwall with his family. We went fishing on one of the boats in the sunshine and had the most wonderful time, eating lobster overlooking the beach and harbour.

John Godden
flyingfishseafoods.co.uk

Newlyn Line-caught Sea Bass

with
shellfish
fondue,
crushed
potatoes
and
seaweed
butter sauce

SERVES 4

SHELLFISH FONDUE

10 vine-ripened tomatoes
2 sprigs of rosemary
2 sprigs of thyme
olive oil, for cooking
2 shallots, sliced
2 garlic cloves, sliced
4 teaspoons chopped
   cooked mussels
4 teaspoons chopped
   cooked cockles
4 teaspoons chopped
   cooked winkles
4 teaspoons chopped
   cooked razor clam
4 teaspoons chopped coriander
4 teaspoons chopped dill
4 teaspoons chopped chives
Maldon sea salt and black pepper

Preheat the oven to 150°C/130°C fan/Gas Mark 2.
Lightly score the tops of the tomatoes with a knife,
then place them on a baking tray and scatter over the
rosemary and thyme sprigs. Season with sea salt and
drizzle over a little olive oil. Roast the tomatoes for about
an hour or until the skins have darkened a little. Remove
from the oven. When cool enough to handle, peel off and
discard the skins. Set aside.

Heat a little olive oil in a heavy-based pan and add the
shallots and garlic. Cook over a medium heat, stirring
frequently, for 5–6 minutes or until the shallots are
translucent. Add the roast tomatoes and stir well. Cook
over a low heat for about 2 hours or until the mixture
is thick, stirring occasionally. Transfer the mixture to
a food processor and blitz until smooth. Pass the purée
through a fine sieve into a bowl. Taste and adjust the
seasoning with salt and pepper. Cover with clingfilm
and keep in the fridge until needed.

Before serving, reheat the shellfish fondue with the
cooked shellfish until warmed through, then stir in the
chopped herbs.

CRUSHED POTATOES

500g Mayan Gold potatoes
400ml Chicken Stock (see
   page 379)

200g unsalted butter
a sprig of thyme
2 garlic cloves
2 spring onions, chopped
100g picked, cooked white
    crab meat
2 sprigs of dill, chopped
2 sprigs of coriander, chopped
1 lemon, for zesting

Peel the potatoes, put them into a pan and add the stock,
butter, thyme, peeled garlic and a good pinch of salt.
Cook for about 15 minutes or until tender. Remove from
the heat and leave the potatoes to cool in the stock. Once
cooled, transfer the potatoes to a bowl using a slotted
spoon (save the stock for later). Lightly crush them with
a fork, then set aside.

Before serving, reheat the crushed potatoes with a little
of the reserved cooking stock, then stir through the
chopped spring onions, crab meat and herbs. Finish with
some lemon zest.

SEAWEED BUTTER SAUCE

200g spinach leaves
200g sea lettuce, thoroughly
    washed
200g unsalted butter, melted
100ml Fish Stock (see page 378)

Bring a pan of salted water to the boil and blanch
the spinach leaves for about 4 minutes or until very soft.
Drain well, then transfer to a blender. Add the sea lettuce
and half the melted butter, and blitz until the mixture is
smooth. Taste and adjust the seasoning with salt.
Set aside.

Before serving, stir in the fish stock and remaining
melted butter and reheat gently.

SEA BASS

olive oil, for cooking
4 x 120g sea bass fillets (skin on)
Lemon Oil (see page 381),
    to drizzle

Cook the fish when you are about ready to serve. Heat a
little olive oil in a wide frying pan until hot. Season the
sea bass fillets with salt, then place them in the pan, skin

side down. Fry for 2–3 minutes or until the skin is golden brown and crisp, and the fish is cooked two-thirds of the way up. Turn the fillets over and cook the other side for 1 minute or less – just until the fish is almost cooked through. Remove the fillets to a plate or tray and leave to rest for a minute before drizzling over some lemon oil.

————————

ASSEMBLY

meat from 4 cooked crab claws
Crab Reduction (see Poached
    Day-netted South Coast Sea
    Bass recipe, page 151)

For each serving, spread a little seaweed butter sauce on a serving plate and place a tablespoonful of shellfish fondue on top. Lay a sea bass fillet on the fondue. Place a portion of crushed potatoes in a separate side bowl and top with the meat from a cooked crab claw. Blend the crab reduction with a stick blender until it is foamy, then spoon a little foam over the top of the crab claw. Serve immediately with the sea bass.

Meat & Game

Cumbrian Suckling Pig
202

Winter Lake
District Lamb
212

Spring Lake
District Lamb
218

Cartmel Valley
Loin of Venison
224

Braised West Country
Ox Cheek
230

Roast Lincolnshire
Rabbit
236

40-day Dry-aged
Lake District Beef Fillet
242

Cumbrian Suckling Pig

with
red cabbage
purée,
stuffed dates
and
lardo-
roasted
potatoes

SERVES 4

SUCKLING PIG RACK & BELLY

1 rack of suckling pig with 8 bones, about 1kg
1 boned suckling pig belly, about 1kg (skin on)
30g pink curing salt
70g fine sea salt
7 cloves
a few sprigs of thyme
1 garlic clove, sliced
olive oil
Maldon sea salt and black pepper

Using butcher's string, tie the rack of suckling pig into even-sized portions, ensuring you have 8 chops of the same size and shape. Set aside in the fridge.

Trim off any sinew from the suckling pig belly, then place it in a deep tray. To make the salt cure, put the pink salt, sea salt and the cloves into a small blender and blitz until fine. Rub this all over the meat and skin. (You need about 100g of salt cure per kg of meat.) Cover the tray with clingfilm and leave to cure overnight in the fridge.

The next day, rinse the salt cure off the pig belly, then place it in a vacuum bag with the thyme, garlic and a little olive oil. Vacuum-seal the bag. Lower it into a sous vide machine (or water bath) heated to 85°C and gently poach for about 10 hours or until very tender. Remove the bag. Place the belly (still in its bag) on a baking tray, skin side down. Put another tray on top and weigh down with a few tins. Keep the belly in the fridge until needed.

When ready to serve, heat a little olive oil a large frying pan. Season the rack with salt and add to the pan. Fry for 6–8 minutes, turning every couple of minutes, until evenly golden brown. Remove from the pan to a warmed plate. Cut the belly into 8 portions, then fry in the same manner as the rack until evenly golden brown all over. Leave the rack and belly pieces to rest.

PORK SAUCE

1kg pork bones
olive oil, for cooking
1 onion, chopped
1 small leek, chopped
1 carrot, peeled and chopped
1 celery stick, chopped
½ bulb of garlic, cloves separated and chopped
½ tablespoon tomato paste
250g streaky bacon (preferably from Alsace), chopped
200ml dry white wine
1 litre reduced Veal Stock (see page 380)
500ml Chicken Stock (see page 379)
2 sprigs of lemon thyme
a few lime leaves

Chop or crush the pork bones into smaller pieces using a heavy cleaver. Heat a little olive oil in a large, heavy-based pan, add the pork bones and fry over a high heat for 6–8 minutes or until evenly browned, stirring occasionally. Remove the bones to a large plate and set aside.

Add a little more oil to the pan followed by the chopped vegetables and garlic. Cook over a high heat, stirring once in a while, for 6–8 minutes or until the vegetables begin to brown. Add the tomato paste and stir well, then fry for another couple of minutes until the vegetables are evenly golden brown. Add the bacon and fry, stirring, for a further 2 minutes. Deglaze the pan with the white wine, scraping the bottom to release any browned sediment. Let the wine boil until reduced by half.

Reserve a few browned pork bones for later and return the rest to the pan. Pour in the stocks and top up with a little water if the liquid does not cover the bones. Bring to a simmer, skimming off any froth and scum that rises to the surface, then leave to simmer for 4 hours. Remove from the heat and leave to cool.

Strain the sauce through a fine sieve into a clean pan. Season lightly with salt and pepper. Taste the sauce and, if necessary, boil it until reduced by a third to intensify the flavour. Strain the reduced sauce again into a clean pan, ready for reheating.

To finish the sauce, return the remaining browned pork bones to the pan along with the lemon thyme and lime leaves. Reheat, then strain. If necessary, boil the sauce to thicken and intensify the flavour.

RED CABBAGE PURÉE

olive oil, for cooking
½ red cabbage, finely shredded
2 Braeburn apples
100g sultanas
1 small cinnamon stick
1 star anise
1 clove
1 litre red wine
1 litre port
50ml Cabernet Sauvignon vinegar
125g unsalted butter

Heat a little olive oil in a large pan over a medium-high heat. Add the cabbage with a pinch each of salt and pepper and stir, then sweat the cabbage, stirring occasionally, for 10–12 minutes or until tender but not browned.

Peel and chop the apples. Add to the pan along with the sultanas and spices. Cook, stirring, for a couple of minutes. Pour in both wines and bring to the boil. Cook until the wine has reduced and the pan is quite dry. Add the vinegar and bring back to the boil. Reduce the vinegar by half before adding the butter. Stir until the butter has melted, then take the pan off the heat.

Transfer the hot cabbage mixture to a blender and blitz to a smooth purée. Taste and adjust the seasoning with salt and pepper. Transfer to a bowl, cool, cover and keep in the fridge until needed. Before serving, reheat the purée in a saucepan until hot.

BRAISED CHICORY

2 large red chicory
250ml fresh apple juice
1 teaspoon ascorbic acid
a sprig of thyme
olive oil, for cooking
a few knobs of unsalted butter
finely grated lime zest

Put the chicory into a vacuum bag with the apple juice, ascorbic acid, thyme and a pinch each of salt and pepper. Vacuum-seal the bag and gently cook in a sous vide machine (or water bath) heated to 88°C for 2 hours. Lift out the bag and submerge it in a bowl of iced water to stop the cooking process. Keep in the fridge, in the bag, until ready to serve.

To finish, drain the braised chicory and pat it dry, then slice each one in half lengthways. Put the chicory halves in a hot pan with a little olive oil and a few knobs of butter. When golden brown and caramelised, grate over a little lime zest and remove from the heat.

STUFFED DATES

4 large Medjool Bonbon dates
olive oil, for cooking
1 shallot, finely diced
250g Italian lardo, finely diced
1 Granny Smith apple, peeled and finely diced
2 sprigs of marjoram, leaves picked and finely chopped
Pickling Liquid (see page 376)

Soak the dates in cold water for a few hours to plump them up, then dry and remove the skins. Cut each date in half and discard the stone. Put the dates between 2 sheets of greaseproof paper and press down with the palm of your hand to flatten them. Leaving them between the paper sheets, put the flattened dates in the fridge to chill and firm up.

Heat a little olive oil in a heavy-based pan, add the shallot and sweat over a medium heat for 5–6 minutes. Stir in the lardo and increase the heat to high. Let the lardo fry in its fat until golden brown. Take the pan off the heat and add the apple, marjoram and some black pepper. Mix well, then leave to cool.

Scoop the lardo mixture into a piping bag. Lay a flattened date on the work surface and pipe a line of lardo filling down the centre. Roll the date to reform its natural shape. Repeat to stuff the rest of the dates. Cover and keep in the fridge until needed.

Before serving, heat up a little pickling liquor in a small saucepan, add the dates and cook for a few minutes or until the dates are glazed and warmed through. Drain.

CABBAGE IN SEAWEED BUTTER

1 Savoy cabbage
Seaweed Butter Sauce (see Newlyn Line-caught
   Cornish Sea Bass recipe, page 196)

Core and dice the cabbage, then blanch in boiling water for 2–3 minutes or until tender but still green. Drain and refresh in a large bowl of iced water. Drain again, then pat dry with a clean kitchen towel.

Just before serving, warm the cabbage in the seaweed butter.

LARDO-ROASTED POTATOES

500g Italian lardo, chopped
500g baby Mid potatoes, peeled
100g unsalted butter
a sprig of thyme
1 garlic clove, chopped

Heat a wide frying pan until hot, then add the lardo. When the lardo has rendered its fat, tip in the potatoes with a little salt and pepper. Pan-roast the potatoes, turning them occasionally, until they are evenly golden brown. Add the butter and, as it begins to foam, spoon it over the potatoes. Add the thyme and garlic to the pan and cook the potatoes for 10–15 minutes or until they are soft (with a similar texture to fondant potatoes).

Drain off the buttery fat and tip the roasted potatoes on to a large plate lined with kitchen paper. (If not serving immediately, allow the potatoes to cool, then keep in the fridge. Reheat them in a hot pan with a little more butter before serving.)

ASSEMBLY

For each serving, spoon or pipe a small mound of red cabbage purée on to the centre of a warmed serving plate. Add 2 pieces of pork belly to the plate. Carve the rack into individual chops and add 2 chops to the plate, resting them against a piece of pork belly so the bones are standing up. Add a braised chicory half, a stuffed date, a couple of roasted potatoes and some Savoy cabbage to the plate. Serve with an individual jug of pork sauce alongside and the potatoes on a side plate.

Lake District Farmers

I still remember my first meeting at Pollen Street Social. I was really nervous going in. The restaurant had built a reputation very quickly. Jason was already well known and you always felt he would excel in his own place. It was obvious that Pollen Street was going to achieve great things, and we wanted to be part of that journey.

Every passionate supplier dreams of having their produce served in the world's best restaurants. For a lucky few of us that dream is realised. Pollen Street Social has become one of the best restaurants in the world and for us, it's an honour to have played our part in that progression.

Herdwick Lamb is my favourite ingredient of all that we've supplied to Pollen Street across the years. It's our flagship product. Our farmers have worked so hard with us to establish it. We knew it was going to be difficult because the lamb takes such a long time to rear – it's a really slow-growing animal. And it's a small animal. Both go against everything that is commercially viable. But with that slow process comes exceptional flavour. To see that recognised by leading restaurants is probably our biggest achievement at Lake District Farmers.

Jason seems to have a very personal relationship with his suppliers, which I think is a big achievement considering how busy he must be. We've done a couple of supplier evenings with him now, which have been great fun. He's a down-to-earth guy. I remember last year receiving a surprise package in the post from him with a few gifts and a card thanking me for the quality of product we supply to Pollen Street Social. I thought it was a classy touch. It made my day.

Dan Austin, Lake District Farmers
lakedistrictfarmers.co.uk

Winter Lake District Lamb

with
lamb hotpot
and
beetroot &
blackcurrant
purée

SERVES 4

LAMB LOIN & FILLET

2 boned short saddles of lamb, about 475g each
    (loins and fillets separated)
meat glue, for dusting
olive oil, for cooking
sprigs of rosemary
unsalted butter, for cooking
Maldon sea salt and black pepper

Trim off any sinews from the fillets, then set aside in the fridge. Carefully cut off the fat covering the loins so that the fat remains as whole pieces. Lay out the fat on a chopping board and bang the pieces with a rolling pin to flatten them out. Arrange the pieces of fat side by side on a large sheet of clingfilm to make a rectangle large enough to wrap around the loins. Rub the loins with a little salt. Sprinkle a little meat glue on the rectangle of fat, then place the loins along one side. Holding the ends of the clingfilm, roll up to wrap the fat around the loins and form a neat log. Unwrap the clingfilm, then tie the loin ballotine with butcher's string.

Put the loin ballotine into a large vacuum bag and vacuum-seal it. Set the bag on a steaming tray and place in a steam oven to cook for 5 minutes. Remove and immediately immerse the vacuum bag in a bowl or tray of iced water to stop the cooking process. Keep in the fridge until needed.

When ready to finish the loins for serving, preheat the oven to 200°C/180°C fan/Gas Mark 6. Heat a little olive oil in an ovenproof frying or sauté pan and sear the loin ballotine for 2 minutes on each side or until evenly browned. Add some rosemary to the pan, then transfer to the oven and roast for a couple of minutes for medium rare. Leave to rest for a few minutes before serving.

To cook the lamb fillets for serving, heat a little oil in a wide frying pan. Season the fillets with a little salt and pepper, then add them to the pan with some rosemary and butter. Sear for about 2 minutes on each side or until evenly golden brown. As they cook, spoon the foaming butter over them to keep them moist and encourage even cooking. When ready, remove the from the heat and allow to rest for a few minutes.

LAMB HOTPOT

100g gros sel (grey sea salt)
a few sprigs of thyme, leaves picked
1 large garlic clove
20g grated lemon zest
1 boned shoulder of lamb, about 2kg
olive oil, for cooking
200g lamb fat
4 large carrots
4 turnips

500g baby silverskin onions, peeled
1 litre Lamb Sauce (see page 375)
2 large Desirée potatoes
125g clarified butter, melted

Start by making a salt cure. Put the salt, thyme leaves, peeled garlic and lemon zest in a small food processor and blitz together. Tip half the mixture on to a baking tray. Place the shoulder of lamb on the tray and sprinkle the remaining salt cure over the top. Rub the cure all over the lamb with your hands. Cover the tray with clingfilm and set aside in the fridge to cure for 4 hours.

Rinse off the salt cure from the lamb shoulder and pat it dry with kitchen paper. Heat a little olive oil in a large pan over a medium-high heat and sear the lamb shoulder for about 2 minutes on each side or until evenly golden brown. Remove to a tray and leave to cool. Once cooled, put the lamb shoulder into a vacuum bag and add the lamb fat. Vacuum-seal the bag, then gently cook the lamb in a sous vide machine (or water bath) heated to 84°C for 8–10 hours. When ready, the lamb should be soft and tender. Remove from the sous vide and leave to cool completely in the bag to prevent the lamb from drying out.

Meanwhile, peel the carrots and turnips and chop into roughly 2cm dice. Heat a little olive oil in a large heavy-based pan over a medium-high heat. Add the carrots, turnips and onions with a little seasoning and fry the vegetables, stirring occasionally, for 8–10 minutes or until tender and golden brown.

Roughly chop the lamb shoulder into 2cm dice. Add to the pan along with the lamb sauce and season well to taste. As soon as the mixture is heated through, remove the pan from the heat. Spoon the lamb mixture into 4–6 individual ovenproof serving pots.

Peel the potatoes and thinly slice them on a mandoline. Pile the slices into short stacks and stamp out neat discs with a 3cm round pastry cutter. Working quickly, before they discolour, arrange the potato discs, overlapping, on top of the lamb mixture in each individual pot. Brush the potatoes generously with clarified butter and season well with sea salt.

When ready to serve, preheat the oven to 160°C/140°C fan/Gas Mark 3. Place the pots on a baking sheet and bake for 15 minutes, turning the pots every 5 minutes to ensure that the potatoes colour evenly. The lamb hotpots are done when the potatoes are golden brown and tender when pierced with a skewer or the tip of a knife.

BEETROOT-STAINED CABBAGE

1 Hispi cabbage
1 bottle beetroot juice (we use 'Beet It')

Trim off the base of the cabbage and separate the leaves. Trim the hard stalk from each leaf, then place the leaves in a pan. Pour over the beetroot juice and bring to a simmer. Partially cover the pan with a lid and simmer for 4–5 minutes or until the cabbage leaves are tender and stained purple colour. Leave to cool completely in the juice.

BEETROOT & BLACKCURRANT PURÉE

7 purple beetroots
250g blackcurrants
150ml red wine
150ml port
50ml raspberry vinegar

Peel and coarsely grate the beetroots, then place in a pan with all the other ingredients. Bring to a vigorous boil and cook, stirring the mixture every once in a while, until the beetroot is soft and the mixture has reduced to the consistency of jam. Transfer the contents of the pan to a blender and blitz until smooth. Season to taste. Pass the purée through a fine sieve into a clean pan, ready to reheat for serving.

PURPLE CARROTS

2 bunches of baby purple carrots, trimmed
a few knobs of unsalted butter

Blanch the carrots in a pan of boiling salted water for about 3 minutes or until they are tender when pierced with the tip of a knife. Use tongs or a slotted spoon to transfer the carrots to a bowl of iced water to cool them quickly and preserve their colour. When you are about ready to serve, lightly season the carrots, then reheat them in a pan of foaming butter for a couple of minutes, tossing occasionally, until warmed through.

ASSEMBLY

a handful of baby bull's blood leaves with stems on
Vinaigrette (see page 376)
Mint Sauce (see page 376)

Slice the lamb loin ballotine thickly and place 2 slices on each serving plate. Cut the lamb fillets into individual portions and wrap each portion in 1–2 beetroot-stained cabbage leaves. Add this to each plate followed by a neat spoonful of beetroot and blackcurrant purée and a couple of purple carrots. Dress the baby bull's blood leaves with a little vinaigrette and garnish the plate with a few leaves. Bring the dish to the table with an individual lamb hotpot and a small serving jug of mint sauce on the side.

Spring Lake District Lamb

with
shepherd's
pie,
cauliflower
& yoghurt
purée
and
mint sauce

SERVES 4–6

LAMB LOIN AND FILLETS

2 boned short saddles of lamb, about 450g each
    (loins and fillets separated)
meat glue, for sprinkling
olive oil, for drizzling
a few knobs of unsalted butter
a few sprigs of rosemary
Maldon sea salt and black pepper

Remove any sinew from the lamb fillets, then set aside in the fridge. With
a sharp boning knife, slice off the fat from each loin of lamb, keeping the fat
in one large piece if possible. Lay out the pieces of fat on a chopping board and
bash them with a rolling pin or meat tenderiser mallet to flatten until evenly
thick. Lightly season the fat with salt, then dust with meat glue. Wrap each
loin in a piece of fat, meat glue side in, and tie with kitchen string.

Put the loins into one large or two smaller vacuum bags and drizzle over
a little olive oil. Vacuum-seal the bags. Place them in a steam oven preheated
to 100°C and steam for 15 minutes. Remove the bags and immediately
immerse in a bowl of iced water to stop the cooking process. Once cooled,
keep the saddles, in the bags, in the fridge until needed.

When ready to roast, preheat the oven to 200°C/180°C fan/Gas Mark 6.
Heat a little olive oil in an ovenproof frying or sauté pan and sear the lamb
loins for 2 minutes on each side or until evenly browned. Add some butter
and rosemary. Transfer the pan to the oven and roast for a couple of minutes
for medium rare (45°C on a meat probe). Place the loins on a warmed plate or
carving board and leave to rest for a few minutes before slicing thickly.

To cook the lamb fillets for serving, heat a little oil in a wide frying pan.
Season the fillets with a little salt and pepper, then add them to the pan with
some rosemary and butter. Sear for about 2 minutes on each side or until
evenly golden brown. As they cook, spoon the foaming butter over them to
keep them moist and encourage even cooking. When ready, remove them
from the heat and allow to rest for a few minutes.

BRAISED LAMB SHOULDER

100g curing salt
a few sprigs of thyme
1 large garlic clove
finely grated zest of 1 lemon
1 x 1kg boned lamb shoulder
olive oil, for cooking

Put the curing salt, thyme, peeled garlic and lemon zest into a food processor
and blitz for a minute. Set the lamb on a roasting tray and rub the salt cure

mixture all over the meat. Cover with clingfilm, then leave in the fridge to cure for 4 hours.

Rinse off the salt cure and pat dry with kitchen paper. Heat a little olive oil in a wide frying pan, add the lamb shoulder and sear for 2 minutes on each side until evenly golden brown. Remove to a plate.

Once cooled, put the lamb shoulder into a vacuum bag and vacuum-seal it. Lower the bag into a sous vide machine (or water bath) heated to 84°C and leave to cook overnight or until the meat is soft and tender. Leave the lamb to cool in the bag.

SHEPHERD'S PIE

500g lamb mince (shoulder and belly)
1 onion, finely chopped
1 carrot, peeled and finely chopped
1 celery stick, finely chopped
1 garlic clove, finely chopped
200g skinned and chopped plum tomatoes
1 litre Lamb Stock (see page 380)
1 litre Veal Stock (see page 380)
a sprig of rosemary, leaves picked and chopped
a sprig of thyme, leaves picked
braised lamb shoulder (see above), cut up or shredded

Heat a wide, heavy-based pan until hot, then fry the lamb mince, in batches, for 6–8 minutes, stirring occasionally, until golden brown; remove to a plate. When all the mince has been browned, wipe out the pan with kitchen paper to remove the excess fat. Return the pan to the heat and add the chopped vegetables and garlic. Sweat for a few minutes, then return the browned mince to the pan. Add the chopped tomatoes and the lamb and veal stocks. Bring almost to the boil, then leave to simmer gently for about 40 minutes or until the mince is tender and the liquid has reduced.

Stir in the rosemary and thyme and season well to taste. Finally, stir in the braised lamb shoulder. Set aside, ready to reheat for serving.

TOMATO PURÉE

olive oil, for cooking
1 onion, chopped
3 garlic cloves, chopped
1 aubergine, peeled and chopped
1 red pepper, deseeded and chopped
1 yellow pepper, deseeded and chopped
1 green pepper, deseeded and chopped
1 red chilli, deseeded and chopped
80g root ginger, peeled and chopped
1 teaspoon mustard seeds

1 teaspoon fennel seeds
1 teaspoon coriander seeds
10 fresh tomatoes (about 1.5kg), chopped
400g can plum tomatoes
reduced balsamic vinegar, to taste

Heat a little olive oil in a large, heavy-based pan, add the onion and garlic, and sweat, stirring frequently, for about 6 minutes or until beginning to soften. Add all the other chopped vegetables with the chilli, ginger and a pinch each of salt and pepper. Sweat the vegetables for 10 minutes, stirring often, until they have softened. Add all the spice seeds and cook for a few more minutes before tipping in the fresh and canned tomatoes. Continue to cook over a medium-high heat, stirring occasionally, for about 20 minutes or until the tomatoes have cooked down and the mixture is quite thick.

Transfer the contents of the pan to a blender and add a splash of reduced balsamic vinegar. Blitz until smooth. Taste and adjust the seasoning with salt and pepper. Pass the purée through a sieve into a clean pan, ready to reheat for serving.

_____

CAULIFLOWER & YOGHURT PURÉE

1 head of cauliflower, cut into florets
250ml whole milk
250ml double cream
500ml full-fat plain yoghurt, hung in muslin overnight
    to drain

Put the cauliflower florets into a saucepan and pour in the milk and cream. Add a little salt and pepper, then cover with a piece of greaseproof paper. Bring the creamy milk to a simmer and cook for 10–15 minutes or until the cauliflower is very soft and will fall apart when pressed. (Try not to overcook the cauliflower to a mush or it will darken.) Drain the cauliflower (discard the creamy milk) and put into a blender. Blitz to a silky-smooth purée. Season well to taste, then transfer to a bowl and leave to cool slightly before stirring in the yoghurt. The finished purée should be pale and thick. Reheat gently in a heavy-based pan before serving.

_____

FENNEL & CORIANDER POWDER

100g fennel seeds
100g coriander seeds

Lightly toast the fennel and coriander seeds in a dry pan until they begin to smell fragrant. Tip them into a spice grinder and add a pinch of sea salt. Grind to a fine powder. Sift this through a drum sieve. Store the cooled powder in an airtight jar (it can be kept for a month).

_____

ASSEMBLY

Mint Sauce (see page 376)
Arbequina olive oil, to drizzle
a handful of baby spinach leaves
Vinaigrette (see page 376)
Olive Oil Mash (see page 371)
small, thin discs of carrot, beetroot, turnip and
    swede, warmed in Pickling Liquid (see page 376)
Lamb Sauce (see page 375)

For each serving, put 2 small spoonfuls of tomato purée on a warmed serving
plate and place a piece of lamb fillet on top of each. Put 2 spoonfuls of mint
sauce on the plate and top each with a slice of lamb loin. Pipe a neat mound
of cauliflower and yoghurt purée on the plate, drizzle over Arbequina olive
oil and sprinkle with the fennel and coriander powder. Lightly dress the baby
spinach leaves with a little vinaigrette and use to garnish the plate.

Spoon a layer of shepherd's pie on to the bottom of a warmed serving bowl,
then pipe olive oil mash over it until completely covered. Top the mash with
pickled vegetable discs. Serve immediately, with the lamb loin and fillet and an
individual jug of lamb sauce alongside.

Cartmel Valley Loin of Venison

with
Jerusalem
artichokes
and
venison &
chocolate
sauce

SERVES 5–6

VENISON

> 1 loin of venison, 1–1.2kg (aged
>   for a minimum of 18 days)
> olive oil, for cooking
> Maldon sea salt and black pepper

Trim the loin of venison to remove any sinew, then slice
it across into 200g portions. Place each piece in a vacuum
bag, season with a little salt and pepper and drizzle over
a little olive oil. Vacuum-seal the bags and keep in the
fridge until needed.

About 25 minutes before serving, cook the venison.
Lower the vacuum-sealed bags into a sous vide machine
(or water bath) heated to 58°C and poach the venison for
15 minutes, then remove the bags and leave to rest for a
few minutes.

Remove the venison from the vacuum bags and pat dry
with kitchen paper. Lightly season the meat, then sear in
a little olive oil in a hot pan for about 2 minutes on each
side or until evenly golden brown. Transfer to a warm
plate and leave the venison to rest again for a few minutes
before serving.

VENISON & CHOCOLATE SAUCE

> 1–1.5kg venison bones
> olive oil, for cooking
> 1 onion, chopped
> ½ leek, chopped
> 1 carrot, peeled and chopped
> 1 celery stick, chopped
> ½ bulb of garlic, cloves separated
>   and chopped
> ½ tablespoon tomato paste
> 10g juniper berries
> 200ml red wine
> 500ml Chicken Stock (see
>   page 379)
> 1 litre reduced Veal Stock
>   (see page 380)
> 10g cocoa nibs
> 10g dark chocolate (with
>   70% cocoa solids)

Roughly chop the venison bones with a strong knife or
cleaver into small chunks. Heat a little olive oil in a large

pan, add the bones and fry over a high heat until golden brown. Remove the bones from the pan and set aside.

Add the chopped vegetables and garlic to the pan with a little more oil. Sweat the vegetables for 8–10 minutes or until softened, stirring every once in a while. Add the tomato paste and juniper berries and stir, then fry for a few more minutes until the vegetables are golden brown. Return the browned venison bones to the pan, then deglaze with the red wine, scraping the bottom of the pan. Let the wine bubble until reduced by half. Pour in the chicken and veal stocks. If the liquid does not cover the bones, top up with water. Bring to a simmer, skimming off any scum from the surface, then leave to simmer gently for about 4 hours.

Strain the sauce through a fine sieve into a clean pan; discard the solids. Taste the sauce and if you find that the flavour is not intense enough, boil it to reduce. Strain again into a clean pan and leave to cool.

Before serving, reheat the sauce with the cocoa nibs and dark chocolate. Simmer for a few minutes, then strain into individual warmed serving jugs.

JERUSALEM ARTICHOKE PURÉE

500g Jerusalem artichokes
a squeeze of lemon juice
125ml Chicken Stock (see
    page 379)
50ml double cream

Peel the artichokes (save the skins to make the artichoke crumb), then drop into a bowl of iced water acidulated with a squeeze of lemon juice, to prevent them from browning. Heat a large pan until it is very hot. Working quickly, grate the artichokes and add them to the pan, then stir-fry over a high heat until any liquid released from the artichokes has evaporated. Add the chicken stock and bring to the boil. Once the stock has reduced, stir in the double cream and bring to a simmer. Simmer for a few minutes, then season to taste with salt and pepper. While still hot, blitz the artichoke mixture in a strong blender to make a smooth, creamy purée. Transfer the purée to a pan, ready to reheat for serving.

ROAST JERUSALEM ARTICHOKES

250g Jerusalem artichokes
a squeeze of lemon juice
50ml extra virgin olive oil

1 carrot, peeled and chopped
2 shallots, chopped
1 small bulb of fennel, chopped
2 garlic cloves, chopped
500ml dry white wine
100ml white wine vinegar
250ml Chicken Stock (see
  page 379)
3 sprigs of thyme
finely grated zest of 1 lemon
a few knobs of unsalted butter

Peel the artichokes (save the skins for the artichoke crumb) and immediately drop them into iced water acidulated with lemon juice. Heat the extra virgin olive oil in a pan over a medium heat. Add the carrot, shallots, fennel and garlic and sweat for 10–12 minutes or until soft, stirring occasionally. Pour in the white wine and let it boil and reduce by half. Pour in the vinegar and bring the liquid back to the boil. Boil for a few minutes or until the vinegar has also reduced by half. Add the chicken stock, thyme and lemon zest and bring the liquid to a simmer.

Drain the artichokes and add them to the pan. Place a cartouche (a round of baking parchment) on top and leave to simmer gently for 20 minutes or until the artichokes are tender. Remove from the heat and allow the artichokes to cool in the pan, then remove them to a tray lined with kitchen paper. Keep in the fridge until needed.

Before serving, cut each artichoke in half, then roast in a hot pan with a little butter and some seasoning. They should only take a couple of minutes on each side to caramelise and heat through.

_____

ARTICHOKE CRUMB

reserved artichoke skins (from
  roast artichokes and purée
  above)
vegetable oil, for deep-frying

Lay out all the skins on one or two baking trays. Place in a dehydrator heated to 75°C and dry out for about 4 hours or until the skins are completely dry. Store in an airtight container until ready to fry.

Heat a pan of vegetable oil to 160°C. Deep-fry the dried artichoke skins until golden brown and crisp. Remove to

a tray lined with kitchen paper and sprinkle with a little
sea salt. Finely chop the skins.

PICKLED ARTICHOKE AND PEARS

100ml olive oil
100ml lemon juice
1 large Jerusalem artichoke
1 large Nashi pear

Put the olive oil, lemon juice and a pinch of salt into
a jug and blitz together using a stick blender until the
mixture has emulsified. Divide this pickling liquid
between 2 bowls.

Very thinly slice the artichoke using a mandoline,
then stack the slices, a few at a time, and stamp out neat
discs using a 4—5cm round pastry cutter. Immediately
put the artichoke discs into one of the bowls of pickling
liquid and toss until every slice is coated with liquid.

Repeat the same process for the Nashi pear, adding
the discs to the second bowl of pickling liquid. Cover the
bowls with clingfilm and set aside to pickle for an hour.

ASSEMBLY

For each serving, spread a generous spoonful of
artichoke purée on a serving plate and arrange a few
roasted artichokes alongside. Sprinkle a little crispy
artichoke crumb over some of the artichoke purée. Slice
a piece of venison loin in half and add to the plate, then
garnish with the drained pickled artichoke and pear
slices. Serve immediately, with the venison and chocolate
sauce on the side.

Braised West Country Ox Cheek

with
beef dashi
and
bone
marrow
crumb

SERVES 4

MEAT BRINE

  1.25 litres water
  125g fine sea salt
  a handful of thyme
  1 bay leaf
  ½ bulb of garlic

Heat the water with the salt in a saucepan set over a high heat, stirring until the salt has dissolved. Take the pan off the heat and add the thyme, bay leaf and garlic. Leave the brine to cool and infuse.

OX CHEEKS

  4 ox cheeks
  meat brine (see above)
  olive oil, for cooking
  ½ carrot, peeled and chopped
  ½ onion, chopped
  ½ celery stick, chopped
  250ml red wine
  750ml Veal Stock (see page 380)
  750ml Chicken Stock (see page 379)
  Maldon sea salt and black pepper

Remove the sinews from the ox cheeks. Put the ox cheeks into a vacuum bag and pour in enough cooled brine to cover. (Keep any excess brine for another dish.) Vacuum-seal the bag, then leave in the fridge for 3 hours.

Preheat the oven to 100°C/80°C fan/Gas Mark low. Remove the ox cheeks from the brine and rinse well, then pat dry with kitchen paper. Heat a little olive oil in a wide ovenproof pan, add the ox cheeks with a little salt and pepper and sear for about 2 minutes on each side until evenly browned. Transfer the cheeks to a plate and set aside.

Drizzle a little more oil into the pan, then add the chopped vegetables. Cook, stirring occasionally, for 8–10 minutes or until the vegetables are golden brown. Return the ox cheeks to the pan and pour in the red wine. Let it bubble until reduced by half. Pour in the stocks and bring to a simmer. Cover the pan with a lid and transfer to the oven. Braise for 8–10 hours, or overnight, until the cheeks are very tender.

Remove the pan from the oven and leave to cool. Lift out the cheeks. For better presentation, trim each cheek to give it a neat round shape. Strain the braising liquid and boil to reduce and intensify the flavour. Vacuum-pack the cheeks with some of the reduced liquid.

Before serving reheat in a sous vide machine (or water bath) heated to 85°C for 10 minutes.

BEEF DASHI

olive oil, for cooking
125g smoked pancetta
2 small shallots, sliced
¼ bulb of garlic, cloves separated and lightly crushed
a handful of thyme
50ml Kombu Dashi (see page 377)
25ml Cabernet Sauvignon vinegar
750ml strained reduced braising stock from the
    ox cheeks (see above)

Heat a little olive oil in a deep pan, add the pancetta, shallots, garlic and thyme, and cook, stirring occasionally, for 6–8 minutes or until the pancetta is golden brown. Add the kombu dashi and vinegar and boil until reduced by half. Pour in the ox cheek braising stock and bring back to a simmer. Take the pan off the heat and strain the dashi through a muslin-lined sieve into a clean saucepan. Set aside, ready to reheat for serving.

CELERIAC & YEAST PURÉE

1 head of celeriac
olive oil, for cooking
200g cold unsalted butter, diced
25g fresh yeast
100ml Chicken Stock (see page 379)

Peel the celeriac and cut into a rough 2cm dice. Heat a little olive oil in a large pan, add the diced celeriac with some seasoning, and cook, tossing the celeriac occasionally, for 8–10 minutes or until it turns light golden brown. Add a few knobs of butter and toss the celeriac in the foaming butter to ensure that it is evenly coated. Continue cooking as you gradually add the rest of the butter until the celeriac has turned a deep golden brown, like caramel. Crumble in the yeast and cook for another couple of minutes, stirring well.

Drain off the excess butter and oil from the celeriac, then tip it into a clean pan. Pour in the chicken stock and bring to a simmer. Gently simmer until the stock has reduced by two-thirds. While still hot, transfer the celeriac and stock to a blender and blitz until smooth. Pass through a sieve into a clean pan. Season to taste, then cover and set aside, ready to reheat for serving.

PARSNIP PURÉE

3 parsnips
500ml whole milk
500ml double cream
1 garlic clove
a sprig of thyme

Peel the parsnips and cut into roughly 2cm dice. Put them into a saucepan with the milk, cream, peeled garlic and thyme. Season well and cover the ingredients with a cartouche (a round piece of baking parchment). Bring to a simmer, then cook gently for 10–15 minutes or until the parsnips are very soft.

Fish out and discard the thyme and garlic. Drain off about two-thirds of the creamy milk from the pan, then simmer the parsnips until the remaining liquid has reduced slightly. Transfer to a blender and blitz until very smooth. Pass the purée through a fine sieve back into a small saucepan, ready to reheat for serving.

PARSLEY & ANCHOVY PURÉE

2 courgettes
olive oil, for cooking
250g baby spinach leaves
2 bunches of flat-leaf parsley, about 200g,
    leaves picked
50ml double cream
50g anchovy paste

Peel the courgettes (save the skins), then grate them. Heat a little olive oil in a pan and add the courgettes with a little seasoning. Sweat them, stirring often, for 6–8 minutes or until they are soft but not coloured and any moisture released has evaporated.

Meanwhile, blanch the spinach with the courgette skins in a pan of boiling salted water for about 3 minutes or until you are able to squeeze and break down a spinach leaf with your fingers. Add the parsley and blanch for a further 30 seconds. Drain the greens in a muslin-lined sieve – squeeze the muslin to wring out any excess water from the greens. Add the greens to the pan containing the grated courgettes. Stir in the cream. Bring the mixture to a simmer, then pour into a Thermomix or strong blender and blitz to a purée. Pass the purée through a fine sieve into a bowl and cool it down quickly to preserve the vibrant green colour. Before serving, stir in the anchovy paste and warm up the purée in a small pan.

BONE MARROW CRUMB

200g stale sourdough bread (without crust)
100g bone marrow fat
100g unsalted butter

Put the bread into a food processor and pulse until coarsely chopped. Tip the crumbs into a bowl and set aside.

Render the bone marrow fat in a pan until fully melted, then add the butter. As the butter begins to foam, tip in the breadcrumbs and stir-fry for a few minutes until evenly golden brown. Tip the crumbs on to a tray lined with kitchen paper to drain off the excess fat. Sprinkle with sea salt. When cooled, store in an airtight container.

ROAST PORTOBELLO MUSHROOMS

2 large Portobello mushrooms, stalks removed
100g beef fat or dripping

Pan-roast the mushrooms in the beef fat in a pan with a little seasoning
for 5–6 minutes, turning over halfway, until golden brown. Transfer the
mushrooms to a chopping board and leave to cool before slicing them very
thinly, as you would a carpaccio. Arrange the slices on a tray lined with
greaseproof paper. Set aside until needed.

THYME & PARSLEY PASTE

a bunch of flat-leaf parsley, about 100g, leaves picked
a bunch of thyme, about 100g, leaves picked
100ml olive oil

Blanch the parsley leaves in a pan of boiling water for 30 seconds, then drain
and immediately cool them down in a bowl of iced water. Drain again and pat
dry with kitchen paper. Put the blanched parsley in a mortar with the thyme
and a little olive oil and grind/pound with the pestle to make a paste. Mix in
the rest of the oil. Transfer the paste to a bowl and cover with clingfilm. Set
aside or keep in the fridge until needed.

ASSEMBLY

For each serving, put a spoonful each of the celeriac and yeast purée, parsnip
purée, and parsley and anchovy purée on a warmed serving plate. Place an ox
cheek on top of the purées. Overlap 3 or 4 slices of Portobello mushroom on
the ox cheek. Spoon a little beef dashi over the mushrooms and ox cheek, then
top with a thin layer of thyme and parsley paste. Add a little bone marrow
crumb to the plate and serve at once.

Roast Lincolnshire Rabbit

with
summer
beans,
courgette &
basil purée
and
langoustine
tails

SERVES 4

SADDLE OF RABBIT

1 boneless saddle of rabbit
5–6 slices of Parma ham
meat glue, for sprinkling
olive oil, for cooking
Maldon sea salt and black pepper

Trim off any sinew from the rabbit. Arrange the Parma ham slices, slightly
overlapping, on a large sheet of oven-safe clingfilm to form a rectangle large
enough to wrap the saddle. Place the saddle on top of the ham. Use the smaller
ends of the loins to fill any gaps along the saddle so that it is of even thickness.
Sprinkle with salt, pepper and a little meat glue. With the help of the
clingfilm, roll up the saddle tightly to form a neat ballotine, making sure that
it is completely covered by the Parma ham and wrapped in clingfilm.

Put the ballotine into a vacuum bag and vacuum-seal it. Lower it
into a sous vide machine (or water bath) heated to 62°C and cook for 25
minutes. Remove and leave in the bag to cool completely. Keep in the fridge
until needed.

When ready to finish the saddle ballotine, preheat the oven to 200°C/180°C
fan/Gas Mark 6. Unwrap the ballotine and sear it in a little olive oil in a hot
ovenproof pan until evenly browned. Transfer the pan to the oven to cook for
2 minutes. Remove from the oven and leave to rest for a couple of minutes
before carving.

RABBIT LEGS

2 boneless rabbit legs
100g Maldon sea salt
1 litre water
2 pieces of pared lemon peel
2 bay leaves
2 sprigs of thyme
300g caul fat
meat glue, for sprinkling

First make a brine. Put the salt and water into a saucepan and stir over
a high heat until the salt has dissolved, then bring to the boil. Immediately
remove from the heat and add the lemon peel, bay leaves and thyme. Leave
to cool and infuse.

Check the rabbit legs and trim out any sinews. Put the legs into a bowl (or a
resealable bag) and pour over the cooled brine. Cover the bowl with clingfilm
and set aside in the fridge for an hour.

Remove the legs and rinse off the brine, then pat dry with kitchen paper. Lay
out the caul fat on a sheet of clingfilm. Arrange the rabbit legs on top to make

an even layer. Dust with a light sprinkling of meat glue and season with a little pepper. With the help of the clingfilm, roll up the rabbit legs into a neat ballotine completely covered with caul fat and wrapped in clingfilm.

Put the ballotine into a vacuum bag and vacuum-seal it. Lower the bag into a sous vide machine (or water bath) heated to 62°C and cook for 25 minutes. Remove the bag and immediately immerse it in a bowl of iced water to stop the cooking process. Keep the cooled ballotine, in the bag, in the fridge until needed.

Before serving, finish the rabbit leg ballotine in the same way as for the saddle ballotine (see above).

SUMMER BEANS

olive oil, for cooking
1 carrot, peeled and chopped
1 leek, chopped
1 celery stick, chopped
1 onion, chopped
2 garlic cloves, chopped
500g fresh borlotti beans, podded
1 litre Chicken Stock (see page 379)
2 sprigs of thyme
2 sprigs of rosemary
2 pieces of pared lemon peel
200g runner beans, blanched for 2 minutes, then cut
    across into rondelles
200g fine white or yellow beans, blanched for 2
    minutes, then cut diagonally into diamonds
20g unsalted butter
50g sun-dried tomatoes, chopped
50g preserved lemons (peel only), chopped
a handful of picked marjoram and chervil leaves

Heat a little olive oil in a wide, heavy-based pan over a medium heat and add the carrot, leek, celery, onion and garlic. Sweat the vegetables, stirring frequently, for 8–10 minutes or until they begin to soften but not colour. Tip in the borlotti beans and pour in the chicken stock. If the stock does not cover the beans, top up with a little water. Bring to a simmer, skimming off any froth from the surface. Lower the heat, partially cover the pan and cook for 20 minutes or until the beans are tender.

Take the pan off the heat and add the thyme, rosemary and lemon peel. Season well. Leave to cool and infuse.

Put 100g of the cooked beans and stock mixture (without the herbs and peel) into a blender and blitz until smooth. Transfer the purée to a bowl and set aside, along with the rest of the bean mixture.

Before serving, fish out and discard the thyme and rosemary sprigs and the lemon peel from the pan of beans. Add the bean purée to the pan along with

the runner beans, fine beans and butter. Season to taste. Heat through, then
stir in the sun-dried tomatoes, preserved lemon and herb leaves.

COURGETTE & BASIL PURÉE

4 courgettes, peeled and grated
olive oil, for cooking
500g baby spinach leaves
4 bunches of basil, about 400g, leaves picked
100ml double cream
50g Parmesan, freshly grated

Peel the courgettes (save the skins), then grate them. Heat a little olive oil in a
pan and add the courgettes with a little seasoning. Sweat them, stirring often,
for 6–8 minutes or until they are soft but not coloured and any moisture
released has evaporated. Transfer to a bowl and set aside.

Meanwhile, blanch the spinach with the courgette skins in a pan of boiling
salted water for about 3 minutes or until you are able to squeeze and break
down a spinach leaf with your fingers. Add the basil leaves and blanch for a
further 30 seconds. Drain the greens in a muslin-lined sieve – squeeze the
muslin to wring out any excess water from the greens. Add the greens to the
pan containing the grated courgettes. Stir in the cream. Bring the mixture to
a simmer, then pour into a Thermomix or strong blender, add the Parmesan
and blitz to a purée.

Pass the purée through a fine sieve into a bowl and cool it down quickly
to preserve the vibrant green colour. Transfer to a squeezy bottle. Before
serving, gently warm the purée by placing the bottle in a bowl of hot water.

DRIED COURGETTE FLOWERS

4 courgette flowers
olive oil, for cooking

Carefully remove the bulbous stigma inside each flower without damaging
any of the petals. Brush the flowers with olive oil and sprinkle over a little
sea salt. Place the flowers on a baking tray lined with a silicone mat, then put
this into a dehydrator preheated to 70°C. Leave for about 4 hours or until the
flowers are completely dried out. Keep in an airtight container until needed.

RABBIT SAUCE

olive oil, for cooking
1kg rabbit bones, chopped
1 onion, roughly chopped
1 small leek, roughly chopped
1 carrot, peeled and roughly chopped
1 celery stick, roughly chopped

½ bulb of garlic, cloves separated and roughly chopped
½ tablespoon tomato paste
200ml dry white wine
1 litre reduced Veal Stock (see page 380)
500ml Chicken Stock (see page 379)
a sprig of lemon thyme
a handful of parsley stalks
pared peel of 1 lemon
50g Browned Butter (see Almond Cake, Cherry
    'Bakewell Tart' recipe, page 355)
100ml double cream

Heat a little olive oil in a large, heavy-based pan over a medium-high heat. Add the rabbit bones and fry, turning occasionally, for 5–6 minutes or until they are evenly golden brown. Remove the bones to a plate and set aside.

Add a little more olive oil to the pan followed by the chopped vegetables and garlic with a little salt and pepper. Cook, stirring frequently, for 8–10 minutes or until the vegetables are soft and golden brown. Stir in the tomato paste and fry for another couple of minutes. Return all but a few browned rabbit bones to the pan and pour in the wine. Boil until reduced by half, then add the stocks. Bring back to the boil, skimming off the froth and scum from the surface. Reduce the heat and leave to simmer for 4 hours.

Let the sauce cool, then strain it through a fine sieve into a clean saucepan. Taste the sauce – if you want a more intense flavour, boil the sauce to reduce it. Adjust the seasoning with salt and pepper.

Before serving, reheat the sauce with the reserved browned rabbit bones, lemon thyme, parsley and lemon peel. Strain again into a clean saucepan, then return to the heat and stir in the browned butter and cream. Simmer until slightly thickened.

ASSEMBLY

8 Grilled Langoustine Tails (see Isle of Mull
    Langoustine recipe, page 119)

Thickly slice the saddle and rabbit leg ballotines and put a couple of slices of each on each serving plate. Add a few small spoonfuls of summer beans to the plate followed by 2 langoustine tails. Pipe a little courgette and basil purée on the plate and garnish with dried courgette flowers. Serve with individual jugs of rabbit sauce.

40-day Dry-aged
Lake District Beef Fillet

with
aubergine &
miso purée,
confit garlic
and
Dorset snails

SERVES 4

DRY-AGED BEEF FILLET

1 centre-cut piece of beef fillet
(preferably dry-aged for 40
days), about 1kg
olive oil, for cooking
30g unsalted butter
3–4 garlic cloves, lightly crushed
a few sprigs of thyme
Maldon sea salt and black pepper

Using a sharp knife, trim any white sinew from the
beef fillet. If there are any bits that are too dry from the
ageing, trim these off too but save the trimmings for the
beef sauce. Roll the trimmed beef tightly in clingfilm to
get a neat log shape, then cut this across into 4 portions.
Wrap each portion again with a little more clingfilm to
cover the cut sides, then keep in the fridge until ready
to cook.

About 20 minutes before cooking, remove the pieces of
beef fillet from the fridge to allow them to come to room
temperature. Heat a little olive oil in a wide frying pan
until hot. Unwrap the beef and season with a little salt
and pepper, then sear for 2 minutes on each side until
golden brown. Add the butter, garlic and thyme. Spoon
the foaming butter over the pieces of fillet constantly as
they continue to cook – use a meat thermometer to test
the beef for doneness: 38–40°C for rare; 42–45°C for
medium rare; 48–50°C for medium; 58°C for medium
well; and 62°C for well done. When cooked to your taste,
transfer the beef to a warm platter and leave to rest for
5–10 minutes.

AUBERGINE & MISO PURÉE

2 aubergines
olive oil, for cooking
1 shallot, chopped
250ml Chicken Stock (see
page 379)
1 packet of squid ink
300g red miso paste (we
prefer Ichibiki brand)
150ml rice vinegar
140g soft brown sugar
175g unsalted butter, melted

Trim off the ends of the aubergines, then roughly chop the flesh. Heat a large pan until very hot, then add a little olive oil followed by the chopped aubergine and a little salt and pepper. Fry the aubergines, turning every couple of minutes, until they are golden brown. Remove to a plate and set aside.

Add a little more oil to the pan along with the shallot. Sweat, stirring frequently, until it begins to soften. Return the aubergines to the pan and sweat the vegetables for 3–4 minutes or until they soften. Add the chicken stock and boil until the liquid has almost completely evaporated.

Transfer the contents of the pan to a blender and blitz until smooth. Add a little squid ink to the blender and blitz again until the mixture is dark and well mixed. Pass the purée through a sieve into a bowl and set aside.

Preheat the oven to 160°C/140°C fan/Gas Mark 3. Spread the miso paste thinly over a silicone mat on a baking tray. Bake for 15–20 minutes or until the miso is a deep golden brown and slightly crisp around the edges. Remove from the oven and scrape the baked miso into a blender. Add the vinegar and sugar to the blender and blitz until smooth. With the machine running, gradually pour in the melted butter. When fully incorporated, pass the mixture through a sieve into a bowl. Weigh the miso mixture (weigh the empty bowl first).

Now weigh the aubergine purée. You want a 2:1 ratio of aubergine purée to miso. So, for example, for 200g aubergine purée, stir in 100g miso mixture. Mix well, then cover with clingfilm and keep in the fridge until ready to serve.

CONFIT GARLIC

1 bulb of garlic, cloves separated
200ml vegetable oil

Put the peeled garlic cloves into a small saucepan and pour over the oil to cover. Place over a low heat and gently cook the garlic for 45 minutes or until it is tender. Transfer the garlic and oil into a clean, sterilised jar and cover. Leave to cool completely before storing in the fridge.

When ready to serve, pan-roast the garlic cloves in a little of the garlicky oil for 1–2 minutes until lightly golden.

CONFIT GARLIC PURÉE

5 heads of garlic
100ml double cream

Preheat the oven to 150°C/130°C fan/Gas Mark 2.
Wrap the garlic in a large piece of foil and place on a
baking tray. Bake for about an hour or until soft. Leave to
cool for a few minutes, then while still warm, squeeze the
soft cloves out of the skins into a small saucepan. Pour the
cream over the garlic cloves and bring to a simmer. Cook
for a few minutes until reduced and thickened slightly,
then tip the garlic and cream into a blender and blitz until
smooth. Season to taste with salt and pepper. Return the
purée to the saucepan, ready to reheat for serving.

BEEF-FAT CARROTS

500ml beef fat
4 large carrots, peeled
3 sprigs of thyme
2 garlic cloves
a few sprigs of flat-leaf parsley,
    finely chopped

Melt the beef fat in a wide pan over a medium heat. Add
the carrots, thyme and peeled garlic, and season with salt
and pepper. Cook the carrots gently for 15–20 minutes or
until they are tender when pierced with the tip of a knife.
Set aside to cool in the beef fat.

For serving, remove the confit carrots from the beef fat
and fry them in a hot frying pan for a few minutes until
they are evenly golden. Transfer them to a chopping
board and cut into shorter lengths so they resemble
barrels. Roll them in the parsley to coat.

DORSET SNAILS

24 ready-cooked shelled
    Dorset snails
100g plain flour
100g unsalted butter
pan-roasted confit garlic cloves
    (see above)

Fry the snails just before serving. Put the flour into a
shallow bowl and lightly season with salt and pepper.
Dust the snails with the seasoned flour. Melt the butter
in a heavy-based pan, add the snails and fry for a few

minutes until they are golden and crisp. Remove them to a bowl and sprinkle with a little sea salt, then toss with the confit garlic cloves. Keep warm in a low oven, if necessary.

———————

ASSEMBLY

For each serving, cut each piece of beef fillet in half and place on a warmed serving plate. Sprinkle over a little sea salt. Add some of the carrot and confit garlic mixture and 2 shallot halves. Squeeze dots of confit garlic purée around the plate. Put a generous spoonful of mash in a smaller side bowl and top it with a spoonful of aubergine and miso purée. Arrange 6 Dorset snails around the bowl. Serve immediately, with individual jugs of beef sauce.

Poultry & Game Birds

Roasted Squab Pigeon
250

Whole Roasted
Goosnargh Duck
260

Roasted Red-legged
Partridge
266

Ribble Valley Chicken
272

Game Pithivier
278

Salad of Wild Duck
282

Soy-glazed
Norfolk Quail
288

Grouse
294

Roasted Squab Pigeon

with
baked
Roscoff
onion, violet
artichoke
barigoule
and
braised ceps

SERVES 4

ROASTED PIGEON BREASTS & CONFIT PIGEON LEGS

  4 squab pigeons, 550–600g each
  a few knobs of unsalted butter
  a handful of thyme
  100g Salt Cure (see Suckling Pig recipe, page 203)
  2 garlic cloves
  about 300ml duck fat
  olive oil, for frying
  Maldon sea salt and black pepper

To prepare each pigeon, remove the head and cut out the neck, keeping
as much skin as possible covering the breast, then trim off any visible sinew.
Carve out the legs, then remove the guts and gizzards. (Reserve the legs, livers
and hearts for later and keep any bones or necks for the sauce.)

Rinse the pigeon breast crowns and pat dry, then place them in vacuum
bags. Season with salt and pepper and add a few sprigs of thyme and a few
knobs of butter to each bag. Vacuum-seal the bags. Lower into a sous vide
machine (or water bath) heated to 71°C and cook for 10 minutes. Remove
the bags and immediately immerse them in a bowl of iced water to stop the
cooking process. Once cooled, keep in the fridge (in the bags) until needed.

Next, confit the pigeon legs. Place them in a small tray and cover with the
salt cure. Cover with clingfilm and leave in the fridge to cure for about 4
hours. Rinse off the salt cure and pat the pigeon legs dry with kitchen paper,
then put them into a large vacuum bag. Add the peeled garlic cloves, the rest of
the thyme and the duck fat, then vacuum-seal the bag. Confit the legs in a sous
vide machine (or water bath) heated to 85°C for 6–8 hours or until the meat is
tender. Lift out the bag and leave to cool, then remove the legs and shred
the meat, discarding skin and sinew.

When ready to serve, remove the pigeon crowns from the bags and fry in
a hot pan with a little drizzle of olive oil for about 2 minutes on each side or
until evenly golden brown. Remove the crowns to a plate and leave to rest
while you finish the other elements of the dish.

PIGEON SAUCE

  1kg pigeon bones (to include any off-cuts)
  olive oil, for cooking
  4 shallots, chopped
  1 leek, chopped
  2 carrots, peeled and chopped
  2 celery sticks, chopped
  1 bulb of garlic, cloves separated and chopped
  1 tablespoon tomato paste
  200ml red wine
  200ml ruby port
  2 litres reduced Veal Stock (see page 380)

1 litre Chicken Stock (see page 379)
2 sprigs of lemon thyme

Heat a drizzle of olive oil in a large, heavy-based pan, add the pigeon bones and fry over a high heat for about 2 minutes on each side or until golden brown. Remove to a plate and set aside. Add a little more oil to the pan followed by the chopped vegetables and garlic. Cook over a medium-high heat, stirring frequently, for about 8 minutes or until the vegetables begin to soften. Stir in the tomato paste and fry for 2 more minutes. Saving a few browned pigeon bones for later, return the rest to the pan, then deglaze it with the red wine and port, scraping the bottom well. Boil the liquid until reduced by half before adding the stocks. Bring back to the boil, then lower the heat and simmer for about 4 hours, skimming frequently at the beginning to remove any froth or scum from the surface.

Strain the sauce through a fine sieve into a clean saucepan; discard the solids. Adjust the seasoning with salt and pepper. If you want a more intense flavour, boil the sauce to reduce it. Set aside in the pan, ready to finish.

Before serving, add the reserved browned pigeon bones and the lemon thyme to the sauce, heat through and strain again.

BAKED ROSCOFF ONIONS

4 Roscoff onions (unpeeled)
olive oil
250g unsalted butter
200g stale breadcrumbs
pigeon hearts and livers (see above)
200g cooked pearl barley (see Pearl Barley Risotto
    recipe, page 372, without the Madeira cream and
    mushroom purée)
2 teaspoons Mushroom Purée (see page 371)
confit pigeon leg meat (see above)
pigeon sauce (see above)
grated truffle, to garnish

Preheat the oven to 180°C/160°C fan/Gas Mark 4. Cut off the top from each onion and very slightly trim the base so that the onion can sit securely upright on a baking tray. Drizzle the onions with a little olive oil and season lightly with salt and pepper. Bake for about 25 minutes or until the onions are soft and slightly caramelised. Remove from the oven and leave to cool.

Carefully peel off the skin from each onion, then scoop out the inner layers to leave a bowl-like onion 'shell'. Save the inner layers for the onion purée and set the onion shells aside on a baking tray.

Melt the butter in a heavy-based pan, add the breadcrumbs and fry over a medium-high heat, stirring frequently, until the crumbs are evenly golden brown. Tip the breadcrumbs on to a tray lined with several layers of kitchen paper to absorb excess butter. Sprinkle with a little sea salt, then set aside.

In the same pan, fry the pigeon hearts and livers with a little oil and a pinch of salt until golden brown. Remove to a plate and cool, then chop finely.

Put the pearl barley, mushroom purée, confit pigeon leg meat and chopped pigeon hearts and liver in a saucepan. Add a splash of pigeon sauce to moisten. Stir well to mix, then taste and adjust the seasoning. Set aside.

Before serving, preheat the oven to 200°C/180°C fan/Gas Mark 6, and reheat the barley and pigeon mixture. Use to fill the onion shells and cover the tops with the fried breadcrumbs. Bake for 2 minutes, then garnish with truffle.

___

ROASTED ONION PURÉE

olive oil, for cooking
1.5kg Spanish onions, sliced
scooped-out baked onion (see above)
250ml Chicken Stock (see page 379)
100ml pigeon sauce (see above)

Heat a little olive oil in a large, heavy-based pan, add the sliced onions with a little pinch each of salt and pepper and sweat, stirring every once in a while, for 10–12 minutes or until the onions are soft and translucent. Add the reserved scooped-out baked onion and continue to cook gently, stirring often, for about 20 minutes or until the onions are deep brown and sticky. Pour in the chicken stock and bring to the boil, scraping the bottom and sides of the pan to deglaze. Add the pigeon sauce and boil until excess liquid has evaporated.

Transfer the contents of the pan to a food processor or Thermomix and blitz to a smooth purée. Taste and adjust the seasoning with salt and pepper. Pass the purée through a fine sieve, then let it cool completely before storing in a squeezy bottle. For serving, warm the onion purée by placing the bottle in a bowl of hot water for a few minutes.

___

VIOLET ARTICHOKE BARIGOULE

1 teaspoon ascorbic acid
5 violet artichokes
finely grated zest and juice of 1 lemon
50ml extra virgin olive oil
1 small bulb of fennel, chopped
1 carrot, peeled and chopped
2 shallots, chopped
2 garlic cloves, chopped
500ml dry white wine
100ml white wine vinegar
250ml Chicken Stock (see page 379)
3 sprigs of thyme
olive oil, for cooking

Stir the ascorbic acid into a bowl of iced water and set aside. Trim each artichoke stalk and snap back the tough outer leaves to expose the pale yellow inner leaves. (Rub all cut surfaces with lemon juice as you work to prevent the artichoke from discolouring.) Use a teaspoon to remove the fibrous 'choke' buried in the centre. As each artichoke heart is prepared, drop it into the bowl of acidulated water.

Heat the extra virgin olive oil in a heavy-based pan, add the fennel, carrot, shallots and garlic, and sweat the vegetables, stirring occasionally, for about 10 minutes or until they soften. Pour in the wine and let it boil until reduced by half. Add the vinegar and boil until the liquid has reduced by half again. Add the artichokes to the pan along with the chicken stock and thyme. Cover the contents of the pan with a cartouche (a round piece of baking parchment), then leave to simmer gently for about 20 minutes or until the artichokes are tender.

Take the pan off the heat and leave the artichokes to cool in their poaching liquid. Once cooled, fish out the artichokes and dry them on a plate lined with kitchen paper. Keep in fridge, covered, until ready to finish.

Before serving, cut each artichoke in half lengthways and lightly season, then fry in a hot pan with a little olive oil for about 2 minutes on each side or until lightly golden brown.

BRAISED CEPS

500g fresh ceps, cleaned
olive oil, for cooking
200g unsalted butter, diced
200ml Chicken Stock (see page 379)
100ml pigeon sauce (see above)
a sprig of thyme
2 garlic cloves

Cut each cep in half through the stalk, then score the cut sides. Place the ceps, scored side down, in a large frying or sauté pan. (Starting with a cold pan helps the mushrooms to caramelise evenly.) Drizzle over a little olive oil and dot with half of the diced butter. Lightly season with salt and pepper. Set the pan over a medium heat and fry the mushrooms for a couple of minutes until golden brown, then flip them over to brown the other sides.

Add the stock, pigeon sauce, remaining butter, the thyme and peeled garlic cloves. Increase the heat and swirl the contents of the pan as the butter melts so it emulsifies with the stock. Let the liquid bubble for a few minutes, then take the pan off the heat and keep warm.

ASSEMBLY

Cherry Purée (see page 384)

Neatly carve out the pigeon breasts from the crowns. Brush the skin of the breasts with warm pigeon sauce. For each serving, put a pigeon breast on a warmed serving plate. Arrange a couple of artichokes and braised ceps over and around the breast. Squeeze some onion purée and cherry purée next to the breast. Serve immediately with a baked Roscoff onion and a little more pigeon sauce on the side.

Johnson & Swarbrick

Johnson & Swarbrick was founded in 1985 and has quickly become the UK's foremost poultry producer. We are a family-owned and operated business, and our motto is 'a happy bird is a tasty bird'.

Our founder, Reg Johnson, put his home village of Goosnargh, Lancashire, on the map when he met a young chef called Paul Heathcote in 1987. Paul had recently moved out of London and was looking for English corn-fed chicken. Reg took up the challenge and invested much time and work in developing the now-famous Goosnargh corn-fed chicken, which has become the benchmark in the industry.

Both our Goosnargh chicken and duck are now supplied to the finest chefs across the country, including to the kitchens at Pollen Street. Our Goosnargh duck is a cross between Aylesbury and Peking duck, giving the best meat to bone balance, with good breast weight in particular.

We have worked with Jason and his team for a good few years. Originally it was always Reg who went to London to meet all our customers, and he and Jason developed a great working relationship. Reg loved what Jason did with our poultry.

Sadly Reg passed away in 2015, but the legacy of this Lancashire food hero lives on through his poultry.

johnson-swarbrick.co.uk

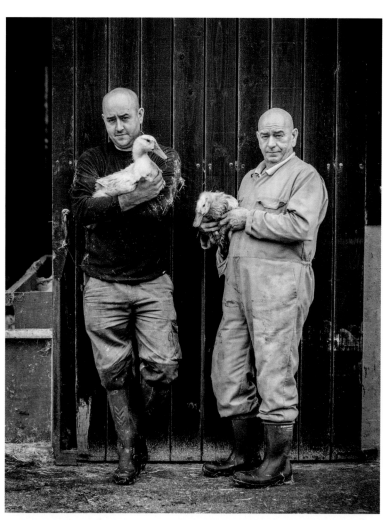

Whole Roasted Goosnargh Duck

with
braised
swede
and
pesto purée

SERVES 2

ROAST DUCK

1 Goosnargh duck, about 1.8kg
500g runny honey
50ml truffle vinegar
mixed lavender, rosemary and thyme, to garnish
Maldon sea salt and black pepper

Ensuring that you leave on as much skin as possible, cut along the base of
the neck to remove it; save the neck for the Duck Sauce (page 374). Remove
any sinew from around the duck breasts. Trim off the wing tips at the elbow
joint; reserve the tips for the sauce. If the duck feet are still attached, cut them
off just above the knuckle joint. Remove the innards from the cavity. Rub all
over the skin and inside the cavity of the duck with salt and pepper.

Use a blowtorch to brown the skin of the duck, moving the flame all over
the duck so that it is evenly golden brown. Next, truss the duck with butcher's
string: run the string from the front to under the wings and finally cross over
to the back to tie the legs together. Place the duck, breast side up, on a wire
rack set over a roasting tray to collect the duck fat as it cooks. Place the tray
in a steam oven heated to 100°C to cook for 15 minutes.

While the duck is steaming, prepare the truffle and honey glaze. Boil the
honey in a heavy-based saucepan until reduced by half and thickened. Stir in
the truffle vinegar and a pinch each of salt and pepper. Set aside.

Remove the duck from the steam oven and immediately cool it down in a blast
chiller. Once cooled, score the skin, taking care not to slice through the flesh.
If preparing ahead, keep the duck in the fridge until you are ready to roast it.

About 25 minutes before serving, preheat the oven to 180°C/160°C fan/Gas
Mark 4. Brush the truffle and honey glaze all over the duck, then roast it for
about 18 minutes, basting it with the glaze every 4 minutes. When the duck is
dark brown and nicely glazed, remove it from the oven and leave to rest.

Transfer the roast duck to a serving tray and stick a mixed bunch of lavender,
rosemary and thyme into the cavity. Present the duck to your guest, then
return it to the kitchen for carving. First, carve out the legs and remove the
meat from the bones, discarding any fat or sinew. Roughly dice the leg meat
for the salad (see below). Then carve out the duck breasts and season with salt
and pepper; keep the breasts warm.

BRAISED SWEDE

1 small swede
olive oil, for cooking
100ml Duck Sauce (see page 374)
20g truffle trimmings

Peel the swede and cut into neat wedges. Use a turning knife around the edges of each wedge to round them. Heat a drizzle of oil in a wide frying pan over a medium-high heat, add the swede wedges with a pinch of salt, and cook for 2–3 minutes on each side until evenly golden brown. Add the duck sauce and lower the heat slightly. Braise the swede for 10 minutes, turning occasionally in the sauce, until tender and nicely glazed. Take the pan off the heat and stir in the truffle trimmings. If preparing in advance, leave to cool, then cover the pan with a lid. Before serving, reheat the swede in the sauce with the truffle trimmings.

PESTO PURÉE

4 courgettes
500g baby spinach
4 bunches of basil, about 400g, leaves picked
50g Parmesan, freshly grated
100ml double cream
100g toasted pine nuts

Peel the courgettes (save the skins), then grate them. Heat a dry non-stick pan over a medium heat, add the grated courgettes and sweat, stirring frequently, until the courgettes are tender but not browned and any moisture released has evaporated. Take the pan off the heat.

Blanch the spinach leaves and courgette skins in a pan of boiling water for about 3 minutes or until soft. Add the basil leaves to the pan and blanch for a further 30 seconds. Drain the greens in a sieve, pressing down with the back of a ladle to remove excess water.

Tip the greens into the pan containing the courgettes. Stir in the cream and return the pan to the heat. As soon as the cream begins to simmer, transfer the mixture to a Thermomix or strong blender and add the Parmesan and pine nuts. Blitz until smooth. Taste and adjust the seasoning with salt and pepper. Pass the pesto purée through a sieve, then transfer to a squeezy bottle or a piping bag fitted with a plain round nozzle and set aside.

ROASTED SEASONAL MUSHROOMS

250g mixed mushrooms, cleaned
olive oil, for cooking
100g unsalted butter, diced
1 garlic clove, chopped
a sprig of thyme
100ml Chicken Stock (see page 379)
100ml Duck Sauce (see page 374)

Cut any larger mushrooms in half lengthways. Heat a drizzle of olive oil in a wide, heavy-based pan until hot. Add the mushrooms, some seasoning and a few knobs of butter, and fry for 4–5 minutes, turning the mushrooms over halfway through the time, until they are evenly golden brown. Add the garlic and thyme to the pan and cook for a further minute. Stir in the chicken stock, duck sauce and the remaining butter, and increase the heat to high. Once

the butter has melted and emulsified with the sauce, take
the pan off the heat. Keep warm or reheat for serving.

DUCK LEG SALAD

olive oil, for cooking and dressing
diced duck leg meat (see above)
20ml runny honey
100ml Spice Water Dressing (see
    page 373)
200g Swede Purée (see Slow-
    cooked Heritage Breeds Farm
    Egg recipe, page 73)
100g bitter salad leaves (such as
    chicory and radicchio)
75g seasonal radishes, sliced
a handful of seasonal foraged
    herbs (such as sorrel) and
    edible flowers
4 croutons

Heat a little olive oil in a wide, non-stick pan, add the
diced duck leg with some seasoning, and fry for 2–3
minutes or until lightly golden brown. Tip the meat on
to a plate. Dab any excess oil from the pan with kitchen
paper, then return the pan to the heat and add the honey.
Heat until it turns to a deep golden brown. Return the
duck meat to the pan along with the spice water dressing.
Scrape the bottom and sides of the pan to deglaze any
browned bits, then season well with sea salt. Boil for a
few minutes. Remove the pan from the heat and keep
the meat warm.

ASSEMBLY

1 celery stick, cut into
    finger lengths
a few knobs of unsalted butter
1 fresh fig
Duck Sauce (see page 374)

Blanch the celery in a small pan of boiling water for
2 minutes. Drain and discard the water. Bring a splash of
water and a few knobs of butter to a simmer in the pan.
Add the celery and simmer for a couple of minutes or
until tender, then remove to plate with tongs.

Cut the fig into wedges and sear in a hot, dry non-stick
pan until slightly caramelised. Remove to a plate.

For each serving, squeeze some swede purée into the
centre of a serving bowl and top with the glazed duck leg

meat. Toss the bitter salad leaves and sliced radishes with a little olive oil, salt and pepper, then pile on top of the duck. Garnish with seasonal herbs, edible flowers and a crouton.

On each of the 2 other serving plates, place a duck breast with a wedge of braised swede next to it. Squeeze a small mound of pesto purée on to the plate and arrange a couple of celery pieces on top of the purée and over the duck. Top the duck breast and swede with a few roast mushrooms and a couple of fig wedges. Serve immediately with the duck salad and a jug of duck sauce alongside.

Roasted Red-legged Partridge

with
mulled
& spiced
beetroot
and
plum jam

SERVES 4

PARTRIDGE

4 oven-ready partridges, with
    hearts and liver
25g unsalted butter, melted, plus
    extra knobs for cooking
a handful of thyme
4 garlic cloves, sliced
duck fat, for cooking
olive oil, for cooking
Maldon sea salt and black pepper

If the necks are on the partridges, remove these, leaving
as much skin as possible attached to cover the breasts of
the birds; save the necks for the sauce. Set the livers and
hearts aside for later. Carve out the legs from the breast
crowns and set aside. Rinse the crowns well and pat dry
with kitchen paper, then place in a vacuum bag and add
the melted butter, half the thyme, half the garlic and a
pinch each of salt and pepper. Vacuum-seal the bag and
keep in the fridge until ready to cook.

Next, confit the partridge legs. Put them into a vacuum
bag with the remaining thyme and garlic and some
seasoning. Add enough duck fat to cover the legs, then
vacuum-seal the bag. Lower the bag into a sous vide
machine (or water bath) heated to 80°C and cook for
4 hours or until the meat is very tender and falling off
the bone. Take the bag out of the water and leave to
cool, then gently remove the partridge legs. Remove the
meat from four of the legs and dice. Leave the other four
whole. Chill until needed.

When you are ready to cook the partridge crowns, lower
them into a sous vide machine (or water bath) heated to
58°C and poach for 12 minutes. Remove the crowns from
the vacuum bag and pat them dry with kitchen paper.
Heat a little olive oil in a wide frying pan. Lightly season
the crowns, then add to the pan along with a few knobs
of butter. Sear the crowns, constantly basting them with
the foaming butter, for 2 minutes on each side or until
evenly golden brown. Remove to a warm plate and leave
to rest for a few minutes before serving.

Season the partridge hearts and liver, then fry in a hot
pan with a little olive oil and a few knobs of butter until
golden brown all over. Remove to a plate and leave to cool
slightly, then chop into small dice.

PARTRIDGE SAUCE

olive oil, for cooking
500g partridge bones (necks,
    carcasses, etc)
2 shallots, chopped
½ leek, chopped
1 carrot, peeled and chopped
1 celery stick, chopped
½ bulb of garlic, cloves separated
    and chopped
½ tablespoon tomato paste
1 star anise
1 cloves
1 small cinnamon stick
100ml red wine
100ml ruby port
1 litre reduced Veal Stock (see
    page 380)
500ml Chicken Stock (see
    page 379)
a sprig of lemon thyme

Heat a little olive oil in a large, heavy-based pan, add
the partridge bones and fry over a high heat until evenly
browned. Remove the bones to a plate and set aside.
Add a little more oil to the pan followed by the chopped
vegetables and garlic. Cook over a medium-high heat,
stirring frequently, for 8–10 minutes or until the
vegetables are tender. Add the tomato paste and spices
and stir well. Fry for a few more minutes or until the
vegetables are golden brown.

Return all but a few partridge bones to the pan and pour
in the red wine and port to deglaze the pan, scraping the
bottom to dislodge any browned bits. Boil until reduced
by half, then add the stocks. Bring back to a simmer,
skimming off any scum and froth from the surface, then
leave to simmer gently for 4 hours.

Strain the sauce through a fine sieve into a clean saucepan.
Taste the sauce and, if you want a more intense flavour,
boil down to reduce and thicken slightly. Season with salt
and pepper to taste. Set aside until needed.

Before serving, add the reserved bones and lemon
thyme to the sauce and boil for a few minutes, then strain
through a fine sieve.

MULLED & SPICED BEETROOT

1.5kg plain flour
200g fine sea salt
2 sprigs of thyme, leaves picked
   and chopped
10g juniper berries, crushed
5g black peppercorns, crushed
5g star anise, crushed
5g cardamom pods, crushed
750ml cold water
2 large or 4 small red beetroots

First make a salt crust. Mix together the flour, salt, thyme
and crushed spices in a large bowl. Add the water, a little
at a time, mixing until the ingredients come together
to make a dough. Knead the dough a few times, then set
aside to rest for a few minutes.

Preheat the oven to 170°C/150°C fan/Gas Mark 3½.
Divide the dough in half (or into quarters) and roll out
each piece into a disc large enough to wrap around a
beetroot. Wrap each beetroot in dough and pinch the
edges to seal. Place the dough-wrapped beetroots on a
baking tray and stick a temperature probe into one of
them. Bake until the beetroots are tender – the probe
will register 75°C. Remove from the oven and leave to
cool, then cut off the salt crusts and peel off the beetroot
skins. Cut the beetroots into neat wedges (we prefer
them to have rounded edges at the restaurant). Set aside
until needed.

BEETROOT & MEAD REDUCTION

500ml beetroot juice
500ml mead (fermented
   honey drink)
1 tablespoon runny honey

Put all the ingredients in a pan, bring to the boil and
reduce to a thick syrup. Set aside.

MARINATED BEETROOT

1 large golden beetroot
a drizzle of olive oil
a sprig of lemon thyme, leaves
   picked and chopped

Peel the beetroot, then slice thinly with a mandoline.
Stack the slices, a few at a time, and stamp out neat discs

using a 3cm round cutter. Put the beetroot discs into
a bowl and drizzle over some olive oil. Season with a
generous pinch each of salt and pepper, add the chopped
thyme and toss to coat. Cover with clingfilm and set aside
to marinate for 20 minutes.

_____

ASSEMBLY

    200g cooked pearl barley (see
        Pearl Barley Risotto recipe,
        page 372, without Madeira
        cream and mushroom purée)
    2 teaspoons Mushroom Purée
        (see page 371)
    butter, for cooking
    Plum Jam (see page 384)

Place the beetroot wedges in a pan with some of
the beetroot and mead reduction and simmer for a few
minutes until the beetroot wedges are hot and nicely
glazed. Keep warm.

Put the cooked barley into a saucepan with the
mushroom purée and some partridge sauce to moisten.
Stir over a high heat until the mixture is hot. Add the
diced partridge legs, hearts and liver and mix well. When
hot, taste and adjust the seasoning, then take the pan off
the heat.

Carve out the breasts from the crowns. Put the breasts in
a pan with some partridge sauce and glaze over a medium
heat, turning the breasts in the sauce.

Heat a few knobs of butter in a pan, and, once foaming,
add the partridge legs. Roast in the butter to crisp up
the skin.

For each serving, arrange some marinated golden
beetroot discs in a concentric circle on a warmed serving
plate. Add a large spoonful of the pearl barley mixture
to the plate and place 2 glazed partridge breasts on top,
and 1 partridge leg. Add 2 or 3 mulled beetroot wedges.
Squeeze little dots of plum jam around the plate followed
by little spoonfuls of beetroot and mead reduction. Serve
immediately, with any remaining sauce on the side,
if desired.

Ribble Valley Chicken

with
braised
leeks,
mustard
purée
and
chicken-fat
mash

SERVES 4

CHICKEN BREASTS

2 chicken crowns
1 litre water
1 lemon, quartered
a few sprigs of thyme
a few sprigs of rosemary
meat glue, for dusting
a drizzle of olive oil, for cooking
1 black truffle, for serving
Maldon sea salt and black pepper

First, prepare the brine for the chicken. Put the water and 100g sea salt into a pan and stir over a medium heat until the salt has dissolved. Take the pan off the heat and add the lemon and herbs. Leave to cool and infuse.

Gently pull the skin off each chicken crown, preferably in one piece; set the skin aside. Very carefully remove the chicken breasts from the crown using a sharp boning knife. If necessary, trim around the chicken breasts to neaten their shape. Put the 4 boneless chicken breasts into a resealable bag and pour in the brine. Seal the bag and set aside in the fridge for an hour.

Meanwhile, scrape off any excess fat from the reserved chicken skins, making sure not to tear them. (Save the chicken fat to use later.) Lay out the chicken skins on a large piece of oven-safe clingfilm to form a rough rectangle, large enough to wrap around the chicken breasts. Lightly dust the chicken skins with meat glue.

Remove the chicken breasts from the brine and pat them dry with kitchen paper. Dust the breasts with a little meat glue, then join 2 breasts together with their opposite ends meeting. Repeat with the remaining 2 chicken breasts. Place the breasts, end-to-end, along the middle of the chicken skin rectangle. With the help of the clingfilm, wrap the skin around the chicken breasts, making sure that the chicken is completely covered by the skin. Roll up tightly in the clingfilm, then chill to set the shape.

Put the chicken, still wrapped in clingfilm, into a vacuum bag and vacuum-seal it. Lower the bag into a sous vide machine (or water bath) heated to 59°C and poach for 45 minutes. Remove the bag and leave the chicken to rest for 10 minutes, then immerse the bag in a bowl of iced water to cool the chicken quickly. Once cooled, keep the chicken in the fridge until ready to finish.

Before serving, heat oil in a large frying pan set over a high heat. Unwrap the chicken breasts, season lightly with salt and add to the pan. Cook, frequently turning and basting the chicken with the hot oil, until it is evenly golden brown and the skin is crisp. Remove to a plate and leave to rest for a few minutes before slicing across into thick pieces (2 per serving).

BRAISED LEEKS

1 medium leek (white part), cut into 3cm chunks
25g unsalted butter
50ml Chicken Stock (see page 379)
a splash of Truffle Dressing (see page 373)

Blanch the leek in boiling water for a minute. Drain and immediately plunge
into iced water to stop the cooking process. When cooled, drain the leek again
and keep in the fridge until needed.

Before serving, heat the butter and chicken stock in a pan over a high heat.
Add a splash of truffle dressing and season well to taste, then add the leek
pieces and simmer for a couple of minutes until hot.

MUSTARD PURÉE

2 large white onions, very finely sliced
1 tablespoon olive oil
100–200ml Chicken Stock (see page 379)
ready-made English mustard, to taste

Gently cook the onions in the olive oil in a heavy-based pan for 10–15
minutes, stirring occasionally. When they are very soft and translucent, but
not browned, pour in just enough chicken stock to cover. Increase the heat
slightly and simmer until the stock has evaporated. Tip the onions into a
blender and add mustard, salt and pepper to taste. Blitz until smooth. Pass the
mustard purée through a fine sieve into a bowl. Transfer to a squeezy bottle.
Before serving, reheat the purée by setting the bottle in a bowl of hot water.

CHICKEN-FAT MASH

500g unsalted butter
500g chicken skins
500g La Ratte potatoes
125ml whole milk
125ml double cream

Melt the butter in a pan and add the chicken skins and a pinch of salt, plus the
chicken fat reserved from preparing the chicken crowns (see above). Fry the
skins in the foaming butter until they are golden brown and crisp. Take the
pan off the heat and leave to cool slightly, then lift out the chicken skins on to
a plate lined with kitchen paper to drain; set aside. Save the chicken-flavoured
butter left in the pan for the mash.

Gently simmer the potatoes in a pan of salted water for 20–25 minutes or
until they are tender when pierced with the tip of a sharp knife. Drain the
potatoes well. While they are still hot, peel off the skins, then use a potato
ricer to mash the potatoes. Pass the mash through a fine sieve into a bowl to
make sure there are no lumps left.

Add the milk and cream to the chicken-flavoured butter in the pan along with a pinch each of salt and pepper. Add the mash and stir until well mixed. Taste and adjust the seasoning. Reheat for serving.

BRAISED MORELS

250g medium morels, cleaned
50g unsalted butter
100ml Chicken Stock (see page 379)
2 garlic cloves, finely chopped
a few sprigs of thyme

Melt the butter in a pan over a high heat, add the morels with a pinch each of salt and pepper, and fry for a few minutes. Add the chicken stock, garlic and thyme. Simmer until the stock has almost all evaporated. Remove the morels to a plate.

ASSEMBLY

For each serving, place 2 pieces of chicken breast on a warmed serving plate. Arrange 5 or 6 pieces of braised leek next to the chicken, then squeeze several mounds of mustard purée around the plate. Garnish the chicken with a few braised morels and shave over a few slices of black truffle. Put the chicken-fat mash in a separate bowl and sprinkle some chopped crispy chicken skin on top. Serve immediately.

Game Pithivier

with
grouse,
pheasant
and
wild
mushrooms

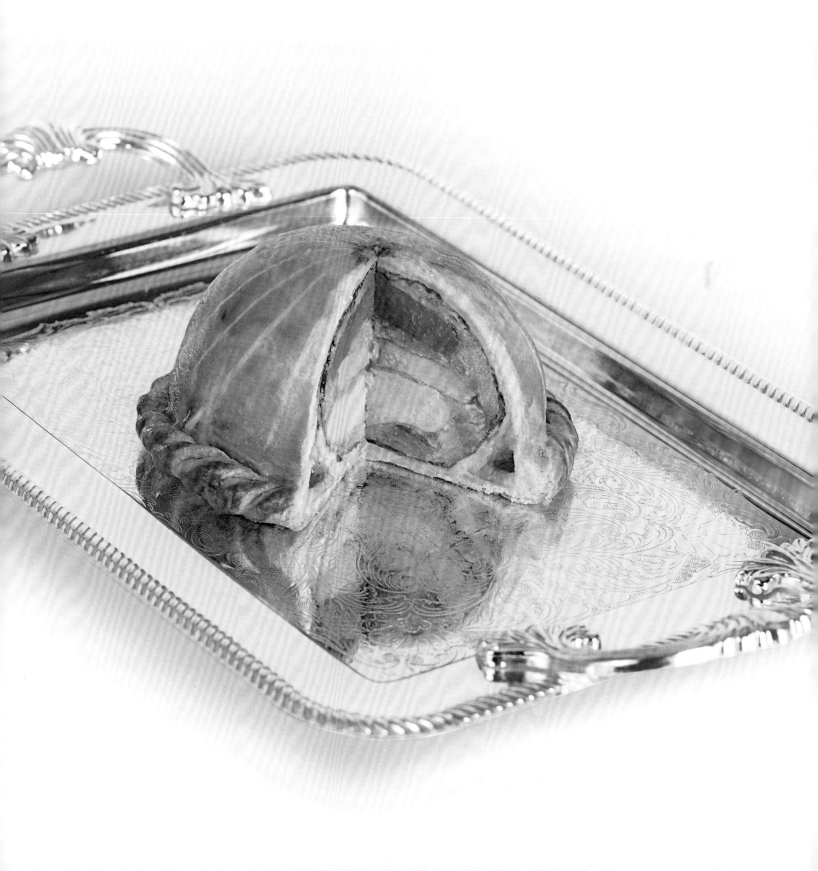

1 oven-ready pheasant
1 oven-ready grouse
Meat Brine (see Braised West Country Ox
    Cheek recipe, page 2322)
100g minced pork
50g lardo (or pork fat), finely minced
200g wild mushrooms (preferably ceps)
olive oil, for cooking
a few knobs of unsalted butter
100ml Game Sauce (see page 375)
2 egg yolks
4 green Savoy cabbage leaves
2 large Crepes (see page 382)
2 x 100g slices of foie gras
200g all-butter puff pastry
3–4 egg yolks, beaten, for the egg wash
Maldon sea salt and black pepper

First, prepare the filling. Use a sharp boning knife to carve out the legs and breasts from the pheasant and grouse. Remove the skin and any sinew from the breasts, then place them in a vacuum bag. Pour in enough meat brine to cover the breasts and vacuum-seal the bag. Chill for 1 hour. Remove the breasts and rinse off the brine. Pat them dry with kitchen paper. Keep covered with clingfilm until ready to cook.

While the breasts are in the brine, remove all the meat from the pheasant and grouse legs (keep all bones, carcasses, hearts and livers for the game sauce). Discard skin and sinew. Finely mince the meat with a chef's knife. Put the game mince into a mixing bowl and add the minced pork and lardo. Season with salt and pepper and mix well. Cover and keep in the fridge until needed.

Clean the wild mushrooms, leaving them whole. Heat a drizzle of oil in a wide frying pan until hot. Add the mushrooms with a little salt and pepper and pan-roast them for a few minutes until any liquid released has evaporated and the mushrooms begin to brown. Flip them over and add a few knobs of butter to the pan. Cook for a further 1–2 minutes. Transfer the mushrooms to a chopping board and leave to cool, then finely chop them. Add the mushrooms to the pork and game mince mixture along with the game sauce, egg yolks and a little more seasoning. Mix well. Cover again and return to the fridge.

Bring a pan of salted water to the boil and have ready a bowl of iced water on the side. Blanch the Savoy cabbage leaves for 1–2 minutes, just until they are wilted but still a vibrant green. Lift out the leaves with tongs and immediately immerse them in the iced water to stop the cooking process. Drain well and pat each leaf dry with kitchen paper.

You can now assemble the pithivier filling. Place a large piece of clingfilm on the work surface. Lay out the crepes on the film, slightly overlapping. Spread the wilted cabbage leaves on top. Cover with a thin layer of mince (about a quarter of it). Arrange the brined pheasant breasts over the mince and top with another thin layer of mince. Place the foie gras slices in a single layer on the mince and lightly season them. Make another layer of mince followed by the brined grouse breasts. Finish with a final layer of mince. Using the ends of the clingfilm to help, roll the cabbage leaves and crepes over to envelop the filling, then wrap well in the clingfilm. Mould into a dome with your hands. Chill for at least 30 minutes to firm up the filling slightly.

Lightly dust the work surface and a rolling pin with a little flour. Roll out the puff pastry to 2–3mm thickness. Using a small plate that is 3cm wider than the filling as a template, cut out a neat round of pastry. Cut out a second round of pasty that is 3cm wider than the first round. Unwrap the filling and place it on the centre of the smaller pastry round. Brush the edges of the pastry with a little egg wash. Drape the larger pastry round over the filling, then pinch and fold the edges to seal, making sure that there are no air pockets. Transfer the assembled pithivier to a baking tray lined with baking parchment. Chill for 20 minutes.

Brush the pithivier with an even layer of egg wash, then return to the fridge to chill for 20 minutes. Repeat the brushing with egg wash and chilling 3 more times. Then use the blunt side of a small knife to lightly score evenly spaced curved lines from the centre top down the sides of the pithivier to the bottom edge. Insert the tip of the knife into the top of the pastry lid to create a small steam hole. Chill the pithivier for a few hours before baking.

Preheat the oven to 170°C/150°C fan/Gas Mark 3. Bake the pithivier, turning the baking tray a few times to ensure that the pastry browns evenly, until the internal temperature registers 38°C on a meat probe. Remove from the oven and leave to rest for 10 minutes. Transfer to a serving tray and slice at the table.

Salad of Wild Duck

with
liver parfait,
walnut &
pear purée
and
crushed
potatoes

SERVES 4

LIVER PARFAIT

150ml red port
75ml white port
150ml Madeira
50ml brandy
100g shallots, finely diced
1 garlic clove, finely sliced
10g picked thyme leaves
300g grade A foie gras
120g chicken livers
4 large eggs
400g unsalted butter
18g Maldon sea salt
2g pink curing salt

The terrine is best served the day after it is made.
Put the red port, white port, Madeira, brandy, shallots,
garlic and thyme into a saucepan and boil until the
liquid has reduced to a syrupy consistency. Leave to
cool completely, then pour into a blender and blitz until
smooth. Set this marinade aside (it can be kept in the
fridge for up to a week).

Remove any large sinews or veins from the foie gras and
chicken livers. Cut them into 2cm dice, keeping the livers
and foie gras separate. Put them into 2 vacuum bags and
vacuum-seal these. Crack the eggs into a third vacuum
bag, add the butter and vacuum-seal it. Lower all 3 bags
into a sous vide machine (or water bath) heated to 55°C
and cook for 10 minutes, just to warm the ingredients.

Remove the foie gras and chicken livers from their bags
and tip into a blender. Pour in the marinade, add the salts
and blitz on high for 30 seconds. Leaving the butter in
the vacuum bag, add the eggs to the blender and blitz
again for 10 seconds, trying not to aerate the mixture
too much. With the blender running, gradually add the
butter from the bag.

Pass the mixture through a fine sieve into a bowl, then
transfer it to a terrine mould. Wrap the mould tightly
in oven-safe clingfilm and place it in a steamer heated to
90°C. Steam the parfait until the internal temperature
reaches 65°C on a probe thermometer. Remove the
terrine and leave to cool for 10 minutes before putting
it into a blast chiller to cool completely. When cold,
transfer to the fridge for storage.

MALLARD BREASTS

2 oven-ready mallards
a few knobs of unsalted butter
2 garlic cloves
2 sprigs of thyme
olive oil, for cooking
Maldon sea salt and black pepper

Use a boning knife to remove the legs from the ducks; save these, with the livers and hearts, to make game sauce (see recipe on page 375) for the truffle sauce (see below). Remove any feathers or excess fat or skin from the duck crowns. Rinse the cavity, then pat dry with kitchen paper. Place a few knobs of butter, a peeled clove of garlic and a sprig of thyme in the cavity of each crown. Put the crowns into vacuum bags and vacuum-seal them.

Lower the crowns into a sous vide machine (or water bath) heated to 58°C and cook for 1 hour. Lift out the bags and leave to rest and cool, then keep the crowns, still in their bags, in the fridge until ready to finish.

For serving, carve the breasts from the mallard crowns and season them with salt and pepper. Heat a little olive oil in a wide frying pan over a medium heat, add the breasts, skin side down, and fry for 2–3 minutes or until golden brown and crisp. Flip the breasts over and cook the other side for 1–2 minutes, just until the breasts are warmed through. Remove to a chopping board and leave to rest for a few minutes before slicing thickly.

WALNUT & PEAR PURÉE

150g unsalted butter
250g fresh wet walnuts
4 Conference pears
50ml water
a dash of Minus 8 vinegar

Heat the butter in a medium pan. When it begins to foam, add the walnuts and sauté for 3 minutes or until they turn a deep golden brown. Meanwhile, peel, core and roughly chop the pears. Add the pears to the pan with the water and simmer for 30 minutes or until the pears are very soft and any moisture in the pan evaporated. Transfer the pears and walnuts to a blender and blitz until smooth. Taste and season with salt, pepper and a dash of Minus 8 vinegar. Set aside.

285

CRUSHED POTATOES

4 large La Ratte potatoes
500ml Duck Stock (see page 380)
a sprig of thyme

Peel the potatoes and place them in a pan with the duck stock, thyme and some seasoning. Bring to a simmer, then gently cook the potatoes for 15–20 minutes or until they are soft. Take the pan off the heat and leave the potatoes to keep warm in the stock.

Before serving, drain the potatoes and break them into small pieces with your fingers.

_____

TRUFFLE SAUCE

200ml Game Sauce (see page 375)
20ml Truffle Dressing (see page 373)
20g Périgord truffle, chopped

Make the sauce just before you are ready to serve. Heat all the ingredients together in a small saucepan, then taste and adjust the seasoning.

_____

ASSEMBLY

1 small head of purple-variegated kale, leaves separated
1 small head of white-variegated kale, leaves separated
candied walnuts, for grating
4 slices of toasted brioche
1–2 Périgord truffles, for grating

For each serving, dollop a spoonful of walnut and pear purée on a serving plate, then place a few slices of duck breast on top. Add a few crushed potatoes to the plate. Arrange a handful of white and purple kale leaves over the duck and potatoes. Drizzle over the truffle sauce and finely grate over a little candied walnut. On a separate side plate, place a slice of liver parfait on a toasted brioche, then grate over some Périgord truffle. Serve immediately.

Soy-glazed Norfolk Quail

with
cured foie
gras roll
and
compressed
apple

GLAZED QUAIL

2 oven-ready quails
300ml Meat Brine (see Braised West Country
    Ox Cheek recipe, page 232)
300ml soy sauce
300ml lemon juice
pared peel of 1 lemon
50ml Jerez vinegar
100ml runny honey
Pistachio Crumbs (see page 381)

Prepare the quails one at a time. Using a sharp knife, remove the head,
cutting at the base of the neck but keeping as much skin as possible on the
bird to cover the breasts. Cut off the wing tips and reserve them for the sauce.
Make an incision down the back of the quail to open it out and flatten the
carcass slightly. Remove the gizzards (save these for the sauce). Rinse the birds
well and pat dry with kitchen paper. Put the quails in a resealable bag and pour
in enough brine to cover. Seal and leave in the fridge for 1 hour.

Remove the quails from the brine and rinse them under cold running water.
Pat them dry again, then place on a tray and let them dry out in the fridge,
uncovered, for a few hours.

Run the flame of a blowtorch over the quails to turn the skin lightly golden
brown all over. Keep the quails in the fridge until needed.

To make the glaze for the quails, put the soy sauce, lemon juice and zest,
vinegar and honey into a small heavy-based saucepan and bring to a simmer.
Give the mixture a stir, then leave to simmer for 5 minutes. Strain through
a sieve to remove the lemon zest, then pour back into the pan. Boil until
reduced to a thick, syrupy glaze. Set aside until ready to serve.

When you are ready to cook the quails, preheat the oven to 200°C/180°C
fan/Gas Mark 6. Put the quails on a roasting tray and brush them generously
with the glaze. Roast for about 8 minutes, turning and basting them
frequently with the glaze, until they are nicely browned and just cooked
through. Remove and leave to rest for a few minutes before carving out the
legs and breasts. Coat the legs and breasts with the pistachio crumbs.

CURED FOIE GRAS ROLL

1 lobe grade A foie gras
150ml brandy
2½ teaspoons fine sea salt
½ teaspoon crushed white pepper
1 teaspoon caster sugar
¾ teaspoon pink curing salt
50ml Jerez vinegar
Pain d'épices Crumb (see page 382)

Allow the foie gras to come to room temperature before you begin to prepare it. Meanwhile, make a marinade by heating the brandy in a small saucepan with the salt, pepper, sugar and pink salt. Stir until the salts and sugar have dissolved, then remove from the heat and leave to cool completely.

Use the back of a spoon and tweezers to remove any veins on the foie gras, then remould it with your hands to roughly its original shape. Put the foie gras into a vacuum bag and pour over the brandy marinade. Vacuum-seal the bag, then leave to marinate in the fridge for an hour.

Remove the foie gras from the bag and rinse off the marinade. Pat the foie gras dry. Put it into another vacuum bag and vacuum-seal it. Lower the bag into a sous vide machine (or water bath) heated to 65°C and cook for 10 minutes. Lift out the bag into a bowl of iced water to stop the cooking process.

Lay out a large piece of clingfilm on a work surface. Remove the foie gras from the bag and slice it into 4 equal pieces. Arrange the pieces, side by side, on the clingfilm. Wrap the foie gras in the clingfilm, then, holding the ends of the film, roll it along the work surface to get an even, tight log. If necessary, wrap the log with another sheet of clingfilm, then lower it into a bowl of iced water. Chill for 8 hours to firm up and set the shape.

Right before serving, unwrap the foie gras and roll it in the pain d'épices crumbs until evenly coated. Cut across into 4 neat slices.

COMPRESSED APPLE

3 large Granny Smith apples
juice of 1 lemon

Peel and juice one apple, then mix the juice with the lemon juice. Very finely slice the remaining 2 apples using a meat slicer or mandoline. Put the slices into a vacuum bag and pour over the juice mixture. Vacuum-seal the bag and leave the apples to macerate for 2 hours.

Before serving, remove the compressed apple slices from the juice. Pile them into short stacks on a sheet of baking parchment and stamp out neat discs using an 8cm round pastry cutter.

ASSEMBLY

1 black truffle, for slicing
Apple & Blackberry Jam (see page 383)

Overlap the compressed apple slices in the centre of each serving plate. Place a roasted quail leg and breast on top. Add a slice of cured foie gras on the side and garnish the foie gras and quail with fresh truffle slices. Finally, pipe a couple of mounds of apple and blackberry jam on to the plate. Serve immediately.

Burnside Farm Foods

Rutherford Estate stands on the banks of the Tweed in the Tweed Valley, six miles from Kelso in the Scottish Borders. This family-run estate has a long history dating back to the 12th century, with Rutherford being one of the oldest Border names.

I took the sense of family tradition and heritage and combined it with a passion for food when, in 1986, I created Burnside Farm Foods on one of the estate farms. We have now been supplying fresh local produce to Scotland and the UK's leading chefs for the last 32 years.

We believe we are probably the only European Commission-approved game processor, processing our own game from our own shoot on our own farm. Our location in the heart of the Scottish Borders gives us access to an abundance of high-quality game from other estates, which we buy to give a constant supply of product. This also allows us to give full traceability on all the game that we supply which is important in today's market.

It is this quality that I know Jason requires for Pollen Street Social to keep to their demanding standards. We understand that the quality has to be consistent week in, week out, and that only the best wild Scottish game will suffice. We work with Michelin-starred chefs across the country and are used to their exacting standards!

Over the years we have developed a good working relationship with Jason and Dale at Pollen Street and they know they can rely upon us for quality and consistency. We feel very honoured to supply such a prestigious chef.

Johnny Rutherford
burnsidefarmfoods.co.uk

Grouse

with
chanterelle-
stuffed
cabbage,
game chips
and
damson jam

SERVES 4

GROUSE

    4 oven-ready grouse
    a few knobs of unsalted butter
    a few sprigs of thyme
    1 garlic clove
    olive oil, for cooking
    Maldon sea salt and black pepper

Prepare each grouse by carving out the legs from the crown (keep the legs for another dish or for the sauce below), then removing any sinew and excess fat around the neck and breasts. Remove the guts and gizzards (keep the liver and heart for later and the neck for the sauce). Rinse the cavity of the crown with cold water, then pat dry with kitchen paper. Place the crown in a vacuum bag and add some butter, thyme, the peeled garlic clove and some salt and pepper. Vacuum-seal the bag and set aside in the fridge.

To cook the crowns for serving, lower the bags into a sous vide machine (or water bath) heated to 58°C and cook for 8 minutes. Leave to rest for a few minutes before carving out the breasts. Sear the breasts in a hot pan with a little olive oil and a few knobs of butter for about 2 minutes on each side – the breasts should still be pink in the middle. Leave to rest for a few minutes before serving.

GROUSE SAUCE

    500g grouse (or other game)
       bones, necks and off-cuts
    olive oil, for cooking
    2 shallots, chopped
    1 small leek, chopped
    1 carrot, peeled and chopped
    1 celery stick, chopped
    ½ bulb of garlic, cloves separated
       and chopped
    ½ tablespoon tomato paste
    1 star anise
    1 clove
    1 small cinnamon stick
    a sprig of lemon thyme
    100ml ruby port
    100ml red wine
    500ml Chicken Stock (see
       page 379)

1 litre Veal Stock (see page 380)
a handful of elderberries

Heat a drizzle of olive oil in a wide pan until hot, add the grouse bones and reserved neck, and sear, turning occasionally, for 5–6 minutes or until the bones are golden brown. Remove them and set aside.

Add a little more oil to the pan along with the vegetables and garlic. Sauté, stirring frequently, for 8–10 minutes or until the vegetables are golden brown. Stir in the tomato paste, spices and thyme and cook for a few more minutes. Return the bones to the pan and pour in the port and red wine. Boil until reduced by half, then add both stocks and bring to the boil, skimming off the scum and froth that rises to the surface. Lower the heat and leave to simmer for 4 hours.

Strain the sauce through a fine sieve into a clean saucepan. If you want a more intense flavour, boil the sauce to reduce it. Season well to taste, then set aside ready for reheating.

Before serving, bring the sauce back to a simmer, then remove from the heat and add the elderberries. Leave to infuse for a few minutes, then strain out the elderberries. Keep the sauce warm.

CHANTERELLE-STUFFED CABBAGE

4 Hispi cabbages
olive oil, to drizzle
50g unsalted butter
1 shallot, sliced
500g chanterelles
200g button mushrooms
100ml dry white wine
100ml double cream
10g Périgord truffle, for grating

Preheat the oven to 160°C/140°C fan/Gas Mark 3. Place the whole cabbages on a baking tray and drizzle over a little olive oil. Sprinkle with sea salt. Bake for 30 minutes or until the cabbages are tender when pierced with the tip of a knife. Remove from the oven and allow to cool, then remove the outer leaves – you want just the tender heart of each cabbage. Trim off any excess stalk, leaving enough to hold the cabbage heart together. Set aside.

Melt the butter in a large pan, add the shallot and sweat for about 6 minutes or until translucent. Add the chanterelle and button mushrooms with a little seasoning. Cook, stirring occasionally, for 5–6 minutes or until the mushrooms take on a little colour and any moisture released has evaporated. Deglaze the pan with the wine and let it bubble until reduced by half. Stir in the double cream, then take the pan off the heat. Tip the contents of the pan into a blender and blitz until smooth. Transfer the creamy mushroom purée to a squeezy bottle and keep warm until ready to serve.

For serving, reheat the cabbage hearts in the oven, drizzled with a little oil.

GAME CHIPS

2 large Maris Piper potatoes
2 teaspoons juniper berries,
   lightly crushed
1 teaspoon Maldon sea
   salt, crushed
about 500ml vegetable oil,
   for deep-frying

Peel the potatoes. Thinly slice them to about 2mm thickness using a French mandoline, alternating 90-degree turns every time to create a criss-cross pattern. To neaten the shapes, stamp discs out of the slices with a 3cm round pastry cutter. Rinse the slices under cold running water until the water runs clear of any starch. Dry the slices well between kitchen towels. Mix together the crushed juniper berries and salt in a small bowl and set aside.

Heat the oil in a deep-fat fryer or a saucepan to 150°C. Fry the potato slices in small batches for 5–6 minutes, turning them halfway so they become lightly golden on both sides and crisp. Remove to a tray lined with kitchen paper to absorb the excess oil. While still hot, sprinkle the chips with the juniper salt. Keep warm in a low oven.

ASSEMBLY

8 fresh ceps
olive oil, for cooking
diced unsalted butter, for cooking
Damson Jam (see page 383)
Pickled Cobnuts (see page 377)
Mulled Elderberries (see
   page 383)

Cut each cep in half through the stalk, then score the cut sides. Place the ceps, scored side down, in a large frying

299

or sauté pan. Drizzle over a little olive oil and dot with butter. Lightly season with salt and pepper. Set the pan over a medium heat and pan-roast the ceps for a couple of minutes until golden brown, then flip them over to brown the other sides.

For each serving, set a baked cabbage heart upright on a side plate and squeeze some creamy mushroom purée into the centre of the cabbage. Grate over some fresh truffle. Place 2 grouse breasts on a warmed serving plate. Pipe small mounds of damson jam around the plate, then dot the plate with a few pickled cobnuts and 2 roasted cep halves. Spoon some mulled elderberries on top of the grouse and drizzle over a spoonful or two of game sauce. Finally, garnish with some game chips and serve immediately, with the stuffed cabbage on the side.

Sweets

Banana Soufflé
302

Pistachio Soufflé
306

Brogdale Pear
310

Forced Yorkshire
Rhubarb
314

Blackcurrant Eton Mess
318

Bitter Chocolate Pavé
324

Hot & Cold Apple Tatin
330

Parsnip Crème Caramel
334

Wild Strawberries
340

Citrus Curd Meringue
344

Chardonnay-
poached Pear
348

Banana Soufflé

with
tempered
chocolate
discs
and
rum & raisin
ice cream

SERVES 3–4

BANANA PURÉE

250g banana purée (we use
    Boivron purées)
scant 1 teaspoon cornflour
1 teaspoon cold water

To concentrate the flavour, simmer the banana purée
in a heavy-based saucepan over a low heat, stirring
occasionally, for 10–20 minutes or until it has reduced
by half. Stir the cornflour and water together to make
a slurry, then add this to the reduced purée. Stirring
constantly, boil the purée for a few minutes until
thickened. Transfer the purée to a bowl and leave to cool.

SOUFFLÉ BASE

10g unsalted butter
110g sushi rice
250ml whole milk
125ml double cream
125ml whipping cream
45g caster sugar
a pinch of Maldon sea salt
½ vanilla pod, split lengthways
    and seeds scraped out
2 tablespoons banana liqueur

Melt the butter in a heavy-based saucepan, add the sushi
rice and stir over a medium heat for a few minutes. Pour
in the milk and both types of cream, then add the sugar,
salt and vanilla pod and seeds. Stir well. Bring to the
boil. Reduce the heat to the lowest possible and simmer,
stirring occasionally, for 20–25 minutes or until the rice
is cooked and the mixture is thick. Take the pan off the
heat, cover with a lid and leave to cool for about an hour.

Remove and discard the vanilla pod, then blitz the rice
mixture in a Thermomix or a strong food processor to a
thick, smooth purée. Pass the purée through a fine sieve
into a large mixing bowl. (You can keep the soufflé base
in the fridge for 2–3 days; before using, warm the base by
setting the bowl over a saucepan of hot water – this will
make it easier to work with.)

MERINGUE

375g egg whites
60g caster sugar

Put the egg whites in the large, grease-free bowl of
a free-standing electric mixer and whisk to stiff peaks.
Slowly whisk in the sugar until you get a meringue that
will hold stiff peaks again.

———————

ASSEMBLY

softened unsalted butter and
    finely grated dark chocolate,
    for the ramekins
8 Tempered Chocolate Discs
    (see Chocolate Pavé recipe,
    page 328)
Rum & Raisin Ice Cream (see
    page 387)
finely grated zest of 1 lime

Preheat the oven to 180°C/160°C fan/Gas Mark 4.
Place a heavy baking tray in the oven to heat up. Brush
the inside of three or four 8cm ramekins with softened
butter, starting with the bottom and using vertical
upward strokes for the sides. Chill the ramekins for a
few minutes, then brush again with another layer of
butter. Dust the inside of the ramekins with the grated
chocolate, tipping out any excess.

Stir the banana liqueur and banana purée into the soufflé
base. Use a large metal spoon to fold in a third of the
meringue. Once the mixture is slackened, add the rest
of the meringue and carefully fold just until the mixture
is evenly incorporated and there are no visible lumps
of meringue. Try not to over-fold or you will lose the
volume whisked into the meringue.

Spoon the mixture into the prepared ramekins until each
is almost full. Level the top with a palette knife, then run
the tip of the knife around inside the rim of the ramekin.
Place the ramekins on the hot baking tray and bake for 6
minutes, then rotate the baking tray quickly (to ensure
that the soufflés rise and brown evenly) and bake for
a further 3 minutes. The soufflés are ready when they
are golden brown and feel a little springy when lightly
pressed on top.

Set each ramekin on a serving plate and place a disc
of tempered chocolate on top of the soufflé. Serve
immediately, with a scoop of rum and raisin ice cream
garnished with a little lime zest.

Pistachio Soufflé

with
tempered
chocolate
discs
and
vanilla ice
cream

SERVES 3–4

SOUFFLÉ BASE

- 10g unsalted butter
- 110g sushi rice
- 250ml whole milk
- 125ml double cream
- 125ml whipping cream
- 45g caster sugar
- a pinch of sea salt
- ½ vanilla pod, split lengthways and seeds scraped out
- 2 tablespoons Amaretto
- 100g pistachio paste

Melt the butter in a heavy-based saucepan, add the sushi rice and stir over a medium heat for a few minutes. Pour in the milk and both types of cream. Add the sugar, salt and vanilla pod and seeds. Stir well and bring to the boil, then reduce the heat to the lowest setting and simmer, stirring occasionally, for 20–25 minutes or until the rice is cooked and the mixture is thick. Take the pan off the heat, cover with a lid and leave to cool for about an hour.

Remove and discard the vanilla pod, then blitz the soufflé base mixture in a Thermomix (or a strong food processor) to a thick, smooth purée. Pass the purée through a fine sieve into a bowl. (You can keep the soufflé base in the fridge for a few days if preparing in advance.)

When ready to bake the soufflé, warm the base in a bowl set over a saucepan of hot water. Add the Amaretto and pistachio paste, and stir until the mixture has loosened.

MERINGUE

- 375g egg whites
- 60g caster sugar

Put the egg whites in the large, grease-free bowl of a free-standing electric mixer and whisk to stiff peaks. Slowly whisk in the sugar until you have a meringue that will hold stiff peaks again.

ASSEMBLY

- softened unsalted butter and finely grated dark chocolate, for the ramekins

309

8 Tempered Chocolate Discs
  (see Chocolate Pavé recipe,
  page 328)
Vanilla Ice Cream (see page 387)

Preheat the oven to 180°C/160°C fan/Gas Mark 4.
Put a heavy baking tray into the oven to heat up. Brush
the inside of three or four 10cm ramekins with softened
butter, starting with the bottom and using vertical
upward strokes for the sides. Chill the ramekins for a
few minutes, then brush again with another layer of
butter. Dust the inside of the ramekins with the grated
chocolate, tipping out any excess.

Use a large metal spoon to fold a third of the meringue
into the soufflé base. Once the mixture is slackened, add
the rest of the meringue and carefully fold just until the
mixture is evenly incorporated and there are no visible
lumps of meringue. Try not to over-fold or you will lose
the volume whisked into the meringue.

Spoon the mixture into the prepared ramekins until
each is almost full. Level the top with a palette knife,
then run the tip of the knife around inside the rim of the
ramekin. Carefully place the ramekins on the hot baking
tray and bake for 6 minutes, then rotate the baking
tray quickly (to ensure that the soufflés rise and brown
evenly) and bake for a further 3 minutes. The soufflés are
ready when they have risen and formed a light crust
on top.

As soon as the soufflés are ready, remove from the
oven and place a disc of tempered chocolate on top. Serve
immediately with a neat quenelle of vanilla ice cream on
the side.

Brogdale Pear

with
milk crisp,
whisky
caramel
and
oat crumble

SERVES 4

___

BROGDALE PEAR

100ml water
100g caster sugar
2 vanilla pods, split lengthways and seeds scraped out
1 ripe pear (we use Brogdale's)
juice of 1 lemon

Put the water, sugar and vanilla pods and seeds into a small saucepan and stir over a medium heat until the sugar has dissolved. Increase the heat slightly and simmer the syrup for a few minutes. Take the pan off the heat and leave to cool, then stir in the lemon juice.

Meanwhile, peel the pears, cut them into quarters lengthways and remove the core. Use a turning knife to give the pear quarters rounded edges, then add them to the vanilla syrup. Set aside to macerate at room temperature.

___

OAT CRUMBLE

135g plain flour
60g rolled oats
5g bicarbonate of soda
45g cold unsalted butter, diced
40g caster sugar
½ teaspoon fine sea salt
½ vanilla pod, split lengthways and seeds scraped out
30g honey

Put all of the ingredients, except the honey, into a large mixing bowl and mix well, rubbing in the butter until the mixture is like crumbs. Add the honey and give the mixture a stir until it comes together as a dough. Wrap the dough in clingfilm and leave to rest in the fridge for a couple of hours.

Roll out the dough between 2 large sheets of baking parchment to about 1cm thickness. Lift on to a baking tray. Chill the dough for a couple of hours.

Preheat the oven to 160°C/140°C fan/Gas Mark 3. Peel off the top layer of parchment, then bake the sheet of dough for 8 minutes or until light golden and set. Remove from the oven and allow to cool slightly; reduce the oven temperature to 90°C/70°C fan/Gas Mark very low. When the dough is cool enough to handle, break it into small pieces on the baking tray, then return it to the low oven to bake for 30 minutes or until the crumble is dry and crisp. Leave to cool completely before storing in an airtight container.

___

HONEYCOMB

150g caster sugar
65ml water

50g liquid glucose
25g bicarbonate of soda

Line a deep baking tray with a silicone mat. Put the sugar, water and liquid glucose into a heavy-based saucepan and stir over a medium heat until the sugar has dissolved. Increase the heat and let the syrup boil to 155°C.

When the syrup has reached the right temperature, take the pan off the heat. Standing back, stir in the bicarbonate of soda. The mixture will immediately foam up and triple in volume. Pour the honeycomb mixture into the lined tray and leave to cool and set. Once set, break the honeycomb into small shards and store in an airtight container.

MILK CRISP

450ml whole milk
150ml liquid glucose

Line 2 dehydrator trays with oven-safe clingfilm and give them a light spray of trenwax. Heat the milk and liquid glucose together in a medium pan until the mixture reaches 80°C. Remove from the heat. Whisk the mixture with a stick blender until a thick foam forms on the surface. Using a large spoon, skim off the foam and place it on a lined tray. Make sure you do not include any liquid milk as you do this. Whisk the milk mixture again, then skim off the foam and place on the tray alongside the first foam. Continue doing this until the milk has almost all been used up and you cannot whisk what remains.

Put the trays into a dehydrator heated to 70°C and leave to dry out for 5 hours or until the foam is crisp and brittle.

Remove the trays and immediately cut the milk crisps into discs while they are still warm (or cool and then break into shards). Store in an airtight container.

WHISKY CARAMEL

250g caster sugar
150ml double cream
75ml peated whisky

Tip the sugar into a wide, heavy-based pan, set over a medium-high heat and allow the sugar to melt and caramelise, swirling it in the pan to get an even-coloured caramel. Meanwhile, warm up the cream in another small saucepan.

When the caramel is a rich golden brown, stand back and pour in the warm cream (take care as the caramel will spit and sputter in contact with the liquid). If there are any bits of hardened caramel, simply stir over a medium heat until melted and the caramel is smooth. Add the whisky and simmer for 2 minutes.

Take the pan off the heat and allow the caramel to cool completely before pouring into a squeezy bottle, ready for serving.

———————

ASSEMBLY

bee pollen
Pear Sorbet (see page 385)
Goat's Cheese Ice Cream (see page 386)

For each serving, lightly crush a handful each of honeycomb and oat crumble with a pinch of bee pollen, then spread the mixture on a serving plate. Place a vanilla-poached pear quarter and a neat quenelle of goat's cheese ice cream in the centre. Use a small spoon to scoop small balls of pear sorbet and place them around the plate. Drizzle over a little whisky caramel. Garnish the ice cream with 2 discs or shards of milk crisp and serve at once.

Forced Yorkshire Rhubarb

with
crème
fraîche
mousse
and
rhubarb &
rose sorbet

SERVES 8

CRÈME FRAÎCHE MOUSSE

80g caster sugar
1 tablespoon honey
1 vanilla pod, split lengthways
    and seeds scraped out
375ml crème fraîche
3 gelatine leaves
375ml whipping cream

Place the sugar, honey, vanilla pod and seeds, and
a third of the crème fraîche in a small heavy-based
saucepan. Give the mixture a stir, then bring to the boil
over a medium-high heat. Meanwhile, soak the gelatine
leaves in a bowl of cold water. When soft, squeeze out
the excess water from the gelatine leaves and add to
the saucepan. Remove from the heat and stir until the
gelatine has melted. Set aside to cool.

Pour the whipping cream into the bowl of a free-standing
electric mixer and whisk on medium speed to soft peaks.
Add the remaining crème fraîche and whisk to combine.
Add the contents of the pan and fold through. Cover the
bowl with clingfilm and keep in the fridge until ready
to serve.

Before serving, whisk the mixture once more, then
spoon into piping bags fitted with plain round nozzles.

RHUBARB COMPOTE

600g forced rhubarb, peeled and
    roughly chopped
40g caster sugar

Put the rhubarb into a bowl, sprinkle over the sugar
and toss together. Leave the rhubarb to macerate for
about 1 hour, to release some of its juice. Tip the contents
of the bowl into a heavy-based saucepan and cook over a
low heat for about an hour until the rhubarb is soft. Leave
to cool before transferring to piping bags fitted with plain
round nozzles. Keep in the fridge until needed.

TUILE

150g egg whites
125g icing sugar, sifted
100g plain flour

100g unsalted butter, melted
½ vanilla pod, split lengthways
  and seeds scraped out

Whisk the egg whites with the icing sugar until they
have tripled in volume and form stiff peaks. Sift over the
flour and fold through gently. Add the melted butter and
vanilla seeds and fold again until evenly combined. Cover
with clingfilm and chill for at least 20 minutes.

At the restaurant, we bake the tuile rings right before
serving but you can bake them in advance and store them
in an airtight container.

Preheat the oven to 170°C/150°C fan/Gas Mark 3.
Line 2–3 baking trays with silicone mats and prepare a
2.5mm-thick stencil to fit the silicone mat. Depending on
the size, cut out 2 or 3 rectangles, measuring 25cm long x
3cm wide, from the stencil. Lay it on a silicone mat. Add
a generous spoonful of the tuile mixture in the centre
of each rectangular shape and spread it out evenly to the
edge, scraping off any excess mixture back into the bowl.
Carefully lift off the stencil.

Bake the tuiles one at a time. They will take about
8 minutes to bake and are ready when they are lightly
golden brown around the edges. Remove from the oven
and leave to cool for a minute or so, then while still hot
and pliable, curl a tuile rectangle around an 8cm round
metal pastry cutter to form a ring (you will need a pastry
cutter for each tuile rectangle on the tray). Leave to cool
and firm up while you shape the other tuile rings from
the tray. If you find that a tuile hardens before you can
mould it, pop it back into the oven for a minute or two
until it is pliable again.

Once the tuile rings have firmed up, slide them off the
metal cutters on to a baking tray. When all the tuile rings
are on the tray, return them to the oven to bake for 1–2
minutes or until they are a little darker and evenly golden
brown. Leave to cool completely.

———

ASSEMBLY

Rhubarb & Rose Sorbet (see
  page 385)
rhubarb powder, for dusting
a handful of edible flowers

Place a tuile ring on each serving plate and pipe in
a layer of rhubarb compote. Add a layer of rhubarb and
rose sorbet. Pipe a generous layer of crème fraîche
mousse on top. Dust with rhubarb powder, then garnish
with a few edible flowers. Serve immediately.

Blackcurrant Eton Mess

with
cassis
fromage
cream
and
clove & miso
biscuit

SERVES 10–12

MERINGUE CUPS

oil, for greasing
125g pasteurised egg whites
1 teaspoon lemon juice
¼ teaspoon cream of tartar
250g caster sugar
freeze-dried blackberry powder,
    for dusting

Preheat the oven to 90°C/70°C fan/Gas Mark low.
Take a large sheet of acetate and cut it into 10–12 strips
measuring 4cm in width and 26.5cm in length. Grease
one side of each acetate strip with a thin layer of oil,
wiping off any excess oil with kitchen paper.

Put the egg whites, lemon juice and cream of tartar into
the bowl of a free-standing electric mixer. Whisk on high
until the whites form soft peaks. Gradually add the caster
sugar, whisking constantly. Once all the sugar has been
incorporated, continue to whisk the meringue to soft
peaks again.

Line several baking trays with silicone mats. Using a
palette knife and a 3mm-thick stencil, spread thin 10cm
discs of meringue on the mats. You will need 10–12 discs.

Arrange the acetate strips side by side greased side up.
Spread meringue thinly over them. Put the remaining
meringue into a piping bag. One at a time, lift up a strip
and wipe off any excess meringue along the edges with
your fingers, then wrap the acetate around a meringue
disc to form a cup. Pipe meringue over any gaps between
the disc and strip.

When all the meringue cups have been shaped, carefully
transfer the baking trays to the oven. Bake for about 3
hours or until the meringue cups are completely dry.
Leave on the baking trays to cool, then carefully peel off
the acetate. Gently turn the meringue cups over and dust
the bases with blackberry powder. If making ahead, store
(upside-down) in an airtight container.

FROMAGE CREAM

250g mascarpone
250g fromage frais
40g icing sugar
625ml whipping cream
125ml whole milk

Mix together the mascarpone, fromage frais and icing sugar in a large mixing bowl. Stir in the whipping cream and milk. Transfer the mixture to an iSi whipper and charge it with one canister of gas. Shake, then keep in the fridge until ready to serve.

CASSIS FROMAGE CREAM

250g mascarpone
250g fromage frais
40g icing sugar
40g blackcurrant syrup

Stir together the mascarpone, fromage frais and icing sugar in a jug. Add the blackcurrant syrup and mix well. Transfer the mixture to one large or 2 smaller piping bags. Keep in the fridge until ready to serve.

CLOVE & MISO BISCUIT

150g unsalted butter, softened
165g light brown sugar
210g plain flour
80g ground almonds
½ teaspoon baking powder
5g fine sea salt
a pinch of ground cloves
a few drops of vanilla extract
9g white miso paste
50ml grapeseed oil
75g egg yolks (about 4 large)

Put the butter and sugar into the bowl of a freestanding electric mixer fitted with the paddle whisk. Beat together until smooth and creamy. Sift all the dry ingredients together and add to the bowl of the mixer. Mix on low speed for about 10 seconds, stopping and scraping the sides of the bowl every once in a while. Add the remaining ingredients and mix just until a dough will form. Do not overwork the dough or the biscuits will be tough. Wrap the dough in clingfilm and chill for at least an hour or overnight.

Roll out the dough in between 2 large sheets of baking parchment to 2mm thickness. Chill in the freezer for at least 20 minutes (or overnight).

Preheat the oven to 160°C/140°C fan/Gas Mark 3. Place the sheet of biscuit dough on a baking tray and peel off the top layer of parchment. Bake the biscuit sheet for 15

minutes. Remove from the oven and stamp out neat discs
using an 8cm round pastry cutter. Remove the off-cuts
from around the discs, then return the biscuits to the
oven and bake for a further 10 minutes or until golden
brown around the edges. Leave on the baking tray to cool
completely before storing in an airtight container.

BLACKCURRANT SAUCE

250ml blackcurrant coulis

For the blackcurrant sauce, simply boil the coulis in a
heavy-based saucepan until thick and syrupy. Transfer to
a squeezy bottle, ready to serve.

CLOVE & BLACKCURRANT FLUID GEL

1 teaspoon blackcurrant syrup
1½ teaspoons caster sugar
¾ teaspoon lemon juice
200ml water
a pinch of ground cloves
2g gellan gum

Put all the ingredients into a Thermomix set to 100°C
and leave for 2 minutes. Pour the mixture on to a cold,
deep baking tray and leave to cool, stirring occasionally.
Once cooled and set, scrape the mixture back into the
Thermomix and blitz until smooth. Transfer to a piping
bag or squeezy bottle, ready for service.

ASSEMBLY

a mixture of seasonal berries
butterfly sorrel (optional)
Blackcurrant Sorbet (see
    page 385)

For each serving, place a clove and miso biscuit in
the centre of a serving plate. Pipe a layer of cassis fromage
frais on the biscuit, then arrange a handful of berries
and butterfly sorrel, if using, on top. Pipe dots of clove
and blackcurrant fluid gel around the berries. Pipe a
layer of whipped fromage cream on top, then pipe dots
of blackcurrant sauce over the cream. Carefully conceal
the dessert with an overturned meringue cup. Serve
immediately with a scoop of blackcurrant sorbet in a
side bowl.

Bitter Chocolate Pavé

with
olive oil
biscuit,
black olive
tuille
and
olive oil
jelly

SERVES 20

OLIVE OIL BISCUIT

150g unsalted butter, softened
165g caster sugar
50ml olive oil
4 large egg yolks
½ vanilla pod, split lengthways
    and seeds scraped out
210g plain flour
80g finely ground almonds
½ teaspoon baking powder
1 teaspoon fine sea salt

Line 2 baking trays with silicone mats. Put the butter
and sugar in a large mixing bowl and beat together with
a wooden spoon or spatula until smooth and creamy. Add
the olive oil, egg yolks and vanilla seeds and stir to mix.
Sift in the flour, ground almonds, baking powder and salt,
and mix until the ingredients come together in a dough.
Divide the dough in half. Roll out each half on the lined
baking trays to sheets about 5mm thick. Chill for at least
30 minutes.

Preheat the oven to 160°C/140°C fan/Gas Mark 3. Bake
the biscuit sheets for 10–12 minutes or until pale golden.
Remove from the oven (leave the oven on for the tuiles,
below) and allow to cool for a couple of minutes, then
while still warm cut into neat discs with an 8cm round
pastry cutter. Leave on the tray to cool completely. Store
the biscuits in an airtight container until needed.

BLACK OLIVE TUILE

200g condensed milk
30g plain flour
50g black olive paste

Blitz the ingredients together using a Thermomix or
a food processor to make a wet paste. Using a palette
knife, spread the paste very thinly on baking trays lined
with silicone mats. Bake for 8 minutes (same temperature
as for the biscuits, above) until crisp and golden brown
around the edges. Leave on the silicone mats to cool
completely, then break into shards and store in between
sheets of baking parchment in an airtight container.

OLIVE OIL JELLY

100g isomalt
50g caster sugar
25g liquid glucose
100ml water
2¼ gelatine leaves
180ml olive oil

Put the isomalt, sugar, liquid glucose and water in
a Thermomix set to 100°C and blitz for 15 minutes.
Meanwhile, soak the gelatine leaves in cold water to
soften. Squeeze out the excess water, then add the
gelatine to the hot sugar syrup and stir until melted.
Gradually stir in the olive oil to emulsify. Strain the
mixture through a fine sieve into a jug.

Pour the jelly mixture into 20 small square moulds
o make a layer 1cm deep. Chill for a few hours until set.
(If you do not have square moulds, simply set the jelly in
a shallow square or rectangular container.) Once set, slice
the jelly into 1cm dice and keep in the fridge until ready
to serve.

CHOCOLATE SPONGE

185g unsalted butter
90g icing sugar
2½ teaspoons cocoa powder
225g dark chocolate (with 70%
   cocoa solids)
7 large egg yolks
9 large egg whites
125g caster sugar

Preheat the oven to 180°C/160°C fan/Gas Mark 4.
Line 2 sponge roll baking trays with baking parchment.
Melt the butter in a small, heavy-based saucepan, then
take the pan off the heat and sift in the icing sugar and
cocoa powder. Stir until well combined.

Put the chocolate into a large heatproof bowl and
set the bowl over a pan gently simmering water. Stir
the chocolate every once in a while until it is melted and
smooth. Take the bowl off the pan, then stir the melted
butter mixture into the chocolate. Whisk in the egg
yolks and one egg white.

Using an electric mixer, whisk the remaining egg whites
with the caster sugar to make a medium-stiff meringue.
Fold the meringue through the chocolate base in several
batches, taking care not to over-fold the mixture. Spread
the sponge mixture in the prepared trays to make a layer

about 1cm thick. Bake for 5 minutes, then rotate the trays (to ensure even browning) and bake for a further 5 minutes. When done, the sponges should feel springy when lightly pressed.

Leave to cool completely before stamping out neat discs with an 8–9cm round pastry cutter. Store the sponge rounds in a sealable container, in between sheets of baking parchment to prevent them from sticking together.

CHOCOLATE MOUSSE

175g dark chocolate (with 70% cocoa solids)
65g unsalted butter
2 large egg yolks
6 large egg whites
50g caster sugar

Melt the chocolate and butter in a heatproof bowl set over a pan of gently simmering water until smooth. Remove the bowl from the heat and stir in the egg yolks. Using an electric mixer, whisk the egg whites with the sugar to medium peaks. Fold the meringue through the chocolate mixture in 2 batches, just until combined; make sure not to overmix or you will lose too much of the volume whisked into the meringue. Chill the mousse until firm, then transfer to a piping bag fitted with a plain 1cm round nozzle. Keep in the fridge until ready to serve.

TEMPERED CHOCOLATE DISCS

250g Valrhona couverture chocolate buttons (with 70% cocoa solids)

Put three-quarters of the chocolate into a microwave-safe bowl. Microwave on medium in three or four 30-second bursts, stirring the chocolate with a spatula between each burst. When almost all the chocolate has melted, take the bowl out of the microwave and stir until all the chocolate has melted and is smooth. (It is important not to overheat the chocolate at the last stage as it can easily burn.) Use a sugar thermometer to check the temperature of the chocolate: it should be 46–49°C.

Add the remaining chocolate to the bowl and stir until melted. Check the temperature again: it should now be about 27°C. If it is too hot, continue to stir for a few more minutes until the chocolate reaches the desired temperature.

Put the bowl back into the microwave and reheat the chocolate on high in 10-second bursts, stirring between each burst, until it reaches 31°C. Make sure not to overheat or you will need to restart the tempering process.

Spread the chocolate on to a metal sheet or marble work surface and allow to cool for a few seconds before cutting out neat discs using an 8cm round pastry cutter. (For decorative purposes, you can also stamp out a few tiny circles of chocolate from each chocolate disc.) Store the discs in an airtight container in a chocolate fridge at 15°C. Any excess chocolate can be re-tempered or used for another dish.

ASSEMBLY

extra virgin olive oil
Olive Oil Ice Cream (see
    page 387)
edible gold leaf

For each serving, place an olive oil biscuit in the centre of a serving plate. Set a chocolate sponge disc on top, then pipe a layer of chocolate mousse on to the sponge. Carefully lay a tempered chocolate disc on top of the mousse. Arrange some olive oil jelly cubes on and around the dessert, then drizzle a few drops of extra virgin olive oil on the chocolate disc. Place a neat quenelle of olive oil ice cream on top of the chocolate disc and stand a couple of shards of black olive tuile around the ice cream. Finish with edible gold leaf and serve immediately.

Hot & Cold Apple Tatin

with
apple crisps
and
Minus 8
vinegar ice
cream

SERVES 4

APPLE PURÉE

4 Granny Smith apples
Maldon sea salt

Peel and finely chop the apples. Put them into a pan, cover with a lid and steam gently for 20 minutes. Remove the lid and lightly season the apples with sea salt. Cook over a medium heat for a few minutes until any liquid released from the apples has evaporated. Transfer to a small blender and blitz until smooth. Tip the purée into a bowl and leave to cool completely before transferring to a squeezy bottle. Keep in the fridge until needed.

APPLE CRISPS

100g soft brown sugar
50ml water
50ml lemon juice
2 Pink Lady apples

Heat the sugar and water in a pan over a medium-high heat, stirring until the sugar has dissolved. Bring to a simmer, then remove from the heat and stir in the lemon juice.

Slice the apples into very thin discs using a mandoline. Lay out the slices on a baking tray lined with a silicone mat and brush them liberally with the lemon syrup. Put the baking tray into a dehydrator set to 75°C and dry out for 45 minutes. Turn the apple slices over and brush with a little more syrup, then return to the dehydrator and dry for another 45 minutes or until the apples are completely dried out and crisp. Cool before storing, in layers between baking parchment, in an airtight container.

HOT APPLE TATIN

juice of 2 lemons
200g caster sugar
1 teaspoon fine sea salt
4 Pink Lady apples
200g all-butter puff pastry
icing sugar, to dust
50g unsalted butter

Combine the lemon juice, 100g of the caster sugar and the salt in a heavy-based saucepan. Warm the mixture over a gentle heat, stirring until the sugar has dissolved. Take the pan off the heat.

One at a time, peel the apples, then use a Japanese-style turning slicer to slice the apple into a long unbroken strip. Working quickly, before the apple discolours, roll the apple strip back to its original shape and place in a vacuum bag. Immediately drizzle over a quarter of the soy and lemon marinade. Repeat for the other apples. Vacuum-seal the bags and leave the apples to macerate while you bake the pastry.

Preheat the oven to 180°C/160°C fan/Gas Mark 4. Roll out the pastry to the thickness of a £1 coin, then transfer to a baking tray. Place another heavy baking tray on top. Bake for 15–18 minutes or until the pastry is lightly golden and 90 per cent cooked through. Remove the top baking tray and dust the pastry with icing sugar, then return it to the oven and bake for a few more minutes. Repeat the dusting with icing sugar and baking 2 more times until the pastry is glazed and golden brown. Remove from the oven (leave the oven on) and leave to cool for a few minutes before cutting the pastry into neat discs using a 7–8cm round pastry cutter. Keep the discs warm.

To make the caramel, put the remaining 100g caster sugar into a heavy-based pan and set it over a high heat. As the sugar begins to melt and colour, swirl it in the pan to ensure that it caramelises evenly. When the caramel has turned a dark terracotta colour, remove from the heat and add the butter. Tip and rotate the pan to mix the butter and caramel together. Return the pan to a medium heat and stir until any hardened bits of caramel have melted. Pour the hot caramel over the bottom of 4 lightly buttered 8cm tartlet tins.

Remove the macerated apples from the vacuum bags. Roll up each apple tightly to its original shape and place in a caramel-lined tartlet tin. Set the tins on a baking tray and bake for 25–35 minutes or until the apple is tender throughout and golden brown. Remove from the oven and leave the caramelised apples to cool for a few minutes.

APPLE SALAD

100ml apple liquor (such as Calvados)
100ml apple juice
juice of 1 lemon
2 Pink Lady apples

Mix together the apple liquor, apple juice and lemon juice in a large bowl. Cut the apples into quarters, remove the core and trim the ends so you have crescent-shaped apple quarters. Finely slice each quarter with a mandoline and place in the apple liquor mixture. Leave the apples to macerate for 1 hour.

ASSEMBLY

apple blossom
wild wood sorrel
Minus 8 Vinegar Ice Cream (see page 386)

For each serving, set a 4cm plain metal ring on a plate and arrange some of the drained apple salad slices in it to resemble a flower. Lift off the ring. Garnish with apple blossom and wild wood sorrel and squeeze dots of apple purée on top. Put a warmed puff pastry disc on another serving plate, then carefully turn out a hot caramelised apple on top. Garnish the apple tatin with apple crisps. Serve immediately with a neat quenelle of ice cream on the side.

Parsnip Crème Caramel

with
blood
orange
granita
and
Pedro
Ximenez-
soaked
raisins

SERVES 10

BLOOD ORANGE GRANITA

1.5 litres blood orange juice
150g caster sugar
juice of 3 lemons

Put the orange juice and sugar into a heavy-based pan
and stir over a medium heat until the sugar has dissolved.
Increase the heat and bring to the boil. Immediately
remove from the heat and stir in the lemon juice. Let the
mixture cool completely, then pour it into a freezerproof
container. Cover and freeze overnight until solid.

PEDRO XIMINEZ-SOAKED RAISINS

50g golden raisins
100ml Pedro Ximenez sherry

Put the raisins into a small bowl or container and pour
over the sherry. Cover and leave to soak overnight. The
following day, strain the sherry into a small saucepan
(reserve the raisins). Boil the sherry until it has reduced
to a light syrup. Pour it back over the raisins and leave to
cool. Keep in the fridge until ready to serve.

CRÈME CARAMEL

750ml whole milk
250g parsnip purée
1 vanilla pod, split lengthways
    and seeds scraped out
5 large eggs
4 large egg yolks
150g caster sugar
a pinch of fine sea salt
250g granulated sugar
75ml water

Put the milk, parsnip purée and vanilla pod and seeds
into a heavy-based saucepan and give the mixture a stir.
Set the pan over a high heat and bring the mixture to
the boil. Meanwhile, beat together the eggs, egg yolks,
caster sugar and salt in a large bowl. As soon as the milk
mixture begins to boil, gradually pour it into the sugary
eggs, stirring constantly. When fully incorporated, place
a sheet of clingfilm on the surface of the crème and leave

to cool, then put the bowl into the fridge to infuse overnight.

The next day, make the caramel for the base. Heat the granulated sugar and water in a heavy-based pan over a medium heat. Once the sugar has dissolved, brush down the sides of the pan with a wet brush, then increase the heat and bring the sugar syrup to the boil. Boil until it turns to a dark golden caramel. Take the pan off the heat and carefully pour the hot caramel into 10 aluminium moulds or ramekins (150ml capacity), tilting each mould so the caramel covers the bottom evenly. Place the moulds on a baking tray and leave the caramel to cool and set.

Preheat the steam oven to 84°C. Stir the crème, then divide it among the moulds. Cover with clingfilm, and steam in the oven for 50 minutes, or until the crème caramels are just set in the middle. Remove and leave to cool at room temperature.

ASSEMBLY

sorrel leaves

Run a thin knife blade around the inside edge of each mould to loosen the crème caramel, then turn it out into a serving bowl. Top the crème caramel with a few sherry-soaked raisins and garnish with sorrel leaves. Scrape the granita with a fork to break it up, then scoop a portion into another individual bowl. Serve at once with the crème caramel.

Mash Purveyors & Secrett's Farm

Mash Purveyors is an independent, family-run London business with over 150 years of industry knowledge and experience. With a passion for the finest fresh produce, we supply the most prestigious restaurants and hotels across London and pride ourselves on a mutual understanding of seasonality, quality and flavour.

We have a great relationship and partner closely with all of our customers and suppliers with the aim of achieving world-class results, while striving to provide the best service, industry wide.

We are synonymous in the Michelin supply chain and work closely with a number of top chefs. Jason contacted us when Pollen Street started and we've been a key supplier ever since.

In turn, Charles Secrett, from Secrett's Farm, approached us to become his London distributor in 2010, and Secrett's have supplied Pollen Street, via Mash Purveyors, ever since.

With Secrett's Farm being local to our offices we are able to offer bespoke grown produce straight from field to fork.

mashpurveyors.com
secretts.co.uk

Wild Strawberries

with
sorrel & sake
granita
and
buttermilk,
cream

SERVES 4

SORREL & SAKE GRANITA

30g caster sugar
180ml water
200g sorrel
100ml sake

Put the sugar and 30ml (2 tablespoons) of the water
into a small saucepan and stir over a medium heat until
the sugar has dissolved. Increase the heat and simmer
the syrup for a few minutes until reduced slightly.
Meanwhile, measure the remaining water in a jug. Pour
in the sugar syrup and stir, then leave to cool completely.

Pour the cooled syrup into a blender. Add the sorrel and
blitz until smooth. Strain the sorrel syrup through a
fine sieve into a wide freezerproof container. Stir in the
sake. Cover the container and freeze for a few hours, or
overnight, until solid.

BUTTERMILK CREAM

4 large egg yolks
500ml whole milk
65g caster sugar
50g cornflour
50g strong white flour
7g agar agar powder
500g plain yoghurt
juice of ½ lemon

Whisk together the egg yolks and 150ml of the milk
in a mixing bowl. Add the sugar, cornflour, strong flour
and agar agar powder and whisk again until the mixture
is smooth.

Bring the rest of the milk almost to a simmer in a
saucepan. Take the pan off the heat and gradually trickle
the warm milk into the bowl, whisking constantly. Once
all the milk has been incorporated, pour the mixture
back into the pan. Set over a high heat and stir with a
whisk until it begins to boil. Continue to cook and stir for
2 minutes to cook out the flour. The mixture will thicken
to a smooth custard.

Spread out the custard on a lightly buttered wide
tray, then cool it down quickly in a blast chiller (or lay
clingfilm on the surface and cool in the fridge or freezer).
Transfer the cold custard to a Thermomix or a strong

blender, add the yoghurt and lemon juice, and blitz until smooth. Pass the mixture through a sieve to make sure that there are no lumps, then spoon into one or 2 piping bags. Keep in the fridge until needed.

WILD STRAWBERRIES

250g wild or alpine strawberries
250g white strawberries
250g Gariguette strawberries

Rinse and hull the wild strawberries, then pat dry with kitchen paper. Put them into a freezer bag or a sealable container and freeze until solid. Hull the white strawberries and Gariguettes and cut them in half.

ASSEMBLY

For each serving, pipe a layer of buttermilk cream into a serving bowl and top it with a mixture of frozen wild strawberries, white strawberries and Gariguettes. Scrape the frozen sorrel and sake granita with a fork to make a coarse grainy texture, then spoon a portion into a small serving bowl. If you wish, set the bowl over a larger bowl filled with ice as we do at the restaurant. Serve immediately.

Citrus Curd Meringue

with
lemon
sponge
and
basil
sorbet

SERVES 12

MERINGUES

>125g egg whites (from 6–7
>   large eggs)
>250g icing sugar
>¼ teaspoon cream of tartar
>finely grated zest and juice of
>   1 lemon

Using an 8–10cm pastry ring as a guide, mark 12 neat circles on 2 large sheets of acetate. Turn the acetate over so the marked circles are on the underside. Place the sheets on 2 baking trays.

Put the egg whites, icing sugar and cream of tartar into the bowl of a free-standing electric mixer. Whisk on low speed until well combined, then increase the speed to high and whisk to a meringue that will form stiff peaks. Add the lemon zest and juice and mix briefly.

Transfer the meringue to a large piping bag fitted with a plain round nozzle, about 1cm in diameter. Pipe little blobs all around each marked circle on the acetate sheets and then inside the piped ring to make a disc. Dry out the meringues in a dehydrator at 75°C (or in a very low oven) for 3–3½ hours or until they are dried but still slightly chewy in the centre. Leave the meringues to cool completely before storing them in an airtight container.

LEMON SPONGE

>200g eggs (about 3 large or
>   4 medium eggs)
>125g caster sugar
>125g strong white flour
>finely grated zest of 1 lemon
>30g unsalted butter, melted
>   and cooled

Preheat the oven to 180°C/160°C fan/Gas Mark 4. Grease 2 baking trays and line with baking parchment.

Using a free-standing electric mixer, whisk the eggs with the sugar until the mixture is light, fluffy and tripled in volume. Sift over the flour in 2 batches and fold into the egg mixture. Fold in the lemon zest and melted butter. Divide the sponge mixture between the baking trays and spread out evenly using a palette knife. Bake for 7–8 minutes or until the sponges have set and are slightly springy when lightly pressed.

Leave to cool completely before stamping out neat discs with the same round pastry ring you used to mark the circles for the meringue. Store the sponge rounds in a sealable container, in between sheets of baking parchment to prevent them from sticking together.

LEMON CURD

110ml lemon juice
2 large eggs, lightly beaten
110g caster sugar
1.5g agar agar powder
140g unsalted butter, diced

Put the lemon juice and eggs into a heavy-based pan. Stir the sugar with the agar agar, then add this to the pan. Set over a low heat and stir the ingredients together as the sugar dissolves. Increase the heat slightly so the mixture is just below simmering point and continue to stir for 8–10 minutes or until it thickens. Remove from the heat and add the butter. Keep stirring until the butter has melted and the mixture is smooth.

Pass the curd through a sieve into a bowl set over a larger bowl of iced water. Stir the curd frequently to cool it down quickly. If you find that a skin has formed on the top, transfer the curd to a blender or Thermomix and blitz until smooth.

Spoon the curd into piping bags fitted with plain round nozzles. Keep in the fridge until needed.

ASSEMBLY

Whole Lemon Purée (see
   page 384)
1 finger lime (optional)
1 lime, for zesting
1 lemon, for zesting
Basil Sorbet (see page 385)

For each serving, place a sponge disc in the middle of a serving plate. Pipe little dots of lemon curd and lemon purée all over the sponge disc. Carefully set a meringue disc on top of the lemon curd and purée. If using the finger lime, cut across the fruit and squeeze out the pearl-like flesh. Scatter these over the meringue, then finely grate over some lime and lemon zests. Serve immediately, with a neat quenelle of basil sorbet alongside.

Chardonnay-poached Pear

with
champagne
granita
and
buttermilk
purée

SERVES 4

POACHED PEAR

400ml Chardonnay wine
200g caster sugar
1 cinnamon stick
1 vanilla pod, split lengthways
    and seeds scraped out
1 tablespoon lemon juice
2 ripe pears

Put the wine, sugar, cinnamon stick, vanilla seeds and
pod into a small saucepan and stir over a medium heat
until the sugar has dissolved. Take the pan off the heat
and leave to cool, then stir in the lemon juice.

Peel the pears, then cut them horizontally into 2cm
thick slices (you should get 2 slices from each pear). Use
a 5cm round pastry cutter to stamp out a neat disc from
each slice of pear. (The pear trimmings can be used for
chutney or smoothies.)

Place the pear discs in a vacuum bag and pour in enough
cooled Chardonnay syrup to cover them. Vacuum-seal
the bag, then lower into a sous vide machine (or water
bath) heated to 60°C. Poach for 40 minutes or until the
pears are tender. Allow to cool. If making ahead, keep
in the fridge. Serve at room temperature.

CHAMPAGNE GRANITA

1 x 75cl bottle of Champagne
185g caster sugar
310ml water

Put all the ingredients into a saucepan and stir over a
medium heat until the sugar has dissolved. Bring to the
boil, then immediately take the pan off the heat. Pour the
syrup into a deep, freezerproof container and let it cool
completely. Once cold, cover the container and freeze for
at least 6 hours or overnight until solid.

BUTTERMILK PURÉE

4 large egg yolks
500ml whole milk
65g caster sugar
50g cornflour

50g strong white flour
7g agar agar powder
500g plain yoghurt
juice of ½ lemon

Put the egg yolks into a large mixing bowl with a third of the milk. Add the sugar, cornflour and strong flour and whisk the ingredients together. Pour the rest of the milk into a heavy-based saucepan and set it over a medium-high heat. As soon as the milk begins to bubble around the edge, take the pan off the heat and slowly stir the hot milk into the egg mixture. Once all the milk has been incorporated, pour the mixture into the pan and stir with a whisk over a high heat until the mixture begins to boil. Add the agar agar and boil, stirring, for 2 minutes. The mixture will thicken to a smooth custard.

Transfer the custard to a wide tray and cool it down quickly in a blast chiller (or lay a sheet of clingfilm on top of the custard and leave it to cool at room temperature). Once cooled, scoop the custard into a food processor or Thermomix and add the yoghurt and lemon juice. Blitz until smooth, then pass the mixture through a sieve to make sure that there are no lumps. Spoon into one or 2 piping bags. Keep in the fridge until needed.

ASSEMBLY

a handful of wood sorrel leaves
olive oil, to drizzle

For each serving, pipe a generous mound of buttermilk purée on to a wide serving bowl. Lay a poached pear disc on top. Garnish with a few wood sorrel leaves and drizzle over a few drops of olive oil. Remove the Champagne granita from the freezer and scrape it with a fork to make a coarse grainy texture. Scoop a ball of granita into a small bowl and serve it alongside the poached pear.

Petit Fours

Cherry 'Bakewell' Tart

with
almond cake
and
cherry jam

SERVES 16

ALMOND CAKE

110g unsalted butter
250g ground almonds
375g caster sugar
45g T45 or plain flour, sifted
310g egg whites (from about 8 large eggs)
flaked almonds, for sprinkling

First brown the butter: put it into a heavy-based saucepan and set over a medium heat. When the butter has melted, continue to heat, swirling the butter in the pan every so often, until it has browned and smells nutty. It should reach a temperature of 140°C. Strain the brown butter through a fine sieve to remove the solids, then leave to cool to about 40°C.

Preheat the oven to 170°C/150°C fan/Gas Mark 3. Mix together the ground almonds, sugar and flour in a large bowl. Put the egg whites into a Thermomix set at 40°C and whisk/blitz until warmed. Fold the egg whites into the dry mixture in 2 stages, then gently fold through the warm brown butter until just combined.

Pipe or spoon the cake mixture into 16 greased non-stick 7cm tartlet tins set on baking trays. Arrange flaked almonds on top of each 'tartlet' in a neat ring. Bake for 20 minutes, rotating the baking tray after about 10 minutes to ensure even cooking, or until golden brown and the cakes feel slightly springy when lightly pressed in the centre. Leave to cool completely.

CHERRY JAM

250g Morello cherry purée
5g agar agar powder

Put the cherry purée and agar agar into a heavy-based saucepan and bring to the boil, stirring. Let the purée boil for 2 minutes or until the agar agar has completely dissolved. Pour into a shallow container and cool, then chill for about an hour or until set. Scrape the mixture into a blender and blitz until smooth. Pass the jam through a fine sieve, then transfer to a squeezy bottle.

ASSEMBLY

icing sugar

Set a tartlet on each serving plate and dust with icing sugar. Pipe a little mound of cherry jam on top and serve immediately.

Clementine & Almond Macarons

with
yuzu &
white
chocolate
crème
pâtissière
and
white
chocolate
discs

SERVES 40

MACARONS

190g finely ground almonds
190g icing sugar
140g egg whites
190g caster sugar
50ml water
10 freeze-dried clementine
    segments, chopped

Combine the ground almonds, icing sugar and half the
egg whites in a large mixing bowl. Stir the ingredients
together to make a wet paste. Set aside.

Put the remaining egg whites in the bowl of a free-
standing electric mixer and start whisking on low
speed. Meanwhile, stir the caster sugar and water in
a small saucepan over a medium heat until the sugar
has dissolved. Increase the heat and bring to the boil.
Insert a sugar thermometer and boil until the sugar
syrup reaches 117°C. As soon as the syrup has reached
the right temperature, increase the speed of the mixer
to high and whisk the egg whites while slowly pouring
in the hot syrup. When all the syrup has been added,
decrease the speed to medium and continue to whisk for
15–20 minutes or until the meringue has cooled to room
temperature and is thick and glossy.

In 3 batches, fold the meringue into the ground almond
mixture, trying not to lose too much air from the
meringue as you do so. Finally, fold through the chopped
freeze-dried clementine. Scoop the macaron mixture
into a piping bag fitted with a 1cm plain round nozzle.
Pipe small rounds (about 3cm diameter) on to baking
trays lined with silicone mats, making sure to leave a bit
of space between each one as the macarons will spread
slightly during baking. Gently tap the baking tray a few
times on the work surface to help the macaron mixture
to settle and to break any air bubbles, then leave to dry
for 10–20 minutes. The surface of each macaron will
become smooth and shiny and a skin will have formed
on top.

Preheat the oven to 150°C/130°C fan/Gas Mark 2.
Bake the macarons for 7–8 minutes or until they feel firm
and have risen slightly. Slide the silicone mats on to a wire
rack and leave the macarons to cool completely. Do not
be tempted to remove them from the mat until they are
cold or you may break them. If made ahead, keep in the
freezer for up to a week.

YUZU & WHITE CHOCOLATE CRÈME PÂTISSIÈRE

250ml whole milk
1¼ teaspoons caster sugar
25g cornflour
25g plain flour
3 medium egg yolks
150g white chocolate
125ml yuzu purée
5g agar agar powder

Gently warm the milk in a heavy-based saucepan until it reaches 80°C. In a large bowl, whisk together the sugar, cornflour, plain flour and egg yolks until the mixture is pale. Slowly stir in the warm milk. Pour the mixture back into the pan and stir over a medium heat until thickened to a custard. Continue to cook and stir for another couple of minutes. Remove the pan from the heat.

Melt the white chocolate in a heatproof bowl set over a pan of simmering water. Heat the yuzu purée with the agar agar in a small saucepan, stirring until the agar agar has completely dissolved. Add the melted chocolate to the custard, then stir in the yuzu mixture until evenly combined. Lay a sheet of clingfilm on the surface to prevent a skin from forming and leave to cool.

Blitz the crème pâtissière in a food processor until smooth, then pass through a fine sieve. Put the crème pâtissière into a piping bag fitted with a 1cm plain round nozzle. Keep in the fridge until ready to serve.

WHITE CHOCOLATE DISCS

250g Valrhona white chocolate
silver dust

Temper the white chocolate (see Tempered Chocolate Discs in the Chocolate Pavé recipe, page 328), then spread the chocolate on to a metal sheet or marble work surface. Allow to cool for a few seconds before cutting out neat discs using a 3cm round pastry cutter. Finish the discs with silver dust.

ASSEMBLY

For each macaron, pipe a layer of yuzu and white chocolate crème pâtissière on a macaron round, then top it with a tempered white chocolate disc. Serve as petits fours to accompany coffee or tea.

Chocolate Ganache

with
Bergamot
purée
and
Pollen Street
Social Blend
Tea

350ml water
10g black tea leaves (we use
   our own Pollen Street Social
   blend tea)
45g Valrhona milk chocolate
   (with 40% cocoa solids),
   chopped
440g Valrhona dark chocolate
   (with 70% cocoa solids),
   chopped
70ml double cream
45ml bergamot purée

Bring the water to the boil in a
saucepan. Add the tea leaves and take
the pan off the heat. Leave the tea to
steep for 10 minutes.

Meanwhile, put the milk chocolate
and 140g of the dark chocolate into
a heatproof bowl and set the bowl
over a pan of gently simmering
water. Stir the chocolate until
completely melted and smooth.
Remove from the heat.

Strain the tea through a fine sieve;
discard the tea leaves. Pour 250ml
of the tea into a saucepan and add
the double cream. Bring to a simmer
over a medium heat.

Put the remaining dark chocolate
into a large bowl. Pour the hot
cream and tea infusion over the dark
chocolate and stir until the chocolate
has melted and the mixture is
smooth. Fold through the melted
chocolate and bergamot purée until
evenly combined.

Pour or spoon the chocolate ganache
into small glasses or cups to serve as
petits fours. Chill for at least an hour
until set.

Dark Chocolate Bon Bons

with
praline &
feuilletine
filling

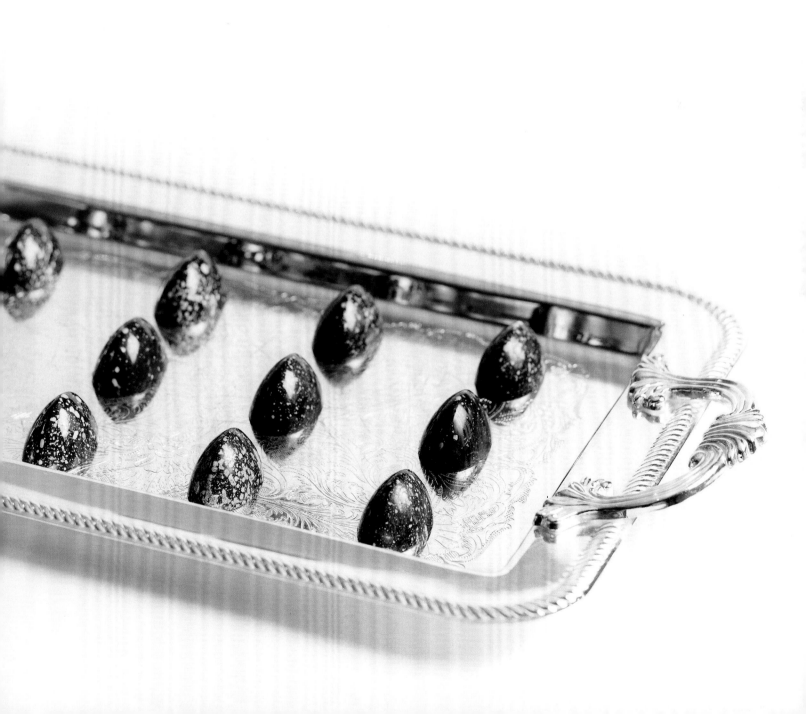

MAKES 30

---

blue and red cocoa butter
food colouring
125g praline paste (we
use Valrhona)
250g ready-made pailleté
feuilletine
1kg Valrhona couverture
chocolate buttons (with
70% cocoa solids)

Separately melt the blue and red
cocoa butters in a microwave set on
high in 20-second bursts, following
the manufacturer's instructions.
Use a spray gun to spray a lining of
cocoa butter into each hole in several
chocolate moulds (half of them blue
and half red), making sure that the
holes are evenly coloured with the
cocoa butter. Chill for 5–10
minutes to set.

Meanwhile, make the filling
for the bon bons. Mix the praline
and feuilletine together, then
transfer the mixture to a piping
bag. Set aside.

Now temper the chocolate. Put
750g of the chocolate into a
microwave-safe bowl. Microwave
on medium in three or four
30-second bursts, stirring the
chocolate with a spatula between
each burst. When almost all the
chocolate has melted, take the bowl
out of the microwave and stir until
all the chocolate has melted and
is smooth. (It is important not to
overheat the chocolate at the last
stage as it can easily burn.) Use a
sugar thermometer to check the
temperature of the chocolate: it
should be 46–49°C.

Add the remaining 250g chocolate
to the bowl and stir until melted.
Check the temperature again: it
should now be about 27°C. If it
is too hot, continue to stir until

the chocolate reaches the desired temperature. This may take 10–15 minutes.

Put the bowl back into the microwave and reheat the chocolate on high in 10-second bursts, stirring between each burst, until it reaches 31°C. Make sure not to overheat or you will need to restart the tempering process.

Pour the tempered chocolate on to the moulds, completely filling the holes to the top. Allow the chocolate to sit for a few seconds, then turn the moulds over and pour out the excess chocolate, back into the bowl containing the rest of the tempered chocolate. Give each mould a few taps on the side of the bowl, then scrape off the excess chocolate from the top of the mould with a pastry scraper. Chill for 5–10 minutes to set the chocolate shells.

Once the chocolate has set, pipe the praline and feuilletine filling into each shell, stopping 3–4mm below the top rim of the shell (this will leave a little space for the tempered chocolate covering).

Pour the rest of the tempered chocolate over the top of the moulds to fill and cover the holes, then scrape off any excess chocolate back into the bowl. Chill for 5–10 minutes or until the chocolates have set.

Twist each mould to loosen the chocolates, then turn it upside down and tap the bon bons out of the mould. Store the chocolates in a cool, dry place. To serve, arrange them on a platter.

La Fromagerie

I have known Jason for many years – from the time he was working with Gordon Ramsay in fact. He was a 'heads-down craftsman' as a young chef, soaking up information and grafting. In the same way I learnt my craft as a 'fromager', absorbing information from cheesemakers and expert refiners of cheese. So I felt a kindred spirit in Jason and was so pleased when he said he wanted to work with us for his cheeseboard and specialist dairy items once he started his own business.

One thing to know about Jason is that he requires 100 per cent from all who work with him, whether in the business or from his producers and suppliers. It is no use having an off-day with Jason. I'm afraid I'm the same! I will always remember early conversations with him and his passion to be the best, his determination to be a success not only for his own personal satisfaction but to show others it could be done and that it was down to hard work and application.

Our cheese technicians keep records of what we supply to Pollen Street Social. Because we're very hands-on with each of his restaurants, we give individual attention, taking notes of the menu and the wine list and talking to the front of house team too. It's all about seasonality when it comes to farmhouse hand-made cheese so regular tastings – with visits to our Cheese Rooms to talk through what's on the shelves and taste groups of cheeses – are vital to both our team and theirs. This enables us all to understand requirements as well as updating knowledge on keeping, cutting and general care of cheese. We

have recently been concentrating on young British cheesemakers who are creating new regional cheeses. Jason has been quick to showcase selections that hold their own alongside their continental neighbours.

Weather patterns and animal welfare at critical times – such as calving and lambing – can accentuate changes to the cheeses and also account for a lack of milk supply. We want our restaurant clients to know all about this and how it affects the choices of cheeses available. For example, goat's cheese will be less available in the winter but will return again in the spring after lambing and when it is warm enough for the animals to go outside (they do prefer to forage for their food rather than stay indoors). Summer milk can start off fresh and grassy, whereas in late summer when the pastures are drier with seeded grasses, the milk will have a spicier, bosky flavour. Deep winter for cattle can mean wetter pastures, which gives milk a dense richness with pronounced vegetal aromas and flavours. All these factors are passed on to the restaurants to make decisions about what to put on their cheeseboard, to keep it harmonious and defined.

Patricia Michelson, Founder
lafromagerie.co.uk

Appendix

Olive Oil Mash

SERVES 6

1kg La Ratte potatoes
250g unsalted butter
100ml whole milk
100ml double cream
200ml Arbequina olive oil
Maldon sea salt and black pepper

Peel the potatoes and place them in a large pan. Cover with cold water and add a generous pinch of salt. Bring to the boil, then simmer the potatoes for 10–15 minutes or until they are tender. Drain well.

Mash the potatoes using a potato ricer, then push the mash through a fine sieve into a bowl. Heat the butter, milk and cream in a heavy-based saucepan. When the butter has melted and the creamy milk begins to simmer, gradually add the mixture to the mash, mixing well; use a stick blender if it is easier. Slowly incorporate the olive oil in the same manner. Taste and adjust the seasoning. Return the mash to the pan and reheat for serving.

Saffron & Garlic Mash

SERVES 6–7

---

5 bulbs of garlic
200ml Arbequina olive oil,
    plus extra for drizzling
1kg La Ratte potatoes
200ml double cream
2g saffron threads
Maldon sea salt and white pepper

Preheat the oven to 150°C/130°C fan/Gas Mark 2. Cut off the top quarter from each bulb of garlic to expose the cloves. Put the garlic, cut side up, in a small baking dish or tray and drizzle over a little olive oil. Roast for 1–1¼ hours or until garlic skins are golden brown and the cloves are soft. Leave to cool slightly, then squeeze out the cloves. Push them through a fine sieve into a bowl and set aside.

Peel the potatoes and cut in half or into quarters so that they are roughly the same size. Put them into a large pan, cover with cold water and add a generous pinch of salt. Bring to the boil, then lower the heat and simmer for 10–15 minutes or until tender. Drain the potatoes and return them to the hot, dry pan. Leave for a few minutes to dry out a little, then mash the potatoes with a potato ricer. Pass the mash through a fine sieve into a clean pan.

In another saucepan, bring the cream to the boil with the saffron. As soon as it boils, take the pan off the heat and blend for a few seconds using a stick blender. Strain the saffron cream, then gradually stir it into the mash. Slowly stir in the olive oil. Finally, mix in 2 tablespoons of the garlic paste (save the remaining garlic paste for another dish) and adjust the seasoning to taste. Reheat before serving.

Mushroom Purée

MAKES ABOUT 150G

---

knobs of unsalted butter
4 large shallots, sliced
1 garlic clove, finely chopped
250g large flat mushrooms, sliced
150ml Madeira
Maldon sea salt and white pepper

Melt a few knobs of butter in a heavy-based pan, add the shallot and garlic, and cook over a medium heat for 4–6 minutes or until they begin to soften. Add the sliced mushrooms and a few more knobs of butter to the pan. Increase the heat and fry the mushrooms until golden brown, stirring every once in a while. Pour in the Madeira and let it bubble until reduced to a syrupy consistency. While still hot, transfer the contents of the pan to a food processor and blitz until the mixture is smooth. Season with salt and pepper to taste, then pass the mushroom purée through a fine sieve into a bowl. Cover with clingfilm and keep in the fridge until needed.

Pearl Barley Risotto

MAKES ABOUT 400G

200g pearl barley
olive oil, for cooking
1 carrot, peeled and
   finely chopped
1 onion, finely chopped
1 celery stick, finely chopped
1 leek, finely chopped
5 garlic cloves, finely chopped
3 sprigs of thyme
800ml Chicken Stock (see
   page 379)
a few knobs of unsalted butter
3 large shallots, finely chopped
150ml Madeira
150ml double cream
150g Mushroom Purée (see
   page 371)
a handful of flat-leaf parsley leaves,
   finely chopped
Maldon sea salt and white pepper

Rinse the barley under cold, running water, then drain well. Heat a little olive oil in a saucepan and add the carrot, onion, celery, leek and 2 of the garlic cloves with a pinch each of salt and pepper. Stir over a medium heat for 6–8 minutes or until the vegetables begin to soften. Tip in the barley and add 2 sprigs of thyme. Cook, stirring, for a few minutes until the barley is lightly toasted. Pour in 500ml of the stock and bring to a simmer, then simmer gently, stirring occasionally, for 25–30 minutes or until the barley is just cooked and tender. (If preparing ahead, cool the barley and keep in the fridge until ready to serve).

Meanwhile, heat the butter in a saucepan, add the shallots and remaining garlic, and season with a little salt and pepper. Stir frequently over a medium heat for 6–8 minutes or until the shallots are soft. Deglaze the pan with the Madeira and add the remaining sprig of thyme. Let

the Madeira boil until reduced to a syrupy consistency. Pour in the remaining 300ml chicken stock and boil until reduced by half. Stir in the cream and bring back to a simmer. Reduce by about a quarter. Remove from the heat and set aside.

Before serving, combine the barley risotto with the mushroom purée and Madeira cream in a saucepan and reheat gently. When hot, stir in the chopped parsley.

Lettuce & Seaweed Powder

MAKES 100G

2 heads of Romaine lettuce,
   leaves separated
200g spinach leaves
10ml soy sauce
10ml mirin
2 sheets of dried nori
1 teaspoon dashi powder

Bring a large pan of salted water to the boil and have ready a bowl of iced water on the side. Blanch the lettuce and spinach leaves for 20 seconds, then drain and refresh them in the iced water until cooled. Drain well. Wrap the leaves in a clean kitchen towel or muslin and squeeze out as much excess water as you can. Spread out the leaves on a baking tray. Place in a dehydrator set to 70°C and dry out for 8 hours.

Combine the soy sauce and mirin in a small bowl. Brush this mixture over both sides of each nori sheet. Lay the sheets on a baking tray and place in the dehydrator with the lettuce and spinach leaves. Leave the nori sheets to dry out for the same amount of time as the leaves.

When fully dried and crisp, break the leaves and nori sheets into smaller pieces and put into a spice grinder. Add the dashi powder and grind the ingredients to a fine powder. Sift the powder using a fine sieve before storing in an airtight container.

Tarragon Mayonnaise

MAKES ABOUT 700G

---

3 bunches of tarragon, about 300g
1 bunch of chives, about 100g
600ml rapeseed oil
60g pasteurised egg yolks
20ml white wine vinegar
Maldon sea salt and black pepper

Roughly chop or snip the tarragon and chives into a Thermomix. Pour in the oil. Blitz at 80°C for 8 minutes or until very smooth. Strain the herb oil through a fine sieve lined with muslin into a bowl. Leave to cool to room temperature.

Put the egg yolks into the Thermomix and blitz until pale. While blending at medium-high speed, gradually add the herb oil. The mixture should emulsify to a thick mayonnaise texture. Add the vinegar and salt and pepper to taste. Blend again, then transfer to a clean jar or squeezy bottle. Keep in the fridge and use within a week.

Spice Water Dressing

MAKES ABOUT 1L

5g cinnamon sticks
5g coriander seeds
5g cumin seeds
5g star anise
5g grated nutmeg
5g curry powder
5g ground turmeric
5g ground ginger
200ml water
440g runny honey
440ml Jerez vinegar
Maldon sea salt

Lightly crush the whole spices and put them into a dry pan with the nutmeg, curry powder, turmeric and ginger. Toast the spices over a medium heat for a few minutes, then pour in the water to cover. Bring to a simmer and cook gently for 10 minutes. Take the pan off the heat and leave to cool and infuse overnight.

The next day, the spices will have settled at the bottom of the pan. Carefully pour the water into a jug, leaving behind the spices and sediment. Add the honey, vinegar and a generous pinch of salt to the spiced water. Blitz the mixture using a stick blender until combined. Pour the dressing into a squeezy bottle and keep in the fridge. Use within a month.

Truffle Dressing

MAKES ABOUT 240ML

50ml truffle vinegar
25ml sherry vinegar
65ml olive oil
65ml truffle oil
30–35g truffle, chopped
a splash of soy sauce, to taste

Put the vinegars, oils and truffle into a jug and blitz together with stick blender. Taste and adjust the seasoning with soy sauce, then pour the dressing into a squeezy bottle. Keep in the fridge and use within a week. Shake well before using.

Beef Sauce

MAKES 750ML

olive oil, for cooking
1kg beef rib bones and trimmings
2 large shallots, roughly chopped
2 carrots, peeled and
    roughly chopped
250g button mushrooms,
    roughly chopped
1½ celery sticks, roughly chopped
1 small leek, roughly chopped
½ bulb of garlic, cloves separated
    and roughly chopped
1 teaspoon black peppercorns
375ml red wine
125ml port
1 litre Chicken Stock (see
    page 379)
1 litre Veal Stock (see page 380)
12g thyme
10g tarragon
a few dashes of Worcestershire
    sauce

Heat a little oil in a large, heavy-based pan until hot, then sear the beef bones for 2–3 minutes on each side or until a deep golden brown. Remove the bones to a tray and set aside. Add any beef trimmings and sear for 2 minutes on each side or until evenly golden brown. Remove to the tray, leaving behind any fat in the pan.

Add the chopped vegetables, garlic and peppercorns to the pan and fry over a high heat, stirring occasionally, for about 10 minutes or until the vegetables are golden brown and caramelised. Pour in the red wine and port and bring to the boil. Boil until reduced by half. Return the browned beef bones and trimmings to the pan and pour over the chicken and veal stocks. If the liquid does not fully cover the bones, top up with a little water. Bring to a simmer, skimming off any froth and scum from the surface, then

partially cover the pan and simmer gently for 2–3 hours, skimming as necessary.

Strain the sauce through a sieve into a clean pot. Bring the sauce back to the boil over a medium-high heat and skim off any excess fat from the surface. Boil to reduce the sauce by half or until the flavour has intensified; the sauce should have thickened enough to lightly coat the back of a spoon.

Strain the sauce once again, but this time through a muslin-lined sieve into a clean saucepan. Add the thyme and tarragon with a few dashes of Worcestershire sauce. Leave to infuse and cool completely before discarding the herbs. Reheat for serving.

Duck Sauce

MAKES ABOUT 1–1.4L

vegetable oil, for cooking
1kg duck bones (necks and
    carcasses), fat removed
1 onion, chopped
1 small leek, chopped
1 carrot, peeled and chopped
1 celery stick, chopped
½ bulb of garlic, cloves separated
    and roughly chopped
½ tablespoon tomato paste
100ml dry white wine
100ml Madeira
1 litre Veal Stock (see page 380)
500ml Chicken Stock (see
    page 379)
a sprig of lemon thyme
Maldon sea salt and black pepper

Heat a little oil in a large pan over a high heat. When hot, add the duck bones and fry, turning occasionally, for 8–10 minutes or until the bones are a deep golden brown. Remove the browned bones to a plate and set aside.

Add a little more oil to the pan and stir in the chopped vegetables and garlic. Fry, stirring every once in a while, for 6–8 minutes or until the vegetables begin to soften. Stir in the tomato paste, then fry for a few more minutes until the vegetables are golden brown. Return all but 4–5 pieces of duck bones to the pan and deglaze with the white wine and Madeira, stirring well. Boil until reduced by half. Pour in both stocks and top up with a little water if the liquid does not cover the bones. Bring to a simmer, skimming off any froth that rises to the surface, then leave to simmer gently for 4 hours.

Strain the sauce through a fine sieve into another heavy-based saucepan; discard the solids. Taste the sauce – if you would prefer a stronger

flavour, boil the sauce to reduce it. Leave to cool, then strain once again and cool. Keep in the fridge until needed.

Before serving, simmer the sauce with the reserved duck bones and the lemon thyme for 2 minutes. Taste and adjust the seasoning with salt and pepper, then strain through a fine sieve.

APPENDIX

Game Sauce

MAKES 2L

olive oil, for cooking
bones and carcasses from game
    birds, around 800g
4 shallots, chopped
1 leek, chopped
2 carrots, peeled and chopped
2 celery sticks, chopped
1 bulb of garlic, cloves separated
    and chopped
1 tablespoon tomato paste
2 star anise
2 cloves
1 cinnamon stick
200ml red wine
200ml ruby port
2 litres Veal Stock (see page 380)
1 litre Chicken Stock (see
    page 379)
2 sprigs of lemon thyme
hearts and livers of game birds
    (such as mallards, pheasants,
    grouse, quail)
Maldon sea salt and white pepper

Heat a little olive oil in a large heavy-
based pan. Add the reserved bones
and carcasses of the game birds and
sear them for 2–3 minutes on each
side or until golden brown all over.
Remove the bones and carcasses
from the pan and set aside.

Add a little more oil to the pan
and tip in the chopped vegetables
and garlic. Season with a little
salt and pepper, then fry the
vegetables, stirring occasionally,
for 8–10 minutes or until they are
soft and light golden brown. Stir
in the tomato paste and fry for
another couple of minutes until the
vegetables are caramelised
and browned.

Add the spices and return all but a
few pieces of bones and carcasses to
the pan (reserve the few pieces to
use later). Pour in the red wine
and port and deglaze the pan,
scraping the bottom and sides to
dislodge the browned bits. Let the
liquid boil until reduced by half,
then add both stocks. If the liquid
does not cover the ingredients, top
up with a little water. Bring to a
simmer, skimming off any froth and
scum from the surface, then leave to
cook gently for 4 hours.

Strain the sauce through a fine
sieve into a clean pan and discard
the solids. Taste the sauce. If you
like, boil to reduce it and intensify
the flavour. Season with salt and
pepper. If making in advance, the
sauce can now be cooled and kept
in the fridge.

When ready to serve, reheat the
game sauce with the reserved bones
and the sprigs of lemon thyme. Pass
the sauce through a fine sieve into
a clean pan.

Heat a little oil in a frying pan
and sauté the reserved game livers
and hearts with a little seasoning
until golden brown all over. Tip the
livers and hearts out of the pan and
finely chop, then add to the game
sauce and gently reheat.

Lamb Sauce

MAKES ABOUT 1L

olive oil, for cooking
1kg lamb rib bones, chopped into
    smaller pieces
1 onion, roughly chopped
½ leek, roughly chopped
1 carrot, peeled and roughly
    chopped
1 celery stick, roughly chopped
½ bulb of garlic, cloves separated
    and roughly chopped
½ tablespoon tomato paste
200ml dry white wine
500ml reduced Veal Stock
    (see page 380)
500ml Chicken Stock (see
    page 379)
a sprig of lemon thyme
a sprig of rosemary
pared zest of 1 lemon
1 dried kombu leaf
Maldon sea salt and black pepper

Heat a drizzle of olive oil in a large,
heavy-based pan, add the lamb bones
and fry over a high heat until evenly
browned. Remove the bones to a
plate and set aside.

Add a little more oil to the pan
and tip in the chopped vegetables
and garlic. Fry for about 8 minutes,
stirring frequently, until the
vegetables begin to soften. Add the
tomato paste and stir well. Fry for
another couple of minutes until the
vegetables begin to brown, then
deglaze with the wine, scraping the
sides and bottom of the pan. Let
the wine bubble and reduce by half.
Return the browned bones to the
pan. Pour in the veal and chicken
stocks, topping up with a little water
if the bones are not immersed
in the liquid. Bring to the boil,
then simmer for about 4 hours,
skimming off any scum and froth
from the surface.

Strain the sauce through a fine
sieve into a clean heavy-based
saucepan; discard the solids. Taste
the sauce. If you want a stronger
flavour, boil to reduce and intensify.
Take the pan off the heat. Season to
taste with salt and pepper and add
the lemon thyme, rosemary, lemon
zest and kombu. Leave to infuse
and cool.

Once cooled, strain the sauce once
more. Reheat before serving.

377

Mint Sauce

MAKES ABOUT 125ML

100ml rapeseed oil
a bunch of thyme, leaves stripped
6 bunches of mint
20ml Pickling Liquid (see
    page 376)
Maldon sea salt and white pepper

Warm the oil with the thyme leaves
in a saucepan. Take the pan off the
heat and set aside to cool and infuse.
Meanwhile, pick the mint leaves and
blanch them in a pan of boiling water
for 10 seconds. With a slotted spoon,
transfer the mint leaves to a bowl of
iced water to refresh them. Drain
the mint. Repeat the blanching,
leaving them in the boiling water for
a few minutes the second time, then
refresh as before and drain well.

Pour the thyme oil into a blender,
add the mint and blitz to a smooth
sauce. Season with salt and pepper
to taste. Transfer to a container,
cover and keep in the fridge until
needed. Mix in the pickling liquid
before serving.

Vinaigrette

MAKES ABOUT 700ML

3 lemongrass sticks
75g demerara sugar
1 bay leaf
20g thyme
100ml white wine vinegar
100ml lemon juice
500ml rapeseed oil
250ml extra virgin olive oil
5g Maldon sea salt

Smash the lemongrass and place
in a pan with the sugar, bay leaf,
thyme and white wine vinegar.
Bring to the boil, then remove from
the heat pour into a bowl. Leave to
infuse overnight.

The next day, strain the vinegar into
a clean bowl and mix with all other
ingredients by blitzing with a hand
blender. Store in a covered container
or squeezy bottles and shake well
before use.

Pickling Liquid

MAKES ABOUT 220ML

125ml Muscatel vinegar
100ml white wine vinegar
100g caster sugar
1 star anise
1 cinnamon stick
3 cloves
1 teaspoon mustard seeds

Put the vinegars and sugar into
a saucepan and bring to the boil.
Immediately remove the pan from
the heat and add all the spices. Leave
to cool and infuse. When cool, strain
the vinegar and discard the spices.
It is now ready to use for pickling
vegetables.

Salt Pickling Liquid

MAKES ABOUT 300ML

100g caster sugar
100ml water
100ml white wine
100ml white wine vinegar
5g Maldon sea salt

Put all the ingredients into a
heavy-based pan and stir over a
medium-high heat until the sugar
has dissolved. Bring to the boil, then
immediately pour into a wide metal
tray or bowl. Place in a blast chiller
to cool the liquid quickly. (If you
don't have a blast chiller, simply pour
it into a wide metal bowl and leave to
cool completely.) Store in a clean jar
in the fridge.

Pickled Cobnuts

MAKES ABOUT 300G

300g cobnuts
100ml dry white wine
100ml water
100ml white wine vinegar
100g caster sugar
5g Maldon sea salt

Peel the cobnuts to reveal their white flesh. Pack them into a sterilised jar. Place all the other ingredients in a pan and heat, stirring until the sugar has dissolved. As soon as the liquid comes up to the boil, pour it over the cobnuts in the jar. Seal the jar and leave to pickle for a few weeks before serving.

Kombu Brine

MAKES ABOUT 2.9L

4 dried kombu leaves
3 litres water
240g fine sea salt

In a large pot, soak the kombu in the water overnight. The next day, heat the liquid to 60°C and add the salt. As soon as the salt has dissolved, remove from the heat and leave to cool completely. If all the brine is not used immediately, any excess can be kept in the fridge. However, do discard the brine after it has been used once.

Kombu Dashi

MAKES ABOUT 950ML

3 large dried kombu leaves
2 litres still mineral water
40g bonito flakes
5 tablespoons aged mirin (minimum 3 years)
1 teaspoon grated citrus zest (such as mandarin, orange, lemon or yuzu)
5 tablespoons white soy sauce
10g peeled and sliced root ginger

Briefly rinse the kombu to remove any white coating, then put it into a saucepan and cover with cold mineral water. Leave to soak overnight.

The next day, set the pan over a high heat and bring to the boil. As soon as the stock begins to bubble, take the pan off the heat. Skim off any froth or scum from the surface of the stock, then strain through a fine sieve and return to the pan. Add the bonito flakes to the hot kombu stock. Cover the pan and set aside to infuse as the stock cools. Once cooled, strain the stock and discard the bonito.

Return the stock to the pan again and add the mirin, citrus zest, white soy sauce and ginger slices. Bring to a simmer over a high heat. As soon as the liquid begins to bubble, take the pan off the heat and leave the stock to cool and infuse for 30 minutes. Strain and discard the solids. The dashi is now ready to use. (It can be kept in the fridge for 3 days.)

Vegetarian Dashi

MAKES ABOUT 1.9L

2 dried kombu leaves
2 x 1.5-litre bottles of mineral water
100g dried shiitake mushrooms
100g dried ceps (porcini)
1 tablespoon white soy sauce

Put the kombu leaves into a saucepan and pour in the mineral water. Cover the pan and leave to soak overnight in the fridge. The next day, set the pan over a high heat and bring the water to a simmer, skimming off any scum from the surface. When the water begins to boil, take the pan off the heat and leave to cool completely. Remove and discard the kombu.

Return the kombu stock in the pan to a simmer, then add the dried mushrooms and soy sauce. Simmer for 2 minutes. Remove from the heat and set aside to infuse for about 5 minutes. Strain the stock and discard the mushrooms. Use immediately or cool and freeze in smaller portions.

Lobster Consommé

MAKES ABOUT 2L

1kg lobster heads, crushed
olive oil, for cooking
1 onion, chopped
2 celery sticks, chopped
1½ carrots, peeled and chopped
1 small leek (white part), chopped
½ bulb of fennel, chopped
1 bulb of garlic, cut in half
    horizontally
½ tablespoon tomato paste
175ml brandy
375ml dry white wine
a handful of thyme sprigs
2 bay leaves
2 star anise
2 litres Fish Stock (see page 378)
a small bunch of basil, about 75g
a small bunch of coriander,
    about 75g

TO CLARIFY THE STOCK
100g egg whites (from about
    3 medium eggs)
1 shallot, chopped
1 carrot, peeled and chopped

Heat a little olive oil in a large stockpot over a high heat. Tip in all but 4 of the lobster heads. Fry the lobster heads, stirring once or twice, for 5–6 minutes or until fragrant and lightly golden brown. Remove to a plate and set aside.

Add the chopped vegetables and garlic to the pan. Fry, stirring occasionally, for 6–8 minutes or until the vegetables are soft and lightly golden brown. Stir in the tomato paste and fry for another couple of minutes until the vegetables take on a deeper colour. Deglaze with the brandy, scraping the bottom and sides of the pan to loosen any browned bits. Pour in the white wine and bring to the boil. Boil until reduced by half.

Return the browned lobster heads to the pan and add the thyme, bay leaves and star anise. Pour in the stock, topping up with water if the ingredients are not covered. Bring to a simmer, skimming off any froth and scum from the surface. Leave to simmer gently for 40 minutes. Remove from the heat and add the basil and coriander sprigs. Set aside to cool and infuse for about 20 minutes.

Strain the stock through a fine sieve into a clean pan, pressing down on the solids with the back of a ladle to extract all the flavourful juices; discard the contents of the sieve. When the stock has cooled to about 30°C, set the pan over a medium heat. While the stock is heating, put the egg whites, shallot, carrot and reserved lobster heads into a strong food processor or Thermomix and blitz to a rough pulp. Stir this pulp into the warm stock, then bring to a simmer, without stirring. As the stock heats up, the egg white mixture will form a raft that will trap all the impurities and clarify the liquid. When the raft has floated up to the surface, remove the pan from the heat.

Use a ladle to transfer the liquid and raft to a fine sieve lined with muslin and strain into a clean saucepan; do not break up the raft. The clarified consommé is now ready to use. It can be kept in the freezer for a month, if making ahead.

Fish Stock

MAKES 2–2.5L

2.5kg bones of flat white fish
    (without heads)
1 onion, quartered
½ head of celery, roughly
    chopped
1 small bulb of fennel,
    roughly chopped
3 white peppercorns
10g fennel seeds
10g coriander seeds
2 small dried bay leaves
3 sprigs of dill
3 parsley stalks
2 sprigs of thyme

Rinse the fish bones to remove any blood until the water runs clear, then put the bones into a large stockpot. Pour in enough cold water to cover the bones. Bring to a simmer, skimming off any froth and scum from the surface. Add all the remaining ingredients and bring the liquid back to a simmer. Skim again, then leave the stock to simmer over the lowest heat for about 40 minutes.

Take the pan off the heat. Ladle the stock into a muslin-lined sieve and allow to strain into a bowl. The stock is now ready to use, or you can cool it, then freeze in smaller amounts.

For **Reduced Fish Stock**, reduce the stock by half over a medium-high heat, which will intensify the flavour.

Vegetable Stock

MAKES ABOUT 4L

2 carrots, peeled
1 celery stick
2 leeks
2 onions
1 bulb of fennel
1 bulb of garlic, cloves separated
4 litres water
20g thyme
20g chervil
20g parsley
20g chives
10g coriander seeds
10g fennel seeds
5g white peppercorns
375ml dry white wine

Finely chop all the vegetables and garlic, then place in a large stockpot and cover with the cold water. Bring to the boil, then simmer for 10 minutes. Add the herbs, spices and white wine. Remove from the heat and allow to cool. Pour into a container and leave to infuse in the fridge overnight. The next day strain the stock through a fine sieve. Keep in the fridge or freezer.

Chicken Stock

MAKES ABOUT 10L

5kg chicken carcasses, broken up roughly
6 onions, roughly chopped
2 leeks, roughly chopped
1 celery stick, roughly chopped
3 carrots, peeled and roughly chopped
2 bulbs of garlic, cloves separated and cut in half
2 bay leaves
50g thyme

Place the chicken carcasses in a large stockpot and cover with 10 litres cold water. Bring to a simmer, skimming off all the froth and scum that rises to the surface. Once the liquid is clear, add the vegetables, garlic and herbs. Leave to simmer for 4 hours.

Strain the stock through a fine sieve. Cool, then keep in the fridge or freezer.

Brown Chicken Stock

MAKES 4L

3kg chicken carcasses
2kg chicken wings
olive oil, for cooking
6 onions, chopped
4 carrots, peeled and chopped
2 leeks, chopped
1 celery stick, chopped
2 bulbs of garlic, cloves separated and cut in half
30g tomato paste
50g thyme
2 bay leaves
Maldon sea salt

Preheat the oven to 180°C/160°C fan/Gas Mark 4. Using a large meat cleaver, chop the chicken carcasses and wings into smaller pieces. Place them in large roasting trays and season with salt. Roast for 45 minutes or until golden brown.

Meanwhile, heat a drizzle of oil in a large stockpot, add the vegetables and garlic, and cook over a medium-high heat until deeply caramelised. Stir in the tomato paste and cook for 2 minutes, then add the herbs.

Remove the bones from the trays and discard the excess fat, then add the bones to the stockpot. Cover the contents with 10 litres cold water. Bring to a simmer, skimming off foam and fat that rises to the surface, then cook for 4 hours. Strain the stock through a fine sieve. Cool, then keep in the fridge or freezer.

Duck Stock

MAKES ABOUT 1–1.4L

vegetable oil, for cooking
1kg duck bones (necks and
    carcasses), fat removed
1 onion, chopped
1 small leek, chopped
1 carrot, peeled and chopped
1 celery stick, chopped
½ bulb of garlic, cloves separated
    and roughly chopped
½ tablespoon tomato paste
100ml dry white wine
100ml Madeira
1 litre Veal Stock (see page 380)
500ml Chicken Stock (see
    page 379)
a sprig of lemon thyme
Maldon sea salt and black pepper

Heat a little oil in a large pan over
a high heat. When hot, add the duck
bones and fry, turning occasionally,
for 8–10 minutes or until the bones
are a deep golden brown. Remove
the browned bones to a plate and
set aside.

Add a little more oil to the pan and
stir in the chopped vegetables and
garlic. Fry, stirring every once in a
while, for 6–8 minutes or until the
vegetables begin to soften. Stir in
the tomato paste, then fry for a few
more minutes until the vegetables
are golden brown. Return the
duck bones to the pan and deglaze
with the white wine and Madeira,
stirring well. Boil until reduced by
half. Pour in both stocks and top up
with a little water if the liquid does
not cover the bones. Add the thyme.
Bring to a simmer, skimming off any
froth that rises to the surface, then
leave to simmer gently for 4 hours.

Strain the sauce through a fine sieve
into another heavy-based saucepan;
discard the solids. Leave to cool,
then strain once again. Keep in the
fridge until needed.

Lamb Stock

MAKES ABOUT 750ML

olive oil, for cooking
1kg lamb rib bones, chopped into
    smaller pieces
1 onion, roughly chopped
½ leek, roughly chopped
1 carrot, peeled and
    roughly chopped
1 celery stick, roughly chopped
½ bulb of garlic, cloves separated
    and roughly chopped
½ tablespoon tomato paste
200ml dry white wine
500ml reduced Veal Stock
    (see page 380)
500ml Chicken Stock (see
    page 379)
Maldon sea salt and black pepper

Heat a drizzle of olive oil in a large,
heavy-based pan, add the lamb bones
and fry over a high heat until evenly
browned. Remove the bones to a
plate and set aside.

Add a little more oil to the pan
and tip in the chopped vegetables
and garlic. Fry for about 8 minutes,
stirring frequently, until the
vegetables begin to soften. Add the
tomato paste and stir well. Fry for
another couple of minutes until the
vegetables begin to brown, then
deglaze with the wine, scraping the
sides and bottom of the pan. Let
the wine bubble and reduce by half.
Return the browned bones to the
pan. Pour in the veal and chicken
stocks, topping up with a little water
if the bones are not immersed in
the liquid. Bring to the boil, then
simmer for about 4 hours, skimming
off any scum and froth from
the surface.

Strain the stock through a fine sieve
into a clean heavy-based saucepan;
discard the solids. Season to taste
with salt and pepper.

Veal Stock

MAKES ABOUT 1.5L

5kg veal bones
olive oil, for cooking
5 onions, roughly chopped
4 carrots, peeled and
    roughly chopped
1 leek, roughly chopped
½ head of celery, roughly chopped
1 bulb of garlic, cloves separated
    and roughly chopped
30g tomato paste
1 calf's foot
50g thyme
1 bay leaf

Preheat the oven to 180°C/160°C
fan/Gas Mark 4. Place the veal bones
in large roasting trays and roast
for about 1 hour or until deeply
coloured. Remove from the oven,
drain off the fat and keep to one side.

Heat a drizzle of oil in a large
stockpot. Add the vegetables and
garlic, and cook over a medium-high
heat until deeply caramelised. Stir in
the tomato paste and cook for
2 minutes.

Add the veal bones, calf's foot
and herbs. Cover with 10 litres
cold water and bring to a simmer.
Simmer for 24 hours, skimming
the stock regularly and adding more
water as the stock reduces. Strain
the stock through a fine sieve into
a clean pan, then reduce by half,
skimming regularly. Strain again.
Cool, then keep in the fridge
or freezer.

Pumpkin & Seaweed Oil

MAKES ABOUT 600ML

200g pumpkin seeds,
   lightly toasted
250g sea lettuce
100ml pumpkin seed oil
500ml light olive oil
200g blanched spinach

Put all the ingredients into a Thermomix set at 70°C and blitz for 8 minutes to make a smooth purée. Transfer to a fine sieve lined with a piece of muslin and set over a bowl, then leave the oil to strain through for a few hours or overnight. Do not press down on the mixture in the muslin, but allow the light green oil to slowly drip through. Store the oil in a sterilised jar or squeezy bottle. It can be kept in the fridge for 3 days.

Black Olive Oil

MAKES 125–150ML

100g dehydrated black olives
   (dried out in a dehydrator at
   75°C for 6 hours)
100ml olive oil

Blitz together the black olives and oil in a strong blender until the mixture is smooth and emulsified. Strain through a fine sieve to remove any pits, stones and pulp, then pour the resulting oil into a squeezy bottle. The oil can be kept in the fridge for up to a week.

Chive & Dill Oil

MAKES ABOUT 400ML

200g chives
200g dill
400ml vegetable oil

Put all the ingredients into a Thermomix set to 70°C and blitz for 8 minutes. Pour the mixture into a muslin-lined sieve. Bring together the edges of the muslin and tie so you can hang up the resulting muslin bag. Allow the oil to drip through slowly for a few hours or overnight. The resulting oil will be very dark – almost black in colour. Transfer to a squeezy bottle. The oil can be kept in the fridge for 3 days.

Lemon Oil

MAKES ABOUT 150ML

zest and juice of 2 lemons
100ml olive oil
a sprig of dill

Combine the lemon zest and juice with the oil and dill in a small pan. Warm to 50°C. Remove from the heat and leave to infuse for an hour. Strain the lemon oil through a fine sieve. Store in an airtight container.

Pistachio Crumb

MAKES ABOUT 280G

1 Granny Smith apple
100g pistachios
100g blanched almonds
50g dried apricots

Peel and core the apple and cut into 1cm dice. Spread out on a baking tray in a single layer. Place in a dehydrator heated to 70°C and leave to dry out for 5 hours or until the apple is completely dried and crisp.

Preheat the oven to 160°C/140°C fan/Gas Mark 3. Spread out the nuts on a baking tray and toast them in the oven for 20 minutes or until golden; toss the nuts halfway through the time. Remove from the tray and leave to cool completely.

Using a large chef's knife, chop all the ingredients together until they resemble fine crumbs. Store in an airtight container.

Crepes

MAKES ABOUT 8

100g plain flour
2 large eggs
250ml whole milk
Maldon sea salt and black pepper

Sift the flour with a pinch each of salt and pepper into a mixing bowl. Make a well in the centre and add the eggs and milk. Gradually mix the dry ingredients into the wet, stirring with a whisk, until the batter is smooth. It should be slightly thicker than single cream. Set aside for a few minutes.

Heat a non-stick pan over a medium-high heat until hot. Ladle some batter into the pan and tilt the pan to move the batter around and make a thin, even layer. Quickly pour any excess batter back into the bowl. Return the pan to the heat and cook the crepe for about 30 seconds or until lightly golden on the base. Flip the crepe to cook the other side for another 30 seconds. Slide the crepe on to a plate. Continue to make crepes with the rest of the batter, stacking them interleaved with greaseproof paper.

Pain d'épices

MAKES 1 LOAF

120g unsalted butter
120g caster sugar
170g runny honey
2 large eggs
25g lemon purée (we use
   Boiron purées)
25g orange marmalade
240g plain flour
5g baking powder
9g pain d'épices spice powder

Preheat the oven to 160°C/140°C fan/Gas Mark 3. Grease a 400g loaf tin and line with baking parchment.

Using a free-standing electric mixer, cream the butter and sugar together until pale and light. Meanwhile, lightly beat together the honey and eggs in a small bowl. With the mixer running at medium speed, gradually add the honeyed eggs to the creamed butter. Add the lemon purée and marmalade and mix well. Sift the flour, baking powder and pain d'épices powder into the bowl and fold the wet and dry mixtures together until well incorporated.

Scrape the mixture into the lined tin and bake for about 25 minutes or until the loaf has set and a skewer inserted into the centre comes out clean. Remove from the oven and leave the pain d'épices to cool for 10 minutes before unmoulding on to a wire rack. When completely cooled, store in an airtight tin and enjoy within a week.

To make **Pain d'épice Crumbs**, crumble a few slices of pain d'épices on to a baking tray. Put the tray into a dehydrator at 75°C and leave to dry for 3 hours. For finer crumbs, pulse the dried pain d'épices in a food processor to the desired texture.

Lemon & Yoghurt Meringue

MAKES 10

70g liquid glucose
100g egg whites (from about
   3 medium eggs)
15g egg white powder
30g lemon purée (we use
   Boivron purées)
a squeeze of lemon juice
20g plain yoghurt

Turn on the oven to the lowest possible setting (about 75°C/50°C fan/Gas Mark very low). Put a splash of water into a small, heavy-based saucepan and add the liquid glucose. Set the pan over a high heat and bring to a rolling boil.

Meanwhile, put the egg whites and egg white powder into the bowl of a free-standing electric mixer and start whisking on high speed. As soon as the glucose syrup is boiling, take the pan off the heat and slowly pour the hot syrup into the egg whites while whisking at medium speed. When the syrup is fully incorporated, continue to whisk the meringue for several minutes until the side of the bowl no longer feels hot. The meringue should have at least tripled in volume. Add the lemon purée and lemon juice and whisk to mix them in, then mix in the yoghurt.

Spread the meringue evenly on 2 baking trays lined with silicone mats to a layer 5mm thick. Bake in the low oven for 2 hours or until completely dry. Remove the trays from the oven and leave to cool completely before breaking the meringue into rough squares. Store in an airtight container, in between sheets of baking parchment.

Mulled Elderberries

MAKES ABOUT 200G

300ml red wine
50ml red wine vinegar
100g demerara sugar
1 star anise
5 juniper berries
1 cinnamon stick
finely grated zest and juice
of 1 large orange
200g elderberries

Put all the ingredients, except the elderberries, into a pan and bring to a simmer, stirring initially to help dissolve the sugar. Remove from the heat and leave to cool and infuse. Meanwhile, wash and dry the elderberries, then pack them into a sterilised jar.

Once the liquid has cooled, strain it, discarding the spices, and return to the pan. Bring back to the boil. Immediately pour the boiling liquid over the elderberries in the jar. Seal and leave to mull for a few weeks before serving.

Apple & Blackberry Jam

MAKES ABOUT 500ML

---

4 Granny Smith apples
500g blackberries
500ml red wine
200ml ruby port
finely grated zest and juice
of 1 orange
1 star anise
1 clove
½ cinnamon stick

Peel, core and finely chop the apples. Place them in a pan and add all the remaining ingredients. Bring to a simmer and cook for about 1 hour or until the liquid has reduced and the jam has thickened. The apples should be stained a deep red colour. Transfer the contents of the pan to a blender and blitz until smooth. Pass the jam through a fine sieve. Store in a sterilised jar, or in a squeezy bottle if serving soon.

Damson Jam

MAKES ABOUT 1KG

1kg damson plums
1kg jam sugar
finely grated zest and juice
of 2 large oranges
20g agar agar powder

Halve the damsons and remove the stones, then cut the fruit into quarters. Put the damsons and sugar into a heavy-based saucepan and set over a medium-high heat. Add the orange zest and juice. Bring to a simmer, stirring to dissolve the sugar, then cook for about 20 minutes or until the damsons are soft.

Transfer the damsons to a blender and blitz until smooth. Pass through a fine sieve into a clean pan. Add the agar agar powder and place the pan on a high heat. Stir constantly as the jam comes up to the boil. After 2 minutes, remove from the heat and leave to cool. Transfer the jam to a bowl, cover with clingfilm and chill until set.

Blitz the jam and pass it through a sieve again to ensure a smooth consistency. Store in sterilised jars (or squeezy bottles) in the fridge and use within a couple of weeks.

Plum Jam

MAKES ABOUT 1.5KG

2kg overripe plums
300g caster sugar

Wash the plums and remove the
stones. Roughly slice the plums,
then place in a large pan with the
sugar. Stir over a high heat until
the sugar has dissolved. Lower the
heat slightly and cook the plums
until they have reduced to a jam
consistency. Transfer the plum jam
to a blender and blitz until smooth.
Pass the jam through a fine sieve into
a bowl. Leave to cool, then store in a
sterilised jar or in squeezy bottles.

Cherry Purée

MAKES ABOUT 1L

1kg Morello cherry purée (we
use Boivron purées)
20g agar agar powder

Put the cherry purée into a pan
and sprinkle over the agar agar.
Bring to the boil over a high heat,
stirring constantly, then boil for a
couple of minutes until thickened.
Pour the purée into a tray and leave
to cool. Chill for 1–2 hours until
the purée has set.

Scrape the set jelly into a blender
and blitz until smooth. Pass the
purée through a fine sieve, then
transfer to a squeezy bottle or jar.
The purée can be kept in the fridge
for up to a week, though you may
need to blitz it before use if it has
hardened and set again.

Whole Lemon Purée

MAKES ABOUT 1L

1kg lemons, cut in half
65ml vegetable oil
100g caster sugar
50ml water
Maldon sea salt

Put the lemons into a pan, cover
with cold water and bring to the
boil. Immediately drain the lemons
in a colander. Return them to the
pan, cover with cold water again and
bring to the boil, then drain. Repeat
the boiling and draining one more
time. (This blanching will help to
remove the bitterness from
the peel.)

Put the blanched lemon halves into
a large vacuum bag. Pour in the oil
and vacuum-seal the bag. Gently
poach the lemons in a sous vide
machine (or water bath) heated to
85°C for 2–2½ hours or until the
lemon peel is tender. Meanwhile,
make a sugar syrup by heating the
sugar and water together in a pan,
stirring until the sugar has dissolved,
then simmering for a few minutes.
Set aside.

Drain the lemons and transfer them
to a strong blender or Thermomix.
Add the sugar syrup and blitz until
very smooth. Pass the purée through
a fine sieve. Store in sterilised jars, or
in sealed vacuum bags, in the fridge.
Use within 2 weeks.

Lemon Purée

ABOUT 300ML

250ml ready-made lemon purée
(we use Boivron purées)
½ tablespoon pectin X58
6g gellan gum
65g caster sugar

Put the purée into a saucepan
and bring to a rapid boil. Add all
the remaining ingredients and
boil for another couple of minutes,
stirring constantly. Pour and spread
the purée on to a baking tray and
immediately put the tray into a blast
chiller (the purée will discolour if
not cooled quickly). When cold,
transfer the purée to a blender and
blitz until smooth. Pass through
a fine sieve, then transfer to a
squeezy bottle.

Basil Sorbet

MAKES ABOUT 700ML

100g caster sugar
2g ice cream stabiliser 2000
140g liquid glucose
juice of ½ lemon
400ml water
80g picked basil leaves

Stir together the sugar and ice cream stabiliser until well mixed. Put the liquid glucose, lemon juice and water into a heavy-based pan and stir over a medium heat until the glucose has dissolved. Bring to the boil. Tip in the sugar mixture and stir until the sugar has dissolved. Bring back to the boil, stirring. Take the pan off the heat and leave to cool completely. (The syrup can be kept in the fridge at this point.)

Bring another pan of water to the boil and have ready a bowl of iced water. Blanch the basil leaves in the boiling water for 10 seconds, then drain and refresh in the iced water. Drain again. Put the leaves into a blender, pour in the cold syrup and blitz until smooth.

Strain the mixture through a fine sieve into an ice cream machine. Churn until the sorbet has almost set, then scrape it into a freezerproof container.

Pear Sorbet

MAKES ABOUT 1.2L

75ml water
75g caster sugar
10g trimoline
1 tablespoon lemon juice
1 litre pear purée (we use
    Boiron purées)

Heat the water, sugar, trimoline and lemon juice in a small saucepan set over a medium heat. Stir until the sugar has dissolved, then let the syrup heat to 80°C. Take the pan off the heat and cool the syrup completely.

Add the pear purée and mix well. Pass the mixture through a fine sieve into an ice cream machine. Churn the mixture until it is almost set, then transfer the sorbet to a freezerproof tray or container. Cover the tray with clingfilm and freeze for a few hours until set.

Blackcurrant Sorbet

MAKES 1.7L

500ml water
175g caster sugar
1 litre blackberry purée
2 tablespoons crème de cassis

Put the water and sugar into a heavy-based saucepan and stir over a low heat until the sugar has dissolved. Take the pan off the heat and stir in the blackberry purée and crème de cassis. Once the mixture has cooled, pour it into an ice cream machine and churn until almost firm. Transfer the sorbet to a freezerproof container, cover and freeze for at least 4 hours or until set.

Rhubarb & Rose Sorbet

MAKES ABOUT 1L

500ml sugar syrup (made
    with 250g caster sugar and
    250ml water)
500ml rhubarb juice
5g super neutrose stabiliser
5g gellan gum
4 drops of rose essence

Put all the ingredients into a Thermomix set to 40°C. Blend at speed 6 for 10 minutes to activate the gellan gum. Pass the mixture through a fine sieve. Churn in an ice cream machine, then transfer to a freezerproof container and place in the freezer until set.

Strawberry Sorbet

MAKES ABOUT 1L

300ml water
1 tablespoon liquid glucose
125g caster sugar
45g dextrose
5g ice cream stabiliser 2000
450g strawberry purée (we use
    Boivron purées) or juice
50g calamansi lime purée or juice

Heat the water and liquid glucose together in a small saucepan to 40°C. Add the sugar, dextrose and stabiliser and stir over a medium-high heat until the mixture reaches 80°C. Remove from the heat and leave to cool completely.

Pour the mixture into a blender and add the strawberry and lime purées (or juices). Blitz well to mix, then strain through a fine sieve into the bowl of an ice cream machine. Churn until almost firm. Scrape the sorbet into a freezerproof container, cover and freeze for at least 4 hours, or overnight, until set.

Goat's Cheese Ice Cream

MAKES ABOUT 1.2L

690ml water
314g trimoline
20g caster sugar
40g dextrose powder
5g superneutrose powder
500g soft goat's cheese
    (without rind)
100g crème fraîche
6ml lemon juice

Heat the water, trimoline and sugar together in a small saucepan over a medium heat, stirring until the sugar has dissolved, then let the syrup heat to 40°C. Add the dextrose and superneutrose and give the syrup a stir. Bring to 80°C, then remove from the heat and cool.

Measure 535ml of the syrup into a Thermomix and add the goat's cheese, crème fraîche and lemon juice. Set the temperature to 80°C and blitz on speed number 3. Pass the mixture through a fine sieve into a large bowl and leave to cool, then churn in an ice cream machine until softly set. Transfer to a freezerproof container, cover and freeze for at least 4 hours or until firm.

Minus 8 Vinegar Ice Cream

MAKES ABOUT 1.3L

750ml whole milk
5 large egg yolks
185g caster sugar
60ml Minus 8 vinegar
200g full-fat plain yoghurt

Pour the milk into a heavy-based saucepan and place it over a low-medium heat. Mix together the egg yolks and sugar in a mixing bowl. When the milk has warmed to about 50°C, take the pan off the heat and slowly pour the warm milk into the sugary eggs, stirring constantly. Return the mixture to the saucepan and stir over a medium heat until thickened to a light custard (about 70°C).

Pour the custard into a bowl set over a larger bowl of iced water. Stir the custard frequently as it cools, to prevent a skin from forming on the surface. Once cooled, transfer the custard to an ice cream machine and add the vinegar and yoghurt. Churn until the ice cream is almost firm. Scrape the ice cream into a freezerproof container, cover and freeze for a few hours until set.

Olive Oil Ice Cream

MAKES ABOUT 1.2L

500ml whole milk
1 vanilla pod, split lengthways
    and seeds scraped out
5 large egg yolks
150g caster sugar
13g dextrose
150ml extra virgin olive oil
250g crème fraîche

Put the milk into a heavy-based saucepan and set it over a medium heat. Add the vanilla pod and seeds.

While the milk is heating, beat together the egg yolks, sugar and dextrose in a bowl. When the milk has reached 80°C, before it begins to boil, take the pan off the heat and slowly trickle the milk over the sugary eggs, whisking constantly. Return the mixture to the pan and stir over a medium heat until the mixture has thickened to a light custard that will lightly coat the back of the spoon.

Strain the custard through a fine sieve into an ice cream machine. Add the olive oil and crème fraîche and stir well. Churn until almost firm, then transfer to a freezerproof container. Freeze for a few hours or overnight until the ice cream has set.

Rum & Raisin Ice Cream

MAKES ABOUT 1 L

175g dark raisins
75ml aged rum (such as Mount Gay)
300ml whole milk
300ml double cream
1 vanilla pod, split lengthways
    and seeds scraped out
8 medium egg yolks
55g caster sugar

Put the raisins into a small saucepan and pour in enough cold water to cover. Bring to the boil and boil for 10 minutes, then drain the raisins in a sieve. Tip them back into the pan. Repeat the boiling and draining 2 more times, then transfer the raisins to a bowl and pour over the rum. Leave to infuse for at least 30 minutes, after which pour the mixture into a blender and blitz to make a smooth purée. Set aside.

Pour the milk and cream into a heavy-based saucepan and add the vanilla seeds and pod. Slowly bring to a simmer. Meanwhile, beat the egg yolks and sugar together in a large bowl. As the creamy milk begins to boil, gradually add it to the sugary eggs, whisking the whole time to prevent the eggs from curdling. Strain through a sieve into a clean pan. Stir over a low heat until the custard has thickened slightly and will coat the back of the spoon. Do not let the custard overheat or it will curdle. Strain through a fine sieve into a bowl. Add the raisin purée and stir well. Lay a piece of clingfilm on the surface of the custard to prevent a skin from forming. Leave to cool.

Once cold, pour the custard into an ice cream machine and churn until almost firm. Transfer the ice cream to a freezerproof container, seal and freeze until firm.

Vanilla Ice Cream

ABOUT 1.4L

500ml double cream
500ml whole milk
100g powdered dextrose
2 vanilla pods, split open and
    seeds scraped out
10 large egg yolks
175g caster sugar

Put the double cream, milk and dextrose into a heavy-based saucepan and add the vanilla pods and seeds. Bring to a simmer, stirring until the dextrose has dissolved. Meanwhile, whisk the egg yolks and sugar together in a large bowl until the mixture is thick and pale. As soon as the creamy milk begins to bubble at the sides, slowly trickle it over the sugary yolks, stirring the whole time to prevent the eggs from scrambling. When all the creamy milk has been incorporated, return the mixture to the pan. Stir constantly over a low heat until it thickens to a light custard that will coat the back of the spoon.

Strain the custard through a fine sieve into a wide bowl and leave to cool, stirring occasionally to prevent a skin from forming on top. Once cold, pour it into an ice cream machine and churn until almost firm. Scrape the ice cream into a freezerproof container, cover and freeze for at least 4 hours or overnight until set.

Index

About the Author

With seasoned experience, having worked under great chefs including Pierre Koffmann, Marco Pierre White, Nico Ladenis and Ferran Adrià, Jason joined the Gordon Ramsay Group in 2001 as the executive chef for Verre in Dubai. In 2005, Jason returned to the UK and opened Maze in the heart of London and then another five Maze restaurants globally, launching what would be the most successful brand in the group.

In 2010, Jason left Gordon Ramsay Holdings to launch his own restaurant company, Jason Atherton Ltd. His flagship Mayfair restaurant, Pollen Street Social, opened in April 2011 and was awarded a Michelin star within just six months of opening, alongside five AA Rosettes and listed as number 3 in *The Good Food Guide*'s 2018 best UK restaurants.

Since then, Jason's 'The Social Company' has grown into a globally renowned restaurant group, with a portfolio of restaurants which include the Michelin-starred Social Eating House, Little Social, Berners Tavern (named 'the defining restaurant of the decade'), Michelin-starred City Social, Social Wine & Tapas, Sosharu and Hai Cenato. Alongside his London restaurants, Jason has also opened critically-acclaimed restaurants in Hong Kong, Shanghai, Dubai and Cebu, and was recently awarded another Michelin star at The Clocktower restaurant in New York.

Jason has written three cookbooks to date, and his recipes and articles have appeared widely in magazines and newspapers including the *Guardian*, *Sunday Times*, *Observer Food Monthly*, *Waitrose Food*, *The Caterer* and *GQ*, as well as appearing regularly on television in the UK and abroad.

Jason and his wife Irha support numerous charities including Action Against Hunger, the MSY Charitable Foundation and the David Nichols Spinal Injury Foundation. In April 2018 Jason was appointed Hospitality Action's principal patron.

Acknowledgements

Jon Croft for the opportunity to work on this project, his belief in the book and support to make it happen. To the rest of the Absolute Press team, Meg Boas, Emily North and Marie O'Shepherd, who have gone above and beyond on many occasions.

Thank you to Dale Bainbridge for all of your hard work on this book while still running a Michelin-star restaurant of the highest standards. And to Kostas Papathanasiou, Alexis Roy Famero and Danny Page for their contributions too.

Thank you to Sarah Hodson for constantly chasing us both to get recipes written, photoshoots arranged and getting everything checked and finished on time.

To John Carey for the beautiful photographs, you always manage to capture the true essence of my dishes and always understand what I am looking for. Your work always takes my breath away.

To Emily Quah and Norma MacMillan for their editing work, Kate Moore for proofreading this huge book and Zoe Ross for indexing.

To my Executive Team: Irha Atherton for your love and support during this adventure we have taken together, Michael West and Laure Patry for your continued loyalty and support on this incredible journey.

To all of the team in the kitchen, front of house, back of house, reservations and head office, whose sheer hard work every single day has created this restaurant.

Credits

Publisher
Jon Croft

Senior Project Editor
Emily North

Photography
John Carey

Production Manager
Marina Asenjo

Proofreader
Kate Moore

Commissioning Editor
Meg Boas

Art Director & Designer
Marie O'Shepherd

Editor
Emily Quah

Copy Editor
Norma MacMillan

Indexing
Zoe Ross

ABSOLUTE PRESS

Bloomsbury Publishing Plc

50 Bedford Square, London, WC1B 3DP, UK

BLOOMSBURY, ABSOLUTE PRESS

and the Absolute Press logo are trademarks of

Bloomsbury Publishing Plc

First published in Great Britain in 2018

A catalogue record for this book is available
from the British Library.

Library of Congress Cataloguing-in-Publication data
has been applied for.

ISBN

HB: 9781472905574

Special Edition: 9781472957870

2 4 6 8 10 9 7 5 3 1

Printed and bound in China by C&C Printing.

To find out more about our authors and books visit
www.bloomsbury.com and sign up for our newsletters.